D1275047

THE PENGUIN
ADOPTION
HANDBOOK

THE PENGUIN
ADOPTION
HANDBOOK

A Guide to Creating Your New Family

Edmund Blair Bolles

The Viking Press   New York

First published in 1984 by The Viking Press
40 West 23rd Street, New York, N.Y. 10010

Published simultaneously in Canada by
Penguin Books Canada Limited

Library of Congress Catalog Card Number: 83-40240

ISBN 0-670-10510-4

Printed in the United States of America
Set in Century Old Style

TO THE NEXT GENERATION

Allison Louise Wiggins
Théophile Jalabert
Harry Tim Bolles

Contents

CONTENTS

Acknowledgments

In writing this book I received the help of many people, including adoptive and foster parents, adoption-agency workers, members of parent organizations, and government officials. Many of these sources were assured of confidentiality and my thanks to them must remain private. To ensure that privacy, the names of adoptive parents and children cited in the book are fictitious; however, in every case they refer to real people. In cases where pronouns refer to children or adults of both sexes, the policy has been to alternate between using masculine and feminine pronouns.

Two sources I am especially indebted to are the Child Welfare League and its wonderful library and the New York Council on Adoptable Children, particularly Mary Talen, who did a lot of work above and beyond the call of neighborliness.

I telephoned so many workers and parents that I could never list them all, but I wish to thank the following institutions, which kindly allowed me to visit them and discuss their operations: Adoption Resource Center (Region II); Adoptive Parents Committee (New York); Agape Social Services (Dallas); American Adoption Agency (Washington, D.C.); Associated Catholic Charities (Diocese of Baltimore); The Barker Foundation (Washington, D.C.); Catholic Social Services (Diocese of Madison, Wisconsin); Committee for Single Adoptive Parents; Dallas Council on Adoptable Children; Families Adopting Children Everywhere (Maryland); Harlem-Dowling Children's Services (New York); Hope Cottage—Children's Bureau (Dallas); Korean Families of Spence-Chapin (New York); Latin American Parents Association (Long Island); LDS Social Services (Gaithersburg, Maryland); Lutheran Social Services of New York; Lutheran Social Services of Wisconsin and Upper Michigan (South Central Area); National Adoption Resource Exchange; National Committee for Adoption; New York Foundling Hospital; New York Spaulding for Children; New York State Department of Social Services; North American Council on Adoptable Children; Pierce-Warwick Adoption Service (Washington, D.C.); Presbyterian Children's Home (Dallas Adoptive Center); The Salvation Army (New York); Spence-Chapin Services to Families and Children (New York); Talbot-Perkins Adoption Agency (New York); and Wisconsin State Department of Health and Social Services. Of course, my thanks and debt does not mean that these groups are responsible for, or even endorse, what I have written.

E.B.B.

Preface

◄───►

Forget the rumors and the scary headlines. You can adopt a child. People say, "Sure, but what sort of child?" The answer depends on you. You can adopt the child you are looking for, whether you are hoping for an infant, a two-year-old, or a ten-year-old. This book explains how the American adoption scene has changed over the last dozen years and how those changes have created widespread confusion. Adopting parents, social agencies, and even many adoption workers have not been able to come to terms with the details of this challenging new situation.

The surprising truth is that adoption is now open to many more people than it used to be. Nostalgia recalls that before 1970 a couple approached an adoption agency, proclaimed their desire, paid their money, and got their baby. That simple picture, however, omits the many people who were turned away. Single people, nonwhites, and the non-middle-class people of course seldom even bothered to try to adopt, but many people who thought of themselves as typical middle-class Americans were turned down as well. Maybe their income wasn't right, or one member of the couple had been divorced, or one had consulted a psychiatrist, or the size of the room available for the adopted infant was too small, or one of the applicants was deemed insufficiently articulate. In those days, stereotypical couples were sought for stereotyped adoptions. Today, however, people who once would have been denied the right to adopt are finding that they can adopt the children they want.

The new adoption scene demands a book that can make sense of the new conditions. Under the old system, the adoption process was so straightforward for those families who qualified that the classic book for people interested in adoption, *Adoption and After* by Louise

13

Raymond (New York: Harper & Row, 1954; revised by Colette T. Dywasak, 1974), was able to devote most of its space to how to raise an adopted child.

Today, if you are thinking about adoption, there are a number of new facts that you must contend with. The role of most adoption agencies has changed dramatically. They now handle a very different sort of child and serve quite a different clientele from the old days. Women giving up their newborn children for adoption are no longer so ready to work with agencies; the method for uniting a baby with adoptive parents is more hit or miss than it used to be. Many new organizations have arisen to serve different participants in this new situation. Some focus on children in need of adoption, some help people hoping to adopt, and a third group represents agency interests. Institutional rivalries and philosophical differences have brought many new pressures into the adoption process.

This book confronts the facts, puts them into a perspective designed to help readers decide what is the best course of action for them, and then suggests how to proceed. The contemporary adoption process has turned into a maze with rules and choices so baffling that many people simply get lost in it and never actually manage a successful adoption. This book will make passage through the maze easier and swifter.

PART I
Thinking About Adoption

1

Why People Adopt

Once, during a conversation about the difficulties of the adoption search, a friend said to me, "Well, at least it must give these families time to think about why they want to adopt." My friend is smart and analytical, but she does not know much about the paradoxes of the human heart. Often the struggle to adopt has the opposite effect from the one she expected: people can become more confused than ever about just why they hope to adopt a child.

The adoption maze presents a host of little practical questions. Should I try this way or that way? Can I trust this information? Do I want to consider such-and-such a type of child? The constant flow of little questions makes it difficult to give much thought to larger questions about the ultimate purpose behind the struggle. Of course, this increased bewilderment makes it still harder to answer all the little questions. And if you forget where you are going, it is impossible to find the best route.

Interviews with adoptive families around the country have convinced me that most searches begin with a reasonably clear sense of purpose. I usually heard something like "We wanted to establish a family," but the purpose of creating a family became lost, or at least blurred, during the search period itself. This confusion can slow down progress, but it can also lead to wrong decisions whose effects last a long time.

Adoption demands a clear head. People usually go through a period of doubt before deciding to adopt. The idea attracts them, but they wonder if it is right for them. They ask themselves if it means settling for second best. They fear it is too unnatural an idea and wonder if it

17

will mark them as different. Then, finally, comes a moment when they push away all doubts and decide that developing their family is the most important thing and they are going to adopt a child.

If applicants could go directly to an adoption agency and be helped straightaway, they might be able to do as my friend suggested and think more fully about their desire for a family. As it is, they become caught up in details. Certainly nobody within the adoption maze is going to remind them of the larger picture. Organizers and social workers know only one step in the whole process, and naturally they have a tendency to mistake their area of expertise for the whole. Instead of talking about families, many adoptive-parent organizations say the purpose of the adoption process is to provide children for those who want them. This view raises protests from people working to find homes for waiting children, because they see adoption primarily as a way to help needy children. Both of these viewpoints focus on the here and now, and neither of them is broad enough to grasp the idea of serving families that won't even exist until the children and adults are brought together. Adoption is an attempt to shape the future, so it is dangerous to base decisions simply on the needs of the moment.

Of course, the nature of a family cannot be stereotyped. Every society cherishes and depends on a family unit, but the form of the family varies from culture to culture and epoch to epoch. Indeed, the shape of the American family is changing rapidly. If the nuclear family—with Mom, Pop, and 2.5 kids—ever was the dominant American family form, that dominance has ended.

The 1980 census illustrated this change with a surprising statistic. The census data show that, as common sense should predict, the number of American families with children increased during the 1970s. The 1970 count had found 26.8 million such families; in 1980 there were 31.5 million. The surprising fact is that the number of two-parent families with children has actually declined. In 1970 there were 25.5 million two-parent families, but by 1980 that figure had dropped to 24.9 million. In other words, the entire increase in families with children is the result of a dramatic rise in untraditional families. This rise may be even more startling than the figures show because the Census Bureau is cautious about probing too deeply into family organization. It asks no questions about adoption or biological connection and makes no distinction between nuclear and extended families that live under one roof. These figures show that American families are moving further away from the Ozzie-and-Harriet stereotype. Family composition is becoming more flexible, and a family's form reflects the individual circumstances and personal history of its members.

Whatever form it takes, a family is the major instrument for orienting individuals toward society. Families define the relationships people can expect to last a lifetime; they determine the way a person is connected to the past, and how one becomes part of the future. A person without any family is confronted by a fearful picture of instability. Where do I come from? Don't know. Who can I count on to be there always? Nobody. What will become of me? Don't know.

Today in America there are hundreds of thousands of children who are without family connections. There are also many adults who, although perhaps not lacking all family relations, miss some of the things only a family can provide. If these adults have no children, they may feel the absence of a link to the future. They may also miss the very important sense of being people whom someone can always depend on and look up to. Adults who do have children have more subtle and varied reasons for wanting to expand their families through adoption. Common reasons are a wish for more children, combined with a feeling that helping those already born is preferable to adding to the world's population, or a sense that the family ought to be larger and it would be better if the new member were not an infant.

Families hoping to adopt are commonly asked by agency workers why they want to do so. The answers given are usually practical and intensely personal. They often begin with the speaker's own situation and then move out to the larger world:

• I have always loved children. I grew up in a family with six children. I had four children of my own. Now they are grown and I have remarried. I would like to start over with raising a family.

• I turned forty-three and realized that although I am not married, I don't have to choose between being single and having a family. I have always wanted children and can give a home and love to a child who otherwise would have nothing.

• I have a child, but feel there is enough love in my heart for another one.

• Both of us want children, but they just aren't coming.

• We have a ten-year-old son who really wants a brother. We'd like another child too, but feel it is best to adopt one, since a baby would be so small that our son wouldn't benefit from its presence.

These are only partial reasons for deciding to adopt. None of us can compress so great and compelling an urge into a few sentences. In talking to adoptive families around the country, I almost always asked about their decision, how they came to it, and why. Some cited a Christian motive of duty and love, some spoke of a personal experience that sparked their action, and others said frankly, "I don't know why we wanted to adopt. We just did."

Even though most of us are not members of anything like a romanticized TV family, when we start to think in the abstract about families, we have to make an effort to break with that image. Biology is responsible for fewer family links than we imagine. This point was made to me with particular strength by a man who had two biological daughters and then adopted a third. He recounted the following phone conversation, in which he told his father and his stepmother of the pending adoption.

ADOPTING FATHER: Dad, you're going to be a grandfather again. M—— and I are adopting a little girl.

FATHER: Oh?

A.F.: Yes, we got the news today.

F.: Well, it won't be the same as it is with K—— and S—— [the two biological daughters]. You can't expect me to love an adopted child the same as I do them.

A.F.: Yes, I can. She's going to be my daughter.

F.: But she won't be my flesh and blood.

STEPMOTHER: Now wait a minute, T——. When I married you, didn't you expect me to love your children even though they weren't my flesh and blood?

F.: Oh, come on. That was different.

S.: No, it wasn't different at all. If I can love your children even though they aren't my flesh and blood, you can love a grandchild who isn't yours.

This particular story had a happy ending. The grandfather saw the wisdom of the argument and quit insisting that flesh and blood make a family. When he met his new granddaughter, he found he could accept her after all.

Happy endings cannot be guaranteed, but often people find that their own prejudices simply disappear if they can get beyond the emphasis on bloodlines. Families are at least as much the invention of society as of biology—a fact that explains why families differ so much around the world. It also explains why adoption is found worldwide. Families are too important, and biology cannot be relied on to provide everybody with a ready-made one.

Books about adoption often suggest, quite falsely, that the adoptive family is a new creation. The modern process, which requires going to a court and getting a legal document, is not universal, but adoption in the sense in which I use the term—making a child a permanent member of a family—is common to all societies, since there are always children in need of help and adults who want to take them in.

I once encountered such a case in a remote African village. I was teaching at the village school when I discovered that one of my students with a Christian name was the brother of two other students with Moslem names. Puzzled by this situation, I asked a friend about it and learned that the Christian boy's biological parents had been killed through some misadventure. When his parents died, a friend of his father's told him, "Because of my love for your father, you are welcome in my family." There were no formal papers, no amended birth certificates, no social workers, and no kinship was involved, but the boy moved into the home of his father's friend.

I revisited the village some years after I had finished teaching there. It turned out that the adoptive father's biological sons had all done so well in school that they had gone on to gain civil service jobs and now lived elsewhere. The adopted son was still in the village; he ran his father's store and was the old man's heir in the business. The boy, who had become a grown man, proudly introduced me to his nephews and nieces, the ones who had been born to his sister since I had left the village. I'm sure it never crossed his mind that they were adoptive nephews and nieces.

The village where this simple adoption took place was unaccustomed to bringing the government into family affairs. No paperwork was ever done, but even in Africa that sort of informal adoption is now likely to become rarer. History shows that as soon as societies begin to formalize their rules, adoption laws appear. The cuneiform laws of the ancient Middle East describe various adoption practices. According to the laws and customs of ancient Egypt, producing offspring was the purpose of marriage and those who could not have children were advised to adopt them. Adoption there was a court procedure.

Our own adoption laws can be traced to the ancient Romans. Many great men of the Republic had no biological sons and adopted heirs as a way of maintaining their family lines. A similar tradition grew up in China and persists to this day. Many Chinese-Americans today adopt children from Hong Kong or Korea as a way of continuing their families. This tradition has been preserved in the United States in the instances of adult adoption. There is no age limit on who can be legally adopted. Adoption is a purely formal process that results in a change of the adoptee's family name and a new status in terms of the inheritance laws.

Because Roman law focused on the matter of inheritance, there is a widespread belief that until recently property concerns were the only reason for adoption. A fuller acquaintance with history makes that idea seem silly; adoption has always served a whole range of family purposes. In many poor societies, for example, one critical role of the extended family is mutual protection. Members are obligated to help one another in times of need. These days it has become common in the Caribbean for that protective role to be satisfied through adoption. A young man comes to a city where he has no kinship connection, is informally adopted by some older woman of the town who puts him up, and then, as he begins to make his way in the world, he gives a part of his income— often a substantial part —to his adoptive mother.

In many preindustrial societies, crafts were passed from father to son. Of course, it often happened that there was no son or the son simply had no talent for the craft. Adoption was the solution.

In short, the family is so important to the functioning of a society, to the welfare of its members, and to the preservation of its traditions that its survival simply cannot be left to biological chance. Only a most unnatural society would allow its needy children to suffer and perish, its adults who want children to yearn without hope, its property titles to fall into confusion, and its traditional knowledge to be lost and forgotten.

Yet many people still think of adoption as an unusual step. This attitude is puzzling because the acceptance of adoption in any particular society usually depends on the society's ideas about bloodlines. In Polynesia, for example, families trace their origins to mythical founders and perpetuate these relationships through rituals. Bloodlines play almost no role in the understanding of a person's identity and place in society, so adoptions are taken for granted.

The American tradition has also been to scorn the claims of blood in favor of experience. Families in America are considered personal rather than public institutions. The members of a family can be very close, but with few exceptions, society does not take much interest in a person's ancestry. Americans have never spoken kindly of the European and British idea that somebody might be judged superior on the basis of the accomplishments of other members of his family.

As one would expect for a country with such ideals, adoption is common in America. It serves our family needs most satisfactorily. There are literally millions of Americans who were adopted into their families, and there cannot be many people who do not know somebody who has adopted or has been adopted. Yet there is a striking contradiction here, for our laws and social workers treat adoption as though it were something extraordinary. Our legal system has a surprising amount of trouble with it, and traditional adoption agencies have never done much to dispel the impression that they are helping people out of an unnatural and peculiar difficulty. The roots of this attitude grew out of British common law, which did not recognize adoption.

The English nobility placed greater stress on the role of blood ties than did practically any other group in history. Property and titles passed directly to the oldest son. If there was no oldest son, the nearest male relation was awarded the land and title. If there were no male kin, the line ended and the title fell out of use. Under this system, adoption was forbidden. It is because of this special emphasis on blood that British literature is full of wards, guardians, foundlings, and illegitimate sons. Informal adoptions were common enough, but adoptions protected by law were unknown and adoptive children were left in a legal limbo.

America's laws and abstract theories about families are based on this feudal custom. Medieval ideas about the primacy of blood relations crop up in contemporary judicial decisions, in movies, in speculation about sociobiology, and even in books about adoption—everywhere except in daily life.

Not surprisingly, this conflict between theory and experience has led to some distorted notions. Parents have sometimes refused to admit, even to themselves, that their child was adopted. Children may reach their late teens before they learn of their adoption and then become obsessed with discovering who their "real" parents are. Relatives may never accept the idea of adoptive kin and may snub them or exclude them from wills.

Some readers may feel this conflict in their own complex attitudes toward the prospect of adoption. Many people come to adoption as a second choice. The natural solution to the absence of biological children is adoption, but often the decision to adopt is reached only after a great deal of anguish. (Readers whose infertility has brought them to the idea of adoption may be interested in contacting a support group for infertile couples. Write to RESOLVE, P.O. Box 474, Belmont, Massachusetts 02178.)

Typically, the suspicion of infertility is greeted by instant denial. *This cannot be!* Efforts to disprove the suspicions grow increasingly desperate. As the truth becomes harder to deny, the couple's mood frequently shifts to anger and sometimes guilt as well. *What did I do to deserve this?* a startled ego asks, while a little voice whispers guilty answers. The imperfections of a lifetime pass before one's eyes. The thought that a couple spent years using contraceptives before deciding to have a baby may be particularly painful. Fortunately, this kind of anger dissipates, and although the disappointment does not go away, it eventually subsides into a duller pain, a sadness that persists but ceases to paralyze.

It is a mistake to suppose that because adoption is often a second choice it is also second best. Both adoption and pregnancy are means to the same end—having a family. I spoke with one woman who went through the whole turmoil—the year of denial and mounting pain, the resigned turning to adoption, the passage of many more months, and finally the day when her daughter was to arrive, in this case by plane ("the modern stork"). It turned out that her social worker could not go with her to the airport because she herself was pregnant and about to give birth. "Your social worker was pregnant?" I asked when I heard the story. "How did you feel about that?"

"I was happy for her," came the sure answer. "My infertility was no longer a problem. I felt pregnant too."

2

The Adoption Maze

It used to be that only one kind of family was recognized by the adoption system: the rare couple whose family was like those portrayed in TV comedies. Adoption agencies loved the Ozzie-and-Harriet world of an ever-present Mom and Dad, two kids who are great pals, a friend who lives just across the way, and perhaps a smallish dog. Applicants who seemed unlikely to provide a child with such a life were routinely turned away. Single people, working-class couples, applicants who had been divorced, working wives, couples who wanted older children, religious minorities, and families who already had children were rejected. Some die-hard agencies persist in hanging on to these prejudices, but the great and happy truth is that almost all these formerly unacceptable applicants can now adopt, and adopt legally.

During the 1970s a series of social changes ended the adoption system's power to demand that couples fit agency stereotypes. Families simply refused to accept the claim that they weren't good enough to raise a child. Unfortunately, the changes that had been developing since the 1960s destroyed the ability of the old adoption system to unite searching parents with waiting children easily. In fact, during the 1970s the agency-dominated system came apart. Today, more than a decade since the agency system failed, most families still begin their attempt to adopt by telephoning the local agencies. Usually these callers are turned away.

The old system was simple: childless couples came to the adoption agencies to find babies, and women with unwanted pregnancies came to the agencies to find families for their children. Agency workers served as the intermediaries, discreetly helping all parties in the matter. The agency role was so important that it provoked resentment among both adopting families and pregnant women, who did not like having their worthiness judged by strangers. During the 1960s, with the great change in sexual mores, the number of unmarried and pregnant women who sought agency help grew dramatically. Resented or not, the adoption agency seemed essential.

Early in the 1970s pregnant women suddenly stopped coming to the agencies. The decline was so catastrophic that in a single year some agencies saw the number of their adoptable babies drop by 75 percent. Many agencies went out of business, and those that survived no longer occupied the dominant position they once had. New organizations, often run by adoptive parents themselves, sprang up. The recovery began slowly, for it took time for families to pool their resources, but by 1980 it began to look as though a new pyramid-shaped adoption system had been built. At the base were hundreds of local parent groups, which could help people locate the sort of children they wanted. The next step up the pyramid was a group of federally funded regional information centers. They had several tasks, including disseminating information about adoption and giving "mini-grants" (usually about one thousand dollars) to parent groups so that they could organize more effectively. At the top of the system were a few national organizations that helped coordinate information among the regions. Almost as soon as the pyramid was capped, however, federal budget cuts overturned the top several layers and returned the system to the disorder it had experienced during the 1970s.

The fundamental problem facing anyone thinking of adoption is that no functioning system exists for creating adoptive families. Instead, there is a maze, which some people master, but only because they are willing to persevere. Fortunately, the urge for a family is so powerful that it has prevailed over the purest chaos, and for those families who persist, the reward is a child they can adopt and love.

Consider, for example, the disturbing story of one woman I'll call Jacobina, because her persistence reminded me of Jacob, who sold himself into bondage for fourteen years in order to marry Rachel. Jacobina was the youngest of thirteen children, and she grew up expecting and wanting a large family, but she and her husband could not conceive a child. She tried desperately to become pregnant, and even though she was not a wealthy woman, she agreed to see if a doctor could end her infertility through surgery. Her doctor was of the caliber that a poor woman could afford, and she became infected

26

and was forced to have a hysterectomy. A divorce followed, but Jacobina still wanted children. One night in the late 1960s she was watching television when the picture of an orphan in need of a family was flashed on the screen. Right then Jacobina swore she would adopt a child.

Jacobina was not the kind of applicant adoption agencies welcomed in 1968. She was black, divorced, age thirty-eight, and living in a deteriorating part of town. She was also hoping to adopt an older child. As a single woman living alone, she wanted a child old enough to be in school while she was at work. In those days, such thinking dumbfounded adoption workers. It was true that Jacobina was also religious and smart, that she had a responsible job, but she was not even close to the middle-class stereotype agency workers preferred. Everywhere she applied she was given a runaround. A private agency would have told her flatly to go away. Public agencies prefer to put people everlastingly on hold, and by chance Jacobina had applied to a city-run agency.

She did not give up. For years and years she was told, "Not yet." She kept calling and pushing. When her friends asked why she kept it up, she explained, "Maybe they are just testing my patience, to see if I really want a child." Others told her that children were just a bother and she should be glad she didn't have any. None of her friends knew anything about the changes going on in the adoption process, so none could give her any practical advice.

By the late 1970s, applicants like Jacobina were no longer so rare. If she had come fresh to the agency, she might have been treated better, but by 1978 her agency had developed a firm habit of giving Jacobina the runaround. Somehow her search came to the attention of an adoptive-parent organization, and she was invited to a meeting. At last she found people she could talk to who would support her and tell her they understood her need. In the twelfth year of her search, Jacobina found a new agency, and, finally, a son was placed in her home. That adoption was such a success that the agency placed a daughter with her only six months later. With determination like Jacobina's, anything can be overcome, but no one should ever have to face so cruel a struggle.

Just why the old system collapsed is a matter of some debate, although the two major results are clear enough: (1) the number of newborn infants being received by agencies kept falling (by the end of the decade it was about 90 percent below what it had been in 1970); and (2) the varieties of families pressing their desire to adopt had multiplied dramatically, including families with working mothers, single parents, and minority families.

Adoption-agency workers explain the decline in the number of waiting newborns as a "baby shortage." It is a phrase that suggests unwanted babies have simply stopped being born. It also discourages families who hope to adopt—they assume that if there is a baby shortage and agencies cannot help, nothing can be done. Let me scotch that idea at once. *There is no baby shortage.* The shortages in the adoption world are shortages of information and organization. The fact that agencies have fewer infants to place has nothing to do with an overall baby shortage. It stems from the fact that many unmarried pregnant women no longer turn to agencies for help. They would rather place their babies privately than endure what they consider a humiliating inquiry into their private lives.

Throughout the 1970s, adoption agencies were facing harder and harder times while at the same time the out-of-wedlock birth rate in this country was rising. Contrary to common assumption, abortion and contraception have not caused a decline in out-of-wedlock births. The federal government estimates that in 1980 almost 600,000 infants were born outside marriage. Even if we assume that 90 percent of these mothers or their families wanted to keep their babies, 60,000 infants in need of adoption would remain. That is about three times the number of babies who were actually adopted into new families during 1980. (A national adoption agency organization estimates that of 20,000 infants adopted in 1980, half were found through agencies and half placed privately.)

Most of the agencies that still function have survived because of their sudden discovery of families who wanted or were willing to adopt children who were not healthy newborns. During the 1960s, people looking for older children or handicapped children had almost no hope of even applying for adoption. The adoption agencies of those days nearly always required that applicants provide medical proof of their infertility and that they express social values that would lead a couple to adopt only a healthy newborn child. Today, however, a number of adoption agencies serve people who want older, handicapped, or minority children. Such applicants continue to be a small percentage of those interested in adoption, but they are now the majority of families served by agencies.

28

It has been left to the searching families themselves to find new ways to adopt infants, so families should speak to a parent organization before they approach an agency. The old apply-and-wait method once favored by agencies is no longer the best way to proceed. But plenty of people have wasted a year or more before they learned about a parent group. During this period of floundering, families are especially vulnerable to misinformation, fraud, or profiteering.

Misinformation is particularly harmful because it discourages and confuses families. In the worst cases, it can even lead to the adoption of a child the parents consider "second best" and whom they will resent. In general, adoptive families should be wary of anyone who tells them that adoption is impossible, or that they must be prepared to settle for a child they would prefer not to raise, or that they must be willing to shave the corners off the law. You *can* legally adopt a child you can love.

Wherever so much desire is mixed with so much confusion, there are bound to be profiteers. Some of them are simple frauds who promise a service, collect some money in advance, and then fail to come through. Such false promises may come from many sources, but be especially cautious of adoption agencies from outside your area that advertise prominently in local phone books. People who find themselves caught in an adoption scam not only lose money and time they could be using to build a family, but, worse, they often lose heart as well, and abandon their searches.

This mixture of despair and misinformation has helped to create a black market in adoptable babies. Word of mouth leads many people to adoption sources that require perjured documents and high prices. In the worst cases, the black market may even involve the kidnapping of children. The black market is not the only means to adopting a baby, but the confusion that dominates the adoption world has made the baby profiteers appear to be a credible source. Many people have come to assume that the only way to find a healthy infant is through a doctor or lawyer whose name is discreetly passed in a whispered tone. Surprisingly, black-market adoptions are no better organized than the legal ones. I have spoken with people who adopted legally and with others who adopted on the black market, and the striking aspect of their stories is that those who used the black market had no easier time of it than those who located an infant elsewhere. The major difference was cost.

Some agencies also profit outrageously in infant adoptions. In 1981 one Canadian-based agency was charging its American customers a flat fee of $17,840. It is an incredible price, but applicants received a form letter with this telling passage: "The biggest difference is that with [us], *it is you, the adoptive parents, who are represented* in your search for a child, rather than an orphan or abandoned child being represented in its search for a good home. . . ." Such an appeal feeds directly on the confusions and misunderstandings created by the collapse of the traditional system. It implies that everywhere else in the adoption world, families are having to settle for whatever kind of child they can get.

One writer about adoption, a clinical psychologist who really ought to have known better, argued, "Selling babies would not work if there was not a need and demand for these services. People are quick to criticize the people involved in selling babies, but . . . if it is meeting a need and no one is hurt, why not sell babies?" Described this way it sounds almost as though the baby market represented free enterprise at its idyllic best.

There is plenty of reason to object to the idea that no one is hurt when babies are sold. The exchange of money is not, of itself, a bad thing. A very likely change in adoption during the 1980s will be that the open payment of money to mothers by agencies will be allowed—payments for expenses, medical costs, and perhaps even some form of "recuperation allowance." Many perfectly legal private adoptions already include such costs, but when a transaction includes the payment of something extra—the baby's price tag—because "after all, there is a baby shortage," a poisonous element enters the process. At this point the baby becomes a commodity. The change is purely subjective, but then, families are subjective institutions. Not many people can pay $10,000 or $15,000 for an item and not have that price tag affect their vision of what they have bought. Families are built on love and experience. They cost a lot of money to maintain, but fortunately most people still understand that families cannot be bought. By turning babies into properties, the black market is eroding families, not helping to create them.

Because the adoption maze contains so many traps, a successful search requires a plan of action. The one described in this book is reasonably direct:
• Begin by selecting a strategy best suited to your family needs and situation (chapter 3).
• Locate a parent organization (chapter 6).

- Contact all possible intermediaries (chapters 6–10).
- Once a child has been found, obtain legal approval of the adoption (chapters 11–13).

The energy to carry you through all these steps must come from the strength of your own motivation. You must find within yourself the willingness to stick with it, even though the process is not easy. There are bound to be periods of profound discouragement. I know one couple who eventually adopted the infant boy they had been looking for, but it took them years, and at one point they simply stopped trying. A year passed, and they began again only after being encouraged by a parents' group. Yet in the end they found a child.

The difference between moving through a system and finding your way through a maze is in the ease of passage. The old adoption system moved automatically. Applicants hooked in to an agency and progressed steadily toward their goal. At the end they had become parents, but it was the adoption system itself that seemed to be the star of the show. It created families. The individual children and the adults who had been brought together seemed to be mere details in a larger process.

A maze, however, is not so readily mastered, and anybody who gets all the way through it deserves a hero's medal. No aspect of adoption has moved me more than the heroic energies of the adoptive parents I have met. The reality and power of love is a visible presence in their world. Looking back on their efforts, even the parents are surprised at themselves. A sentiment I have heard many times is "I knew I had enough love in me, but I was surprised by my stamina."

In contrast with the determination of the parents is the helpless desperation of the children. Many are born and sucked instantly into a terrifying system. The old agency-centered system provided families only for healthy newborns. Cumbersome as the current adoption process is, it is doing better by the children. Many who used to be ignored are now finding homes. Some of them have severe handicaps, but most of them have simply been unlucky. They are the ones who are not retarded, not handicapped, not even neurotic, but because of their parents' problems, they have found themselves trapped in a morass of welfare rules and legal indifference. It is a lucky child who can escape repeated observation by social workers without having some unflattering diagnosis appended to her dossier. Recently these unlucky children have been finding families and moving out of the welfare system into permanent homes.

Is adoption worth the labor? It must be. I have listened to many people describe what labor they went through in order to adopt, but when they reach the end, the speakers smile and often say they expect to adopt again. They have found out that, hard as the work is, they can do it. So can you.

Useful Books

Although there are mountains of books and articles about adoption, very few of them focus on the concerns of people thinking about adoption. Some helpful ones are:

Baker, Nancy C. *Baby Selling: The Scandal of Black Market Adoptions.* New York: Vanguard Press, 1978.

Day, Dawn. *The Adoption of Black Children.* Lexington, Mass.: D.C. Heath, Lexington Books, 1979.

Erichsen, Jean and Heine. *Gamins: How to Adopt from Latin America.* Minneapolis, Minn.: Dillon Press, 1980.

Jewett, Claudia. *Adopting the Older Child.* Harvard, Mass.: Harvard Common Press, 1978.

Kravik, Patricia, ed. *Adopting Children with Special Needs.* Washington, D.C.: North American Council on Adoptable Children, 1976.

Ladner, Joyce A. *Mixed Familes: Adopting across Racial Boundaries.* New York: Doubleday, Anchor Books, 1978.

Menning, Barbara Eck. *Infertility: A Guide for the Childless Couple.* Englewood Cliffs, N.J.: Prentice-Hall, 1977.

Van Why, Elizabeth Wharton. *Adoption Bibliography and Multi-Ethnic Sourcebook.* Hartford: Open Door Society of Connecticut, 1977.

3

How *You* Can Adopt

Even in the old days no single approach to adoption worked best for everybody. Today it is even more complicated, and people's stories about their ultimate success usually reflect this bewildering tangle. The purpose of this chapter is to help adoptive parents bypass the floundering stage and lead them directly to the strategy most suitable to their needs.

Some readers will already know whom they want to adopt, for most adoptions do not involve unrelated strangers. Relatives take in orphans; stepparents adopt their stepchildren; fathers legitimize out-of-wedlock children. These cases which compose the majority of adoptions, are discussed in the section of this chapter "Adoptions Through Established Ties" (see page 48). Foster parents hoping to adopt their foster children should see chapter 15.

If you do not have a particular child in mind, the focus of your strategy will be on finding an adoptable child. Before doing anything else, then, you must decide what sort of child you would be willing to adopt. Most people come to adoption with the thought of adopting a healthy baby of their own race and background; however, waiting children come from so many cultures and groups that people deprive themselves of many opportunities if they do not at least consider what they want from an adoption. Some people find that their initial impulse was correct, while others realize they would be perfectly happy, or maybe even happier, with an older, foreign-born, or handicapped child. The strategy that is best for you will depend on the sort of child you hope to adopt.

Because the adoption world is always changing, you should keep up to date with developments. In the list "Sources for Current Information" at the end of this chapter, you will find subscription services available to families hoping to adopt. Every family should subscribe to *OURS* magazine; each issue has many articles written by members of adopting families and gives a broad picture of contemporary adoptions. Other sources of adoption information are also important, but they are more specialized in their appeal.

Traditional Clients

Different approaches work best for different people. The simplest strategies are open to those people who were traditionally served by adoption agencies; however, only a minority of families meet the traditional criteria. To be considered a traditional client, you must satisfy the following eight requirements:

1. Traditional agency clients are couples who have been married for several years. They have demonstrated their commitment to the family through their marriage and its stability. If either member of the couple was previously divorced, the reason for the divorce cannot have implied that family commitment took second place to some other interest.

2. Traditional clients are financially well off. The husband's income is sufficient to promise that a child could be raised in a comfortable home and without material deprivation. If the wife is working, she is planning to give up her job once she adopts a baby or, if she adopts an older child, to cut back on her work hours. Her focus is on raising the family while her husband provides the income.

3. Good health is also important. Traditional clients are healthy enough to expect to live the full three score years plus ten. There should be no reason to wonder if both parents will still be on hand when their child's high-school graduation arrives. Physical disabilities, weight problems, and chronic diseases are not welcome.

4. Both members of the couple should be under forty.

5. Educational background is strong. Usually traditional clients have a college education; they should definitely be culturally aware and reasonably articulate.

6. The traditional applicants are churchgoers, or else they can explain the moral "structure" they plan to give their child.

7. Bluntly put, traditional clients were also white, but these days that ugly rule is not enforced as readily. If they are traditional in all other respects, nonwhite clients can be considered traditional clients so long as they restrict their search to children of their own racial background.

8. If the applicants hope to adopt a healthy infant of their own race, there is one further criterion. Traditional clients are biologically infertile. Traditional clients are not so deeply committed to theories of zero population growth that they are willing to forego becoming biological parents. Vasectomies and tubal ligations are not acceptable explanations for infertility unless there was a medical reason for them.

If one or more of these points do not apply to you, the strategy best suited to your situation is described in the following section, "Untraditional Clients." If you are a traditional client, you have only one further question to ask yourself: Why do you wish to adopt?

In the old days, the adoption system was designed specifically to serve traditional clients who had no children and who wanted healthy babies of their own race and background. Today it is so much more difficult to adopt that traditional clients ought to examine their ambitions closely. If you are a traditional client, chances are that you can adopt quickly if you are willing to adopt either an older child or a foreign-born infant. If you decide that only a healthy newborn American will do, the "Step by Step" section on page 61 outlines the basic strategy you should pursue. Your primary focus should be on agency or independent adoption. You may find that some agencies are willing to work with you although they refuse to accept applications from other families; however, this advantage is only partial, because many agencies no longer restrict themselves to traditional applicants.

If you are the traditional type of agency client but do not wish to adopt a healthy newborn American, you are likely to have the easiest time of it. All the people I know who have straightforward stories about recent adoptions fall into this category. They wanted a Korean infant, or an older child, or a biracial one—something different from the newborn who looks just like them. You may need to do no more than contact the best-known agency in your area and describe the child you are seeking. Usually the process is not quite that simple, but the strategy is reasonably direct: (1) contact your local parent association and discuss your desires; (2) use an agency if at all possible. Most agencies were established to serve people with your background, and despite the many changes of the past dozen years, they are still most comfortable with clients who fit that background. Some agencies will rather blatantly favor you over less traditional clients.

Untraditional Clients

If you are like most people, you did not get all the way through the list of traditional characteristics without finding a detail or two that eliminated you. That finding carries both bad news and better news. The bad news is that adoption is going to be harder for you than it will be for some other people. The better news is that today adoption is possible. Before 1968 few people in your situation could have much hope of adopting at all; now, if you persist, you can adopt the child you want.

To select the right strategy for you, first determine what kind of child you want to adopt. You must also consider how you differ from a traditional agency client (see the chart "Adoption Strategies for Untraditional Clients").

Social status (strategies A and B). If your social status is untraditional, your primary difficulty is that you are competing with many equally qualified families. The director of a small midwestern agency once said to me, "We get four-hundred inquiries a year and ninety-five percent of those families would provide perfectly fine homes for the children." The trouble is that the agency has only thirty healthy infants available each year. In other words, that agency, which serves primarily a rural and small-town populace, gets enough calls in a single year to keep its waiting list full for the next thirteen years. Some agencies reduce the competition by maintaining "good standards," as they put it, refusing to serve most untraditional applicants. Other agencies acknowledge that you don't have to be rich to create a good family, but they end up in the position of the director I quoted; they are overwhelmed with qualified applicants. Thus, the agencies that will work with your family already have a long list of families ahead of you.

This same situation applies to almost every other intermediary you might approach. Independent and international adoption routes that are available to you are also crowded with a lot of other people. Indeed, even if you were to decide to try an illegal adoption, you would find that the black market also has an enormously long waiting list and will not provide speedy service.

Adoption Strategies for
Untraditional Clients

	(I) I want to adopt *(circle one)*	
	a healthy newborn	all other children
(II) I am an untraditional agency client because of my 1. *social status*	A	B
2. *religious or ethnic background*	C	D
3. *personal situation*	E	

1. *Social status.* People in this group are untraditional clients because they do not satisfy at least one of the requirements involving working wives, family income, or educational background. If you meet all the other requirements of a traditional client, select strategy A or B on page 36–40.

2. *Religious or ethnic background.* Religious minority, black, Hispanic, Indian, and Oriental peoples who do not have the social standing of traditional agency clients do best if they pursue a strategy that focuses more on their background than on their social status. Select either strategy C or D on page 40–44.

3. *Personal situation.* This catchall category of personal situation includes single people, families who are not biologically infertile, people over forty, gays, nonchurchgoers, and just about anybody else who does not fall into one of the two other categories. See strategy E on page 44–48.

Everyone wanting to adopt in your group, including those looking for an older child, has to prepare for a long-term effort. You cannot expect to accomplish your adoption quickly. Because the process will take so long, you ought to be especially alert to changes in the adoption picture. I recommend that everyone use parent associations and the subscription services listed under "Sources for Current Information" at the end of this chapter; they are especially important for people in your group. They will keep you posted on new adoption sources that may appear after you have begun your quest. They can also alert you to any changes at established sources.

The most painful part of the search is the length of time needed to locate a child. Some readers will be lucky and have a child within six months of reading this chapter, but for most it will take much longer. If you hope to adopt a healthy white baby, it may take as long as five years. It may take as long as two years to locate other children, although a year or a year and a half is more likely.

To maintain a search that can last for years, you have to avoid turning your quest into an obsession. The point of an adoption is to enrich your life, not make it an endless cause for complaint. Persistence does not mean that every moment must be focused on adoption. Pick a weekday—say, Wednesday—and make that "Adoption Progress Day." That day can be the one you use to contact agencies and other sources. If you can keep up that pace for as many Wednesdays as it takes, you will be able to boast of your persistence and still keep from reducing your life to an unending struggle to adopt.

Strategy A. I have spoken with many adoptive parents who finally succeeded in adopting infants. Their stories have a recognizable pattern: the family set forth naively thinking that it would not take long and then they began to encounter reality. Agencies either turned them away or put their names at the end of a waiting list. They grew frustrated and desperate. They tried everything they could think of, and when they had just about given up all hope, a miracle happened and a baby became available to them. Your purpose, in a nutshell, is to increase the possibilities of miracles.

Tell everyone you know that you are hoping to find a baby. Persist, persist, persist. People who try to take the adoption maze by storm soon grow tired and discouraged, but if you just keep working, you will win over the long run. If you have already approached every knowledgeable person and agency in your area, call them again.

Contact a parent association. It can give you an indication of the adoption possibilities in your area and can serve as a continuing source of contacts in the adoption world. It can also make you a full member of your local adoption community, and as new sources of infant adoption become available, you will learn of them before the ten thousand other searching families in your area.

Contact agencies. Some agencies keep open waiting lists and will immediately add your name. Others reserve their lists for approved applicants. Contact any open-list agencies in your area right away. The sooner you call them, the sooner they will get back to you. A more patient approach is necessary with reserved list agencies. Call a couple of them each week. When you have contacted all the agencies in your immediate area, search for others that will place children in your town. If you live in a large state, there may be agencies in other parts of the state that are willing to work with you. If you live near a giant state such as Texas or New York, agencies there may be willing to place children across state boundaries.

At the same time, cultivate and promote independent contacts. This independent search should go on while you try to woo an agency. International possibilities should also be considered, but if you insist on adopting a child with your own racial background, this route is none too promising. (See chapter 8 for information about international adoptions.)

Strategy B. Your strategy is comparable to that of a fisherman who casts, reels in, and casts again. He knows that eventually there will be a bite. The shocking truth is that today there is a child waiting to be adopted who would be a welcome member of your family. But the adoption maze is in such chaos that it may be two years before such a child arrives in your home, so be ready for a long day's casting.

The chief virtue required of a fisherman is the patient confidence born of the certainty that success must finally come. The fisherman's strategy almost inevitably leads to a few near-catches that get away. The same will be true for you. The adoption world is full of horror stories of the needy child who was not adopted, despite the wishes of a searching family.

The worst such story I have heard concerned a thirteen-year-old quadriplegic girl. One family wanted to adopt her and was not frightened by the fact that she was permanently paralyzed from the neck down; however, the adoption was barred by the girl's social worker because the girl was a Catholic and the adopting family was Mormon—as though families were lining up for this unfortunate girl. You probably won't have a story that terrible to tell, but you can expect that by the end of your search, you too will have found a child who needed you but who was not allowed to escape his predicament. What do you do then? Just keep casting. That Mormon family eventually found a child; you will too.

Because the adoption of waiting and foreign-born children is so much more difficult than it should be, ask yourself if you are willing to adopt a newborn child. (Waiting children are those caught in the welfare system.) Believe it or not, I know a number of people who were looking for waiting children but encountered such agency foot dragging that they ended up adopting infants instead. If you are willing to adopt an infant, pursue that line at the same time that you are searching for a waiting child. Use only independent and international sources in your search for an infant. If you tell an agency that you are interested in a waiting child and then say you are also interested in any newborns that become available, the agency worker is likely to suspect that you really want an infant and may refuse to help you.

For the untraditional part of your quest, your primary source will be agencies. Although it is not always easy to find an agency that is willing to help, it usually can be done. Even after you are accepted, your work is not over. You have to keep looking, trying to learn about available children, bringing particular ones to the attention of your agency worker. This repeated effort is what I mean by a strategy of casting. You learn of a child and express an interest only to discover that she has been adopted, or somebody doesn't think this child is right for you, or the way is blocked by a wall as impenetrable as it is inexplicable.

The chief means of learning about waiting children is through the various adoption exchanges and their photo books. You should go through these books fairly regularly, at least once every two months. Adoption-group newsletters often include a few listings of waiting children.

The length of time for all this casting varies, but you should be prepared for a long search. Once, while I was interviewing an agency director about the length of time required for the adoption of a waiting child, she blushed and reported that it was often four or five months before a child could be placed in the home. Though it was rude of me, I could not help but laugh at her embarrassment. In this world, four months of waiting counts as a very swift adoption.

Religious or ethnic background (strategies C and D). The distinguishing characteristic of the adoption quest for families in the category of untraditional religious or ethnic background is the limited number of available children. Nonwhites are seldom allowed to adopt white children, and non-Christians have a lot of trouble adopting Christians. There is regional variation in the ease of adoption by any particular group, depending on the size of a group's local population, the scope of local efforts to recruit adoptive minority families, and the dominant group's willingness to adopt minority children. The general situations for particular groups are:

Religious minorities. Jews, Jehovah's Witnesses, Christian Scientists, Moslems, and other members of faiths outside the standard Catholic/Protestant categories face one of the most difficult adoption situations in the country. Only a limited number of agencies will work with them. Many agencies have religious restrictions for their applicants, and even those that do not are suspicious of unusual faiths. Groups that put limits on the medical care their members can receive undergo particularly harsh scrutiny. A Jehovah's Witness said to me, "I go in there [to the agency] to discuss a child and all she [the worker] wants to talk about is religion."

Further complications are state laws that impede the placing of children across religious lines. Infants are commonly labeled Catholic, Protestant, or Jewish, and a family who does not fit neatly into one of those categories is at a disadvantage. States without such laws do not necessarily make matters easier. Texas has no such law, but most agencies there will not accept Jewish applicants. The adoption director of a "Christians only" agency told me she has placed a number of Jewish infants with Christian families.

Of course, any children of minority religions who become available for adoption may be placed in the homes of parents of matching religion, but these children are not available in numbers proportional to their population. For these groups, the problem of finding available infants is much older than the general crisis. They must explore independent and international routes if they hope to find babies.

If you are interested in adopting a waiting child, you have two possibilities: your parent association may help find an agency that will work with you (commonly a public agency) or you can use your church connections. Because this problem is common to the whole religion, church officials have often developed a service to help resolve it. The Greek Orthodox church has been especially energetic in finding Orthodox homes for Orthodox children.

Blacks. The situation is contradictory. On the one hand, there is a large national effort under way to recruit black families for adoption. (See "Information Sources for Black Families" at the end of this chapter.) Many of the waiting children are black, and few nonblack families would adopt them, even if they were allowed to do so. (Many agencies specifically forbid such adoptions.) These facts suggest that black families should have an easy time trying to adopt, but logic has little to do with anything as human as adoption. Few agencies are sympathetic to black families who are not solidly middle class. Most social workers have no experience with or understanding of black families, and despite their pretensions to scientific training, the workers are thoroughly subjective in their consideration of families. Thus, formal adoption for blacks, as for everybody else, is more difficult than it should be.

The availability of black babies varies considerably. In some areas, such as the Northeast, black families have as hard a time finding a black newborn as whites have finding a white infant. In other areas— Colorado is a good example—black babies can be found quickly. Infant girls are always more sought after than infant boys, especially black infant boys. In a number of states, families who insist on adopting a newborn girl find that they face a long wait, while infant black boys are classified as hard to place and go begging for homes. Whenever you call an agency about an infant, be sure the agency understands that you want a black infant. Agencies have turned callers away because they assumed the callers were white and were asking about white infants.

Very few black families seem to have turned to international adoptions to find infants. It is a route to consider. There are a lot of black and black-Indian children in the Caribbean and Latin America. Predictably, these children are the ones least likely to be adopted by white Americans who adopt internationally. There are no regular adoption connections with Africa. Of course, a question about the morality of adopting abroad arises when so many black children in America are in need of adoption. A similar question occurs among whites, but I believe that as long as the American adoption scene remains in its present chaotic state, it is pure fantasy to suppose that your adoption is a contribution to society. You are helping yourself and one child, not rescuing America. If the idea of an international adoption attracts you, proceed with a clear conscience.

Older black children can be adopted reasonably quickly, if you approach the matter carefully, following these guidelines: (1) check the list "Information Sources for Black Families" and contact one of the sources named; if there are no local offices in your area, the national offices on the list can help; (2) contact a local parent organization; by and large, these are white-run groups, and some of them have very limited acquaintance with black families, but most of them know about waiting black children and know which agencies have the best track record in placing them; (3) having gotten a picture of your local situation, begin contacting agencies.

Hispanic. The outlook for Hispanic families varies considerably, depending on the region. There is even a lot of arguing over whether such an ethnic group exists. In New York City, the notion of a separate Hispanic identity is firmly implanted in official adoption circles, but I have seen Hispanic applicants storm out of orientation meetings, deeply insulted by the idea that they were to be lumped into some special category. In practice, this category does offer protection to specific groups in certain regions. In New York, Florida, Texas, and California, a number of Hispanic children enter the foster-care system or are given up for adoption. If families are judged in the traditional way, most of these children would be adopted by financially successful "Anglo" families (to use the Texan term). The addition of an extra label allows Puerto Rican, Cuban, and Mexican communities to ensure that there is not a continual movement of their young population toward an Anglo culture and that Hispanic families who want to adopt are not denied a fair opportunity.

American Indian. Any American Indian families who cannot find a waiting Indian child in their area should contact agencies in the plains states. South Dakota especially has a catastrophic number of waiting Indian children who, by federal law, can only be placed in Indian homes. The Rocky Mountain Adoption Exchange in Colorado is another good source of information (see the list "Regional Adoption Exchanges" at the end of chapter 9). You can also contact the native American Program and Referral Services of Jewish Family and Children's Services, 2033 North Seventh Street, Phoenix, Arizona 85006. Telephone: (602) 257-1904.

Indian infants are another story. If local agencies and independent sources cannot help you, you should consider an international adoption. Many Indian infants are adopted from Latin America.

Oriental. The situation for Oriental adoptions would probably be even tighter than it is for religious minorities were it not for one thing: there are good international connections for finding Oriental children, both infant and older. Pursue the international route.

Strategy C. Despite the great differences in the needs and prospects for different ethnic groups, certain strategies for finding an infant are common among them. If the typical local agencies are unwilling or unable to serve you, there should be a specialized source that focuses on your group. Parent associations usually do not focus on ethnic needs, but they may have heard about some useful sources. In many cases, international sources for adoption are particularly promising. Many countries that are unwilling to allow their children to be placed in American homes change their attitude when a child is to be adopted by a family with ethnic ties to those countries. For example, Irish-Americans can sometimes adopt children born in Ireland. Your first step is to locate promising sources—chiefly international and domestic agencies—and then follow the process outlined in chapter 5.

Strategy D. Waiting children are often considered hard to place specifically because of their ethnic background. You should make as much use as possible of the adoption-exchange listings (discussed in chapter 9). You are like someone looking for a pearl in a mountain of rubies. There are not as many pearls on hand, but because everyone else insists on getting a ruby, you will be more quickly helped. I know of many families in this situation who were speedily successful. It is almost guaranteed that right at this moment there are several children from your ethnic background waiting to be adopted. The trick is finding them; the closest one may be five states away. Contact as many adoption exchanges as you can.

Personal situation (strategy E). In recalling how she became a single adoptive parent, Faith Dorian told me that the idea suddenly came to her in the form of a question. She said she had never supposed adoption was even possible for her until she read about a single woman in California who had adopted. "I suddenly asked myself, 'Why not me?'" During the past dozen years a lot of people who previously were denied all chance of adoption have wondered "Why not me?" and many kinds of families are now being formed that previously would never have been considered.

Single people. Probably the largest new group of adoptive parents are unmarried ones. The idea, however, is a lot more popular with singles than it is with agencies. Some agencies will not accept applications from single people, no matter what sort of child they are seeking. Many agencies will accept your application if you are waiting for a hard-to-place child. Almost no agency will accept an application if you are looking for an infant. Indeed, I would say flatly that no agency will accept your application, except that I do know of a few agency placements of black infants with single black women. The best information source for you is the Committee for Single Adoptive Parents (see the list "Sources for Current Information" at the end of the chapter).

Almost all agency workers agree that singles do not want babies. There is plenty of evidence to the contrary, but the idea is the received dogma of agencies and it harmonizes conveniently with the fact that agencies have no intention of placing infants in single-parent homes. If you wish to adopt a baby or a toddler, you are going to have to adopt either independently or internationally, probably the latter. (To adopt internationally, single parents must be at least twenty-five years old.) The international scene keeps changing, of course. At one time, many single parents were adopting Korean children, but now Korea has barred such adoptions. These days the majority of single-parent adoptions of babies and preschoolers originate in Latin America.

If you are interested in adopting a waiting child, your basic strategy is simple: contact a local parent association and find out about single-parent adoptions in your area; persuade an agency to work with you; seek out waiting children through the adoption exchanges. This approach is the same as that of a couple looking for a waiting child, but for single parents there are usually more difficulties to be overcome. Although single-parent families are nothing new to society, agency attitudes bring all kinds of distortions into the single person's quest for a child. Even though one-fifth of all American families today are single-parent families, you have to convince a worker that you can be a real parent, capable of real love.

Male applicants have an even more difficult time getting an agency to take them seriously. On the old TV show, Ozzie used to run down to the malt shop while Harriet stayed on watch back home. Agencies want to be sure that male applicants won't keep dashing off to some malt shop. They speculate freely about the motives of a male who wants to become an adoptive father, yet once an agency decides to work with a man, the commitment to help often seems more profound than that shown to single women applicants. Single men must make a particularly strong effort to overcome an agency's initial resistance to their applications, but once accepted, males often discover that their agency workers are eager to help. Single women find it relatively easy to be accepted by an agency, but they must then work hard to avoid having their cases drift aimlessly for a long time.

Almost every agency that is willing to consider a single person's application will want to know about backup support, particularly about the extended family. Agencies like to hear that there is a brother or sister on hand who is eager to act as a baby-sitter. If there is no family member close by, there ought to be a good friend. It doesn't do much good to challenge agencies on this issue by pointing out that they don't worry about how married couples are going to find baby-sitters. Agencies push for a clear answer on this issue.

Sexuality is another matter confronting single parents, and it is a real catch-22. If you have an active sex life, then your suitability as a model parent is certainly suspect. On the other hand, if you lead a life of perfect chastity, the worker may doubt your ability to form warm and intimate bonds. Here is an area where men have an advantage over women. A man who says "Yes, I have a girl friend, but if she objects to my adoption, she can lump it" gets a smile from agency workers, while a woman applicant who says her boyfriend can like it or lump it gets a doubting look.

The answers most favorably received are, yes, you do go out, but at the moment there is no one special, or if there is someone special whom you see frequently, you maintain separate apartments. In most jurisdictions, cohabiting or common-law couples are not allowed to adopt.

Previously divorced or separated couples. The traditional adoptive couple has had a stable marriage for several years and has never been divorced. These days previous divorce is more acceptable, but most agencies will want to take a hard look at what happened, in the hope of being sure it won't happen again. If you hope to adopt an infant but have only been married a short time, you will have to adopt either independently or internationally. Some of the more imaginative agencies will agree to put you on the waiting list immediately, knowing that by the time it can place an infant in your home, you will be an old married couple.

Separated couples usually cannot adopt. Courts want to see either a successful marriage or a single parent. Naturally, people often try to hide the fact of separation, but the truth is usually uncovered. Most agencies react to the discovery by withdrawing all offer of services and, if a child has been placed in the home, by reclaiming him. I do know of an agency that learned the truth and helped arrange a package deal—divorce plus a single-parent adoption—but don't count on being given that kind of assistance.

Nonchurchgoers. There are many agencies that will flatly turn you away if you don't attend a church. Other agencies are willing to work with you if you are articulate enough to explain your moral philosophy and your plans to "socialize" any child you adopt. If you plan to adopt through an agency, you have two choices: either restrict yourself to the agencies that will work with you or join a church.

Disabled parents. The most effective way to get past agency prejudices against the disabled is to turn them around. For example, agencies are very reluctant to place a healthy child in the home of a dwarf, but they will freely place a dwarf in that home. If analyzed logically, the thinking behind such behavior reduces itself to a very ugly set of principles, but prejudice is not based on logic. Many of these prejudices can be handled this way: the blind adopt the blind, the deaf the deaf, and even people with a shortened life expectancy can sometimes adopt children with serious health problems.

In the case of families where the father is in a wheelchair, adoption is unlikely unless the father has a successful professional career. If the mother is in a wheelchair, almost no agency will be interested in your application. Your best hope is in finding a very good parent group with a most sympathetic agency contact.

Older parents. If you are over forty and looking for an infant, you will almost certainly have to adopt internationally or independently. Agencies may agree that you are vigorous now, but they will wonder what you will be like when the child is sixteen.

Homosexuals. You may have read in the newspapers about acknowledged homosexuals being allowed to adopt. These stories make the papers because they are less common than moon walks. You will have to pioneer your own strategy here. Very few agencies will work with you, and they will probably accept your application only if you hope to adopt a terribly hard to place waiting child. No matter which route you follow, in the end you are going to have to persuade a judge to endorse your adoption. It won't be easy.

Families with other children. If you have other children and want to adopt a healthy infant, you are going to have to find an independent or international source. The one exception to this rule is if you have one other child who was adopted as an infant. Traditionally, adoption agencies expected to place two children in a family, and some of the more conservative agencies have maintained that custom despite the great decline in available infants. These agencies will place a second infant with you if they placed the first one. Otherwise, you cannot expect to find a healthy infant through an agency. Hard-to-place infants, of course, are a different matter.

If you want to adopt older children, agencies will be quite willing to work with you. Your children will be included in the study process, and if they are of school age, their attitudes toward the prospective adoption will be given a lot of weight. As a general rule, agencies like to place older children with families that already have children, as long as the new child will not become the oldest child in the family. The theory is that people who have experience at being parents are more likely to know what they are getting into when they try to adopt. (It's a theory open to some question. Your adopted child may place a whole new set of demands on you.)

Zero population growth. If you are fertile but want to adopt because you believe adoption is preferable to biological reproduction, almost no agency will place a baby with you. You will almost certainly have to adopt internationally or independently or adopt a waiting child.

Adoptions Through Established Ties.

The easiest and most common adoptions are adoptions of relatives and stepchildren. Typically you seek out a lawyer, explain your desire, and have the lawyer initiate a routine court procedure. Some states require an evaluation by a social worker; some do not. The one common difficulty comes from other relatives, who may raise objections.

Precisely because it is so easy, adoption within families often gets little of the thought it should. There is a controversy in professional adoption circles about adoption by relatives. The most important issue is the thinking that leads people to seek such adoptions. While there are many practical reasons for adopting a child who is already part of the family, there may be a lot of destructive motives as well. Often the adoption is a symbolic action, a quest for a "real family" just like the one everyone else's family is imagined to be.

Stepfamily adoptions. Stepfamily adoptions are the most common and most controversial of all adoptions. Among the many reasons given in favor of them are: (1) they give the stepparent the legal authority to act as a parent, enabling her to sign medical consent forms, driver's license applications, and the like; (2) they assure family stability in case of the death of the biological parent (stepparents have no legal standing in custody controversies, and if the biological parent dies, the stepparent is likely to lose all contact with the surviving children); (3) they are a public demonstration of a personal commitment and affection. The process can be quite important to the adoptive children, helping to resolve their doubts about their situations and to provide emotional security, just as marriage can for adults.

The objection is that stepparent adoptions can be crude attempts to transform the family structure into a more standard Ozzie-and-Harriet form. There are two basic sources of extra tension in the stepfamily. First, the child has known one adult longer than the other, and all involved may feel the unevenness of this relationship. The other issue is loyalty. A child may feel like the worst kind of traitor if he accepts a new parent in place of the old. Taking a new last name often makes the process even more discomforting. The complex issues of stepfamilies are presented in *Making It as a Stepfamily: New Rules, New Roles* by Claire Berman (New York: Doubleday, 1980).

Stepparent adoptions are usually simple legal processes. See a lawyer. In most cases, if the biological parent is still living, he or she will have to consent. However, in some jurisdictions the consent of a divorced parent with no custody rights is not required. That rule has such painful ramifications that the situation ought to be thoroughly discussed with both a lawyer and the biological parent before the rule is invoked. The legal procedure from petition to final decree is described in chapter 11.

Relative adoptions. Adoptions by relatives can be very easy or insanely difficult. It is important to have legal guardianship over any relatives you raise. This status gives you the legal powers and responsibilities of a parent. Formal adoption, complete with court decree, may seem unnecessary and even distasteful. Whether you obtain guardian status or seek a full adoption, you will be taking a legal step that calls for a lawyer.

The simplest adoptions involve orphans whose parents named close relatives as the children's guardians. These adoptions are slightly more complicated if there is no such clause in the will and one has to establish a relationship in court.

The situation grows even more complex if the children fall into the care of the public welfare system before you can bring them into your home. If the welfare office is unsympathetic, you may need a lawyer's help before you can receive the children.

The matter becomes a legal and psychological nightmare if the biological parents are still alive. The process involves a termination of parental rights. (See chapter 13.)

Illegitimate children. If a father wants to acknowledge paternity and responsibility for his illegitimate children, the process is easy. Indeed, if all adoptions were as easy as legitimating a child, this book would be a magazine article. The father simply declares that he is the father. In some states you don't even have to go to court—a newspaper advertisement will serve. The hardest state is California, where, if the father is married, his wife must consent to the legitimation.

Sources for Current Information

OURS magazine
20140 Pine Ridge Drive
Anoka, Minn. 55303
$11, one year; $19, two years; $27, three years

OURS is published by a parent group focusing on international adoptions. This bimonthly magazine is full of accounts of recent adoptions. These reports are usually written by the parents during the euphoric period shortly after the child's arrival, but they are still informative and, taken as a whole, the magazine provides a strong sense of what is going on right now in the world of adoptions. Even if there is no *OURS* group in your area, the periodical is still worth subscribing to.

Committee for Single Adoptive Parents
P.O. Box 4074
Washington, D.C. 20015
$10 membership (18 months)

Members of this committee are sent a list of sources for single-parent adoptions, and periodically (approximately every six months) they receive updated listings. The committee also sells a *Handbook for Single Adoptive Parents.*

International Concerns Committee for Children
911 Cypress Drive
Boulder, Colo. 80303
$5 donation

This committee publishes a directory of foreign-adoption resources that lists adoption agencies and agents in the United States plus a mountain of current information about countries where babies are available, including waiting time, costs, and local laws. There is also some information about adopting older foreign-born children. This basic list is updated nine times a year.

Information Sources for Black Families

NATIONAL

National Black Child Development Institute, 1463 Rhode Island Avenue, N.W., Washington, D.C. 20005. (202) 387-1281

National Urban League, Attention: JoAnne Dixon, 500 East Sixty-second Street, New York, N.Y. 10021. (202) 310-9000

LOCAL (arranged by state)

Black Family Adoption Outreach Unit, Arkansas Social Service, 1700 West Thirteenth Street, Little Rock, Ark. 72202

Tayari Project, San Diego Department of Public Welfare, 4235 National Avenue, San Diego, Calif. 92113

Open Arms Adoption Project, P.O. Box 15254, San Francisco, Calif. 94115

Denver Minority Parents, 3144 Gaylord Street, Denver, Colo. 80205

Black Adoption Program and Services of Kansas Children's Service League, 1125 North Fifth Street, Kansas City, Kans. 66101

St. Augustine's Center, 1600 Fillmore Avenue, Buffalo, N.Y. 14211

Nassau/Suffolk Adopt Black Children Association, 15 North Franklin Street, Hempstead, N.Y. 11550

COAC Black Child Advocacy Program, 875 Avenue of the Americas, New York, N.Y. 10001

Black Adoption Task Force, P.O. Box 21542, Greensboro, N.C. 27406

Akiba Homes for Black Children, 1225 Lauton Street, Akron, Ohio 44320

Rhode Island Urban League Recruitment Project, 246 Prairie Avenue, Providence, R.I. 02905

South Carolina Black Adoption Committee, P.O. Box 2516, Columbia, S.C. 29202

Advocacy for Black Adoption, P.O. Box 26262, Dallas, Tex. 75226

Adopt Black Children Committee, 8602 Allwood, Houston, Tex. 77016

4

Adoption Around the Country

Local peculiarities of law or custom will force some readers to modify the strategies outlined in the preceding chapter. Adoption is a state matter, and the states disagree about how to proceed. In some states independent adoptions are barred. International adoptions can also be legally difficult. The federal government has developed a model act that, in theory, all states could pass, but in practice it merely serves as a classic illustration of what goes wrong when laws are proposed by social theorists rather than by politicians. The act has no constituency and will probably never be passed by a single state. As long as there is such confusion, some strategies for adopting may not be easy or even possible for certain readers.

These regional issues show how sharply adoption cuts into everyday life. It forces people to ask themselves where they stand with regard to particular families and specific children. Everybody everywhere is for the idea of the family, but there are bitter disputes about which real families are desirable. Everybody is pro-child, but controversy quickly arises when the interests of an individual child seem to collide with legal precedent, or with social theory, or with professional prestige, or with the desires of a particular family.

These rival attitudes have blocked a national consensus on how to respond to the recent changes in adoption. Individual states have often been quite imaginative: South Carolina created the first citizens' review board to try and cut through many of the bureaucratic issues that prevent waiting children from being adopted; Iowa developed a way of controlling independent adoption without promoting the black market; New York introduced subsidized adoptions to help in the adoption of waiting children. All these reforms have drawn a lot of praise and done a great deal to help families, but they have been slow to spread. Not many state officials have much of a sense of what is happening outside their own jurisdictions. Indeed, once as I was concluding an interview, a state official expressed her unhappiness at the thought that readers of this book might learn about what is happening in other states.

With fifty states and fifty separate sets of laws that change as often as tide levels, it is impossible to be on top of every regional, state, and county idiosyncrasy. Be sure you learn about the peculiarities and possibilities in your state. The list "State Adoption Offices" at the end of this chapter identifies the office responsible for enforcing and interpreting the adoption laws in each state. These offices often have pamphlets explaining the state laws. At the very least they can supply copies of the laws themselves.

In an effort to help organize the adoption community, the federal government's Adoption Reform Act of 1978 established ten regional Adoption Resource Centers. The primary task of each center was to identify the resources—parent groups, information exchanges, agency programs—of an area and to encourage their further development. Each of the centers developed a directory of the resources in its region. These directories are as invaluable to the field of adoption as phone books are to telephone users. Borrow a copy from your parent group, an agency, or the center itself and study it. Jot down all listings that look promising.

When the centers were established, they were expected to be long-term facilities; however, recent changes in the federal budget have made their future uncertain. Their operation has been combined with that of several other child-welfare projects, and overall funding has been reduced. The list "Family Resource Centers" at the end of this chapter gives the locations of these centers.

During the past dozen years, state responses to changing adoption conditions have focused almost entirely on the matter of waiting children. Practically nothing has been done to help families who are searching for infants, and very few politicians have taken up the cause of families hoping to adopt. The sharpest regional differences seem to concern the tension between the hopes of families and the procedures of adoption professionals.

Independent adoptions. Adoption bureaucracies are agreed that independent routes, which are largely outside their control, are undesirable. Some states absolutely forbid them. For years only Delaware and Connecticut outlawed nonagency adoptions, but during the 1970s, as independent adoption became the major way of locating infants, many more states passed laws against it. Often the effect of these laws is to bar infant adoptions by untraditional families. In Connecticut, for example, agencies have some of the most elite standards in the nation, and families who would be served routinely by an agency in the Midwest find they cannot get through the front door. Apart from moving, there is little to be done for those who wish to adopt American infants. Families in these states who cannot persuade an agency to help them may adopt internationally or adopt waiting children. They can also arrange independent adoptions in a state with no residence requirement. Too often, though, this last choice means giving business to racketeers.

International adoptions. Many states have a strong feeling that local children are to be preferred over outside ones. Michigan has the oldest tradition of making the adoption of out-of-state children difficult, and Wisconsin still has the toughest law on international adoptions, even though it has been liberalized recently. Readers who live in states that make international adoptions difficult have two choices if they wish to persist. They can take the extra time and spend the extra money necessary to complete the adoption abroad. If a family can gain a legal document good enough to persuade the federal government to let the child into the country, the state cannot bar her admission. The other choice is to establish residence in some other state and complete the adoption there, but it is not easy to establish residence for purposes of an international adoption.

Studies. Almost every adoption ultimately requires an evaluation of the adopting family. These studies are made by licensed social workers and are a routine part of every agency adoption; even if you do not adopt through an agency, a study is required. For an international adoption, a study is necessary before a foreign child can be given a visa to enter the United States. Independent adoptions cannot be settled until a court receives word that the study has been completed and the family has been approved. In many parts of the United States, especially in rural areas, families hoping to adopt from abroad or independently find major difficulties in locating a licensed professional to conduct the necessary study. The problem is acute in the farmland of Pennsylvania, in Texas, in many of the plains states, and in the desert states of the Southwest. This problem is the most serious one a family can face, because failure to complete a study is an absolute impediment to legal adoption. A solution is obvious. Adoption is a state responsibility so the states must appropriate the money necessary to support the service, but when states don't provide the funds, residents are stuck. Parent associations in these problem states devote a lot of time to trying to obtain studies for their members.

Out-of-state prejudice. Residents of many of the large-area but low-population states, such as Alaska and the Dakotas, find that it is hard to adopt children from other states because out-of-state workers fear it will be bad for a child to grow up in the wide-open spaces. A South Dakota farmer may think nothing of driving a child 150 miles for some important service, such as a hospital test, but a worker in St. Louis might be stunned by the thought. This problem can usually be overcome by making it clear in your contacts with the out-of-state worker that services are available and that traveling long distances is commonplace in your region.

State Adoption Offices

ALABAMA: *Department of Pensions and Security, Bureau of Family and Children's Services,* 64 North Union Street, Montgomery, Ala. 36130.
(205) 832-6150

ALASKA: *Department of Health and Social Services, Youth Services,* Pouch H-01, Juneau, Alaska 99811.
(907) 465-3170

ARIZONA: *Department of Economic Security, Division of Aging, Family, and Children's Services,* 1717 West Jefferson Street, P.O. Box 6123, Phoenix, Ariz. 85005.
(602) 255-3981

ARKANSAS: *Division of Social Services, Adoption Services,* P.O. Box 1437, Little Rock, Ark. 72203.
(501) 371-2207

CALIFORNIA: *Department of Social Services, Adoptions Branch,* 744 P Street, Sacramento, Calif. 95814.
(916) 445-7964

COLORADO: *Department of Social Services, Adoptions,* 1575 Sherman Street, Denver, Colo. 80203.
(303) 866-5275

CONNECTICUT: *Connecticut Adoption Resource Exchange,* 170 Sigourney Street, Hartford, Conn. 06105.
(203) 566-8742

DELAWARE: *Department of Services for Children, Youth and Their Families, Division of Child Protective Services,* 1901 North Dupont Highway, New Castle, Del. 19720.
(302) 421-6786

DISTRICT OF COLUMBIA: *Committee on Social Services, Department of Human Services and Placement Resource Branch,* 500 First Street, N.W., Washington, D.C. 20001.
(202) 727-3161

FLORIDA: *Department of Health and Rehabilitative Services, Family and Children's Services,* 1317 Winewood Boulevard, Tallahassee, Fla. 32301
(904) 488-1060

GEORGIA: *Division of Family and Children's Services,* 878 Peachtree, Atlanta, Ga. 30309.
(404) 656-6700

HAWAII: *Department of Social Services and Housing, Family and Children's Services,* P.O. Box 339, Honolulu, Hawaii 96809.
(808) 548-5846

IDAHO: *Department of Health and Welfare, Adoption,* State House, Boise, Idaho 83720.
(208) 384-3340

ILLINOIS: *Department of Children and Family Services, Office of Adoptions,* 1 North Old State Capitol Plaza, Springfield, Ill. 62706.
(312) 793-6862

INDIANA: *Division of Child Welfare, Social Services,* 141 South Meridian Street, Indianapolis, Ind. 46225.
(317) 232-5613

IOWA: *Department of Human Services, Adoptions and Foster Care,* Hoover State Office Building, Des Moines, Iowa 50319.
(515) 281-6100

KANSAS: *Department of Social Rehabilitation Services, Child Protection and Placement, Smith Wilson Building,* 2700 West Sixth Street, Topeka, Kans. 66606.
(913) 296-4652

KENTUCKY: *Cabinet for Human Resources, Department of Social Services, Adoption,* 275 East Main Street, Frankfort, Ky. 40621.
(502) 564-2136

LOUISIANA: *Department of Health and Human Resources, Adoptions,* P.O. Box 3318, Baton Rouge, La. 70821.
(504) 342-4029

MAINE: *Department of Human Services, Substitute Care,* State House, Augusta, Maine 04333.
(207) 289-2971

MARYLAND: *Maryland Adoption Resource Exchange, Social Services Administration,* 300 West Preston Street, Baltimore, Md. 21201.
(301) 576-5313

MASSACHUSETTS: *Department of Social Services, Adoption,* 150 Causeway Street, Boston, Mass. 02114.
(617) 727-0900

MICHIGAN: *Department of Social Services, Adoption,* 300 South Capital Avenue, P.O. Box 30037, Lansing, Mich. 48909.
(517) 373-3513

MINNESOTA: *Department of Social Services, Adoption Unit*, Centennial Office Building, St. Paul, Minn. 55155.
(612) 296-3740

MISSISSIPPI: *Department of Public Welfare, Adoption Unit, Social Services Department*, 515 East Amite Street, P.O. Box 352, Jackson, Miss. 39205.
(601) 354-0341

MISSOURI: *Department of Social Services, Foster Care and Adoption*, Broadway State Office Building, Jefferson City, Mo. 65102.
(314) 751-3221

MONTANA: *Department of Social and Rehabilitation Services, Community Services Division*, P.O. Box 4210, Helena, Mont. 59601.
(406) 444-3865

NEBRASKA: *Department of Social Services, Foster Care and Adoption*, P.O. Box 95026, Lincoln, Nebr. 68509.
(402) 471-3305

NEVADA: *Department of Human Resources, Welfare Division, Adoption*, 251 Jeanell Drive, Carson City, Nev. 89710.
(702) 885-4771

NEW HAMPSHIRE: *New Hampshire Division of Welfare, Program Development*, Hazen Drive, Concord, N.H. 03301.
(603) 271-4419

NEW JERSEY: *Division of Youth and Family Services, Adoption Unit*, P.O. Box CN 717, Trenton, N.J. 08625.
(609) 633-6902

NEW MEXICO: *Department of Human Services, Adoption*, P.O. Box 2348, Santa Fe, N. Mex. 87503.
(505) 827-2285

NEW YORK: *Bureau of Children and Family Services, Adoption Section*, 2 World Trade Center, New York, N.Y. 10047.
(212) 488-5290

NORTH CAROLINA: *Department of Human Resources, Adoptions Unit*, 325 North Salisbury Street, Raleigh, N.C. 27611.
(919) 733-3801

NORTH DAKOTA: *North Dakota Department of Human Services, Division of Children and Family Services, Adoptions*, State Capitol, Bismarck, N. Dak. 58505.
(701) 224-2310

OHIO: *Department of Public Welfare, Bureau of Children's Services*, 30 East Broad Street, Columbus, Ohio 43215.
(614) 466-2208

OKLAHOMA: *Department of Human Services, Adoption Section*, P.O. Box 25352, Oklahoma City, Okla. 73125.
(405) 521-2475

OREGON: *Department of Human Resources, Adoptions Unit*, 318 Public Service Building, Salem, Oreg. 97310.
(503) 378-4452

PENNSYLVANIA: *Department of Public Welfare, Adoption,* P.O. Box 2675, Harrisburg, Pa. 17120.
(717) 787-4882

RHODE ISLAND: *Child Welfare Services, Adoption,* 610 Mount Pleasant Avenue, Providence, R.I. 02908.
(401) 277-3945 ext. 3470

SOUTH CAROLINA: *Department of Social Services, Adoption Unit,* P.O. Box 1520, Columbia, S.C. 29202.
(803) 758-8740

SOUTH DAKOTA: *Department of Social Services, Adoption,* State Office Building, Illinois Street, Pierre, S. Dak. 57501.
(605) 773-3227

TENNESSEE: *Department of Human Services, Adoption,* 111 Seventh Avenue North, Nashville, Tenn. 37203.
(615) 741-5938

TEXAS: *Department of Human Resources, Adoption,* John H. Reagan Building, Austin, Tex. 78701.
(512) 835-0440

UTAH: *Department of Social Services, Adoption,* 150 West North Temple Street, Salt Lake City, Utah 84110.
(801) 533-7123

VERMONT: *Department of Social and Rehabilitation Services, Adoption,* State Office Building, Montpelier, Vt. 05602.
(802) 241-2150

VIRGINIA: *Department of Social Services, Adoption Reports Unit,* 8007 Discovery Drive, Richmond, Va. 23288.
(804) 281-9431

WASHINGTON: *Department of Social and Health Services, Adoptions,* State Office Building 2, Olympia, Wash. 98504.
(206) 753-2178

WEST VIRGINIA: *Department of Human Services, Adoption,* 1900 Washington Street, East Charleston, W. Va. 25305.
(304) 348-2400

WISCONSIN: *Office of Children, Youth and Families, Division of Community Services,* P.O. Box 7851, Madison, Wis. 53707.
(608) 266-2701

WYOMING: *Division of Public Assistance and Social Services, Adoption,* Hathaway Building, Cheyenne, Wyo. 82002.
(307) 777-7561

Family Resource Centers

REGION 1
Serves: Connecticut, Maine, Massachusetts, New Hampshire, Rhode Island, Vermont
Judge Baker Guidance Center, 291 Longwood Avenue, Boston, Mass. 02115. (617) 232-8390

REGION 2
Serves: New Jersey, New York, Puerto Rico, Virgin Islands
Cornell University, E-200MVR Hall, Ithaca, N.Y. 14853. (607) 256-7794

REGION 3
Serves: Delaware, District of Columbia, Maryland, Pennsylvania, Virginia, West Virginia
1218 Chestnut Street, Suite 204, Philadelphia, Pa. 19107. (215) 925-0200

REGION 4
Serves: Alabama, Florida, Georgia, Kentucky, Mississippi, North Carolina, South Carolina, Tennessee
1838 Terrace Avenue, Knoxville, Tenn. 37916. (615) 974-2308

REGION 5
Serves: Illinois, Indiana, Michigan, Minnesota, Ohio, Wisconsin
University of Wisconsin (Milwaukee), School of Social Work, P.O. Box 786, Milwaukee, Wisc. 53201. (414) 963-4184

REGION 6
Serves: Arkansas, Louisiana, New Mexico, Oklahoma, Texas
2609 University Avenue, Suite 314, Austin, Tex. 78712. (512) 471-4067

REGION 7
Serves: Iowa, Kansas, Missouri, Nebraska
Institute of Child Behavior and Development, University of Iowa, Oakdale Campus, Oakdale, Iowa 52319. (319) 353-4791

REGION 8
Serves: Colorado, Montana, North Dakota, South Dakota, Utah, Wyoming
Graduate School of Social Work, University Park, Denver, Colo. 80208. (303) 753-3464

REGION 9
Serves: Arizona, California, Hawaii, Nevada, American Samoa, Guam
5151 State University Drive, Los Angeles, Calif. 90032. (213) 224-3283

REGION 10
Serves: Alaska, Idaho, Oregon, Washington
School of Social Work, University of Washington, 4101 Fifteenth Avenue, Seattle, Wash. 98195. (206) 543-1517

5

The Children

Newborns

The confusion in the adoption world has led many people who desperately want a baby to pretend otherwise. They fear they must hide the truth if they are to succeed. One director of adoption services at a very posh agency said to me, "Whenever a couple tells me that they will only consider a healthy infant, I am always grateful for their honesty and openness." Grateful, yes, the director is that, but not helpful. Such honest people are usually turned away. Naturally it becomes tempting to say, "Yes indeed, I am interested in an older child," with the hope of getting your foot in the door and then somehow switching the agency around. If you are a skilled con-artist and have luck on your side, you may be able to get away with it, but remember, the agency has seen plenty of other people with the same idea and has grown mighty suspicious.

Another temptation is to misrepresent yourself, on the theory that "If agencies want young professionals, I'll tell them I'm a young professional." Once again, if you are experienced in the swindler's craft, you may be able to bring it off, but most people fail. The executive director of one exclusive agency (it rejects 80 percent of all applicants) told me, "People will say anything to get in here," but the chief result of the rise of lies has been to make the agencies even more wary and even more demanding for documentation that proves people are who they claim to be.

You may also find that your desire for a baby is directly challenged by people who consider it immoral to adopt anyone other than a waiting child. People can be quite straightforward about this, asking bluntly, "What's wrong with you that you can only accept a baby?" You are just going to have to remind yourself, "The people who can love the waiting children are one kind of person; I'm another kind and I like who I am." If you don't tell yourself something of this sort, this steady challenging can become rather wearing.

The resentment and self-doubt provoked by attempts to steer applicants away from babies is doubly offensive because most people who wish to adopt still want to adopt babies, preferably newborn babies. Even many of the new types of families hoping to adopt want babies. I once spent an evening with the director of the Committee for Single Adoptive Parents going through lists of single-parent adoptions she had learned about. "The reason so many of them are international adoptions," she told me, "is that single people are just like everybody else. They too want babies." It was true. Contrary to all the stories I had heard from agencies in this country, the majority of single people on her lists were adopting infants or toddlers.

People who build large families through the adoption of waiting children are also drawn to babies. One afternoon in Texas I met with three adoptive mothers who, among them, had adopted almost twenty children. They were talking cheerfully about what had led them to the adoption of older, disabled, or minority children. Suddenly one of the mothers said, "You may have noticed that although we adopted older children, we all have babies now." Each one of them had recently adopted an infant, and while we talked, there was a steady stream of distractions as infants were soothed, changed, and quieted.

"We all love being around babies," one of the mothers added. Their preference for waiting children had not kept them from adopting infants. There is just no getting around it: babies are something special. The 4 A.M. feeding is a nuisance, but it has rich compensations. The relationship is also enriched if the parent has known the child since infancy. An inevitable part of biological parenthood is raising a baby, so adoptive parents want that experience too. This quest for a baby remains the central fact for most people who want to adopt.

Step by Step

Locating a baby. Here is a lulu of a step. Locating a baby is the hardest of all adoption tasks, and you should use to the fullest all the resources described in part II. Only the most traditional of clients can limit themselves to agency adoptions. International sources should be investigated by every family. Independent sources should be developed unless they are completely forbidden in your state. If traditionally oriented agencies will not serve you (and they are bound to reject most readers), you may be in for quite a long search. Persistence pays, however, and I am confident that readers who follow the steps in part II can find a baby.

Placement. Finally the long-sought treasure is there: a baby who needs you. The minimum time between birth and arrival in the home varies from state to state and agency to agency. The largest source of delay is the need to protect the legal rights of the biological parents. In some jurisdictions it is enough if the parents sign a notarized document stating that they surrender for all time their rights and privileges as parents. Other places require the biological parents to appear before a judge and terminate their rights in court. Naturally, this second procedure increases the waiting time considerably.

Agencies also like to postpone placement for a couple of weeks after birth in order to get a good look at the baby and to make sure that his health is good. Back in the 1960s some agencies would wait until the baby was six months old before placing the infant with a family, just to make sure that everything was developing normally, but these days there is a lot of emphasis on "bonding" and such long delays are not common.

Trial period. You cannot immediately complete the adoption of a newborn infant; there is always a waiting period to see how it works out. During this trial period you may have questions you fear to bring to the agency lest it conclude that the placement is going badly and that it should reclaim your child. Chapter 6, which deals with parent associations, discusses groups that can be both helpful and neutral in this situation.

Final decree. The typical court session on an infant adoption takes less than five minutes, but a memorable few minutes they are. "For the first time in months, I'm completely relaxed," one woman told me after the judge approved her petition and awarded the adoption decree. After all the time of searching, after the excitement of the arrival and the months of loving care, the final legal act was done. Her time of wandering through the adoption maze was over.

Waiting Children

Anybody who contemplates adopting a waiting child soon discovers that the fate of children who fall into the grip of the child-welfare system is one of the great scandals in America. The results are so cruel, so devastating, so hard to undo, and the damage is done so quickly that adoptive families can hardly believe what they observe. Who could imagine that today in the United States, preschool children are being brought into a child-welfare system that, within a few years, will have destroyed their self-respect and crippled them socially? Over half a million children are ensnared in this system; more than one hundred thousand of them are currently free for adoption, and perhaps a further quarter-million ought to be free.

The scandal gets worse: many recruiting organizations have been formed to find permanent homes for the children. These groups seek out families interested in adopting waiting children, and they let families know about specific children who are currently waiting to be adopted. However, when the families thus recruited apply to agencies, they get a runaround that can last for years. Naturally, many interested families give up trying to adopt.

The scandal grows still worse: attempts to reform the laws and the bureaucracies are met with ferocious opposition from a strange alliance of conservative preachers and liberal social workers.

The scandal has its irony: it is perpetuated in the name of protecting families and helping children. Here are a few examples of what can happen.

• A child, age three, is found abandoned in a New York subway station and placed in foster care. During the next seven years he visits his parents once (they have no interest in seeing him), but parental rights are not terminated until he is finally, at age ten, placed in a home where he will be adopted if the parental rights can be ended. By then the child-welfare department psychiatrist has him taking "downers" three times a day, every day.

• A woman in Connecticut goes to the state's office concerned with protective services for children to say she and some friends are interested in developing a foster-care program for children who are terminally ill. The state office refuses to listen to the proposal.

• An agency in Texas holds an orientation session for people who are interested in adopting children age seven or older. During the session, families learn there are plenty of waiting children. Several couples want to know how long the adoption process will take. They are told that the agency is seriously understaffed and it may take many months before the process can even begin.

• A midwestern judge holds a hearing to determine whether a child might be freed for adoption. He rules that no, the child is to stay within the system because the biological father has kept up an interest in the child—he sent the boy a Christmas card last year.

• A western family adopted a black child and now wants to adopt a second waiting black boy. They are told that no, present agency policy does not permit placement of black children with white parents. Okay, say the parents, they will adopt a waiting white child. No, says the agency, it is against their policy to place white children in families with nonwhite children.

I heard horror stories like these six times a week, every week, while working on this book. At first they surprised me, then they made me sick. Finally, these stories left me with a kind of numbness. How can you possibly reform fifty such problems in fifty separate states?

Yet the children do not go away. They exist and they need families, because, for the most part, they are children their parents could not raise. In some cases, they were born with disabilities serious enough to persuade the biological parents to abandon them immediately. In other cases, the children are older when they enter the system. Sometimes this parental abandonment is the result of birth defects that were not visible at first—mental retardation, deafness, epilepsy. Usually, however, the abandonment is more clearly the result of parental neglect. Perhaps the mother is a fifteen-year-old girl who at first wanted to keep her baby but then began to leave her alone for hours at a time. Perhaps the child's mother suddenly died and the father no longer wished to raise the child. In some cases the parents have abused or neglected the child so badly that the law intervenes and removes him from the home.

Quite predictably, most of the children in the child-welfare system come from the poorest and lowest rungs on the social ladder. In New York City, black and Hispanic children are most commonly caught in the system. In the rural Maryland counties along the Mason-Dixon line, white children from mining families predominate. In South Dakota two-thirds of the children in the system are American Indians. In Alaska 80 percent of the children are native Alaskans (including

Eskimos, Indians, and Aleuts). These poor families are the ones whose resources are so tightly stretched that many snap. It is the children who are sent flying.

The idea behind the child-welfare system is to protect the children who are victims of their families' limitations. A child who is seriously neglected or abused or who is simply too much for the family to handle any longer is placed in foster care. While the child is there, the welfare system studies the situation and judges whether the child can return to the family or whether it would be better to terminate parental rights and put the child in an adoptive home.

The plan sounds reasonable, but, really, few decisions are made. Bureaucrats vacillate, or, to use their euphemism, they "keep all options open." Nobody takes responsibility. Most of the children who enter the system are reasonably young, reasonably sane, and reasonably healthy. At that point they are very attractive candidates for adoption. Many families would welcome them and could care for them. However, everyone keeps postponing making the decision on what to do. The children stay in limbo for years—sometimes ping-ponging back and forth between parents and foster home, sometimes parading through a series of foster homes. When, after long years, somebody finally says "Enough already" and the children are freed for adoption, they are no longer so young, no longer so secure about their place in the world, and they have a long string of medical labels appended to their names.

Who are the waiting children? The question is natural, inevitable, and quite misguided. They are the whole range of what children are and can be. They are individuals who suffer from having been labeled too much. Even children with Down's syndrome, who are commonly discussed as though they were interchangeable units of a standardized tragedy, are individuals with different personalities. The only way to find out what the waiting children are like is to meet a few.

Consider the story of Aida. She was classified as a typical harder-to-place child. Indeed, the family who finally adopted her belongs to an unpopular religious minority and was allowed to adopt Aida only because she was considered so hard to place that a so-called better home for her could probably not be found. Aida was placed in foster care at the age of six months. Her parents' rights over her were not terminated, and she stayed in foster homes. A family snapshot taken at the time she entered the foster system shows a fat, normal baby with striking eyes. A picture of Aida taken at age five, after four and a half years in the foster system, shows a terribly thin child with no fun in her eyes and no pleasure in a smile that reveals she is missing her two front teeth.

Aida continued in foster care. Her second-grade report card tells of growing troubles—an inability to concentrate. She was not working hard at her lessons and her grades were *U*s and *F*s. Sometime during this period she began telling fantasy stories about her importance— that she was a professional athlete, that she was rich, that everyone admired her. She remained in foster care until she was nine years old, when her parents' rights were ended and she finally became available for adoption. The foster family that had had Aida for several years was given the opportunity to adopt her, but Aida overheard her foster mother expressing doubts about an adoption. Aida is Hispanic, with brown skin, and her foster mother was reluctant to adopt a child who wasn't light-skinned. Aida developed a new problem—she began trying to wash the color off her skin. She scrubbed her arms until they bled.

So here is Aida when she is finally listed as available for adoption: age ten; "emotionally handicapped"; does poorly in school; tells lies; does physical harm to herself; and has a poor attention span (diagnosed as hyperactivity). Her photo is unflattering; she is still too thin and she does not smile. The one quality that might catch attention are her beautiful, haunting eyes, but they are partially hidden behind glasses that she began wearing in the third grade.

The Lopez family saw Aida's listing and something in the photo led Mrs. Lopez to say "Maybe." Mr. Lopez had his doubts because the description of the child was so disturbing, but he agreed to take a look at Aida with his wife. It was love at first sight, at least for the Lopezes. Aida had been around long enough to know you don't give your heart so fast, not if you wish to survive. "Here we go again" is what she thought when she saw the Lopezes peeking at her from across the room. A visit to the Lopez home was arranged. Aida came for the weekend and never left.

Inevitably there were problems, especially with the Lopezes' biological children, all boys. Two of the boys were slightly older than Aida and one was four years younger, but the problems were overcome. When I met Aida, she had been with the Lopezes for slightly over a year. I found a very intelligent, very articulate, pretty girl of eleven years. Her schoolwork had improved to the point where she was a candidate for special classes for the intellectually gifted. She had put on weight and, while still on the slender side, looked perfectly healthy. She was no longer a worrisome collection of skin and bones. The need to make up stories about her importance had passed. Her eyes were still beautiful, but now there was a lovely smile as well.

You cannot know the waiting children until they are a breathing reality. The Lopezes had met several other children before Aida, but none of them worked out. Like Aida, the Lopezes also had to think about adoption in personal and practical terms. Every reader who looks at waiting children will find that there are some children you can pity, but not raise. However, there are over one hundred thousand waiting children currently available for adoption, and there may well be some whom you could love enough to bring into your family.

Looking at Aida, I asked myself why on earth did it take so long for this beautiful child to be adopted. Of course, the answer has nothing to do with Aida. It was like asking why a beautiful child has been the one to be hit by a truck. Nobody can adopt a child whose parental rights have not been ended. Nobody can blame a child when, in the name of protecting the family, she is allowed to float in limbo for nine years.

Euphemisms. It is hard to find a term that can cover half a million kids in foster care and still not apply to the rest of the world's children. At one time the popular term was "unadoptable." It had a certain bluntness to it, but it sounded like a death sentence and it discouraged social workers from making much effort on the children's behalf. (Why work to find a family if a child is simply unadoptable?) These days they are commonly called children with "special needs," as though there were some children who did not have special needs. Since we all understand that no child can be raised without attention being paid to her individual needs and characteristics, the euphemism frightens families. People think to themselves, "Boy, this kid's needs must really be *special,* to get that label," so they don't even consider adopting such a child.

I have used the term "waiting children" because it focuses on the one unique quality that characterizes the group—their family status is unsettled and they are waiting to find out what is to happen to them. Any child, from birth on up, can fit into this category if he has been removed from the parents' home and is now in the guardianship of the child-welfare office. Many agencies don't like a category so broad as this. In speaking with agency workers and other adoption professionals, I have often heard contemptuous references to what the general public imagines as "special needs" or "older" children.

These workers restrict those terms to the oldest and hardest of all to place.

Until the close of the 1960s, agencies and parents called anyone six months old an "older child," but during the seventies many of these children began to be adopted readily. The purely practical issue of availability persuaded agencies to raise the age at which children were classed as "older." By the early 1980s most agencies did not consider a child to be older until he reached school age or a little beyond. Age seven is the common cut-off point, although at some specialized agencies a child may not be called older until age ten. (Black boys, however, may be classed as older at around age three.)

There are no new psychological insights supporting this redefinition. The issue is simply one of availability. For many agencies, providing a healthy four-year-old is as difficult as locating a healthy newborn.

In the same way, "special needs" children are defined on the basis of which are the hardest to place. Children with physical handicaps like club feet and withered arms are often not considered special-needs children, so many families are willing to adopt them. These days some specialized agencies don't even consider children with Down's syndrome to be special-needs children until they turn eight or nine years old. The ones who are generally thought of as the hardest to place are children who have become emotionally disturbed after growing up in foster care, the mentally retarded, or those with multiple disabilities.

Of course, it comes as a shock to families thinking about adopting a waiting child to find that some agencies dismiss their inquiries with a cavalier response—"We don't consider that to be a special-needs child"—but such things are typical of the adoption maze. Do not naively assume that agencies will welcome you with warm embraces. Always approach a parent organization first to learn the details pertinent to your area and to get some sense of how you will be received.

Adjustment. Adopted children always need time to get used to their new status. Some who have been in many homes commonly have to be assured that this time it is different and this adoption really will be permanent. Others have forgotten or never really knew that they were waiting, they have been in a particular foster home so long. They have to get over the shock of one unexpected change and then understand that similar surprises will not come in the future. Parents should not expect to find children who will not go through this transition period. Even families who adopt waiting babies that are only a few months old have found that neglect has been so severe that it takes months for the babies to accept and respond to the love they suddenly receive.

You and the waiting children. Be practical; do not adopt a waiting child simply because you want to do a good deed. Many adoptive parents are so stunned by what they learn about the waiting-child scandal that they become actively involved in trying to reform it. Their interest is commendable, but I don't think we can adopt our way out of this problem. There are too many legal and procedural difficulties along the road.

What the family offers. In determining the age range of the child you could seek to adopt, consider what your family has to give, what strains your family can endure, and what your family needs. The first issue calls for a stark self-examination. Why should any child want to be adopted by you? What kind of child would be most likely to say that yours is the sort of family he can most benefit from?

Keep in mind that the older the child, the stronger and more healthy the family must be. Almost any loving parents are able to supply a six-month-old child with the means to survive and grow, but the needs of older children include more abstract elements. At six months, most needs are physical. At age three, the physical needs remain, but the child also needs friends of the same age. At age seven, the child still needs food and clothing, still needs friends, but needs a clear set of moral principles as well. Inevitably, the more a child needs, the more the parents must give. The more a child needs to eat, the more parents must be able to buy. The more a child needs discipline, the more disciplined the parents have to be. Parents of older children have to be more sure of themselves and of their values than do parents of younger children. In the normal course of events, parents grow with their children. They get used to teaching and disciplining an infant and then are ready to teach and discipline a school-aged child. Families who begin by adopting an older child need that extra measure of self-confidence right from the start.

Remember too that the older the child, the less prominent the family presence becomes. School, friends, and recreation take up more of the child's time. On one side, this fact may make adoption seem easier. After all, if the parents work the increasing independence of the child is a benefit. However, the neighborhood has to be able to fill in for the parents, supplying the friends, schooling, and activities the child seeks outside the family. Parents with growing children frequently move to new neighborhoods in accordance with changing family needs. The sudden arrival of an older child in your home is almost certain to force a reconsideration of your neighborhood.

In practical terms, this weighing of what your family has to offer a child leads to the following sort of reckoning: we both work during the day, so we ought to find a child old enough to go to school; our neighborhood seems to have many childless homes, so friends outside the home might not be plentiful; however, the Cub Scout group at our church has a strong and energetic leader plus a good-sized membership. Perhaps the kind of child who could best benefit from our home is a Cub Scout–age boy.

This kind of calculating is approximate and largely instinctive, but it usually marks the first time a family consciously seeks to determine what sort of child it could best serve.

What the family can endure. Families may be elastic, but they cannot be stretched infinitely. It is time for some honest thinking about how much the family can change and adapt. If a child of one sex is adopted, will the spouse of that same sex become jealous? For example, a wife may be delighted by a seven-year-old girl but troubled by a thirteen-year-old.

A particularly strong issue is the presence of other children in the family. Many of the failed older-child adoptions I know of ended because one of the children already present made success impossible. Other children in the family can be a powerful benefit, for they provide an example of what sort of behavior is expected and tolerated, but if children feel seriously and unremittingly threatened by a new arrival, there is going to be lasting trouble. In part this question depends on how secure the children are about their own positions, but there are other factors as well. It is a mistake to assume that the greater the children's maturity, the easier the placement will be. Often the arriving child is quite immature and behaves in ways that simply baffle the other children.

Ideally, the arriving child should not be older than any of the children already present and most agencies insist that the new child not be older than the oldest. I think it is a good rule even though I know many adoptive families who broke it and survived. All of them went through a difficult period of adjustment. One woman who adopted a boy older than two of her girls said to me, "Even though it finally worked out for us, I absolutely discourage the idea of mixing up the age structure. There are just too many problems of every sort."

What the family needs. The need to be a parent has many aspects; a major one is the need to be important—the need to feel that someone can and does depend on you, the sense that someone is learning what you have to teach and admires what you do. Waiting-child adoptions can be especially rewarding in this regard because the child really needs what the family has to give.

At the same time, almost any child who has been repeatedly rejected will defend herself by rejecting you first. The intensity of this self-defense depends on the child and the stability she has encountered, but everyone who adopts a waiting child must be prepared for rejection. There is a powerful contradiction here—parents want to adopt because of their need to help a child, but at the same time they must be strong enough to accept outright rejection. If they aren't hurt by the child's turning away, then their own need to adopt a child probably is not strong; however, if their need is so strong that the child's rejection is devastatingly painful, then the adoption isn't right either.

Along with a desire for a family, parents adopting waiting children need to be mature enough to understand clearly that they are the parents and the child is the child. The child needs love and support; the parents need to give love and support. Parents who look to their children for gratitude, praise, and reassurance are mixing up roles. To keep the family roles straight, adoptive parents of waiting children have to feel certain about their own worth and their own values.

Almost all the issues central to the adoption of waiting children focus on the question of identity—the children's and the parents'. The adoption of a waiting child changes the identity of everyone concerned. This two-way change is not always appreciated. The waiting child takes on membership in your family, but your family also becomes intimately involved in the history and nature of your new child.

In a conversation with a woman who had adopted many waiting children, some white and some biracial, I asked, "How have such adoptions affected your family?" She replied with a story about an incident that had happened a few days earlier. She had been walking across a parking lot with two of her sons, one white and one mixed, when a voice behind her hollered, "Nigger lover!" The white son then said cheerily, "That's what everybody at school calls me." It was a simple fact of identity for him. You may like it, you may hate it, but

71

you must face it: the adoption of a waiting child redefines the identity of the whole family.

Transracial adoptions. Most of the children in the welfare system belong to racial or cultural minorities. Most of the families hoping to adopt belong to the majority group—white, middle class, usually Protestant. One of the touchy questions of present-day adoption is whether these families should be allowed to adopt minority children. The issue was forced onto the table by the National Association of Black Social Workers, which loudly opposes the placement of black children into white homes. The main arguments against such adoptions are that they deprive black children of their cultural identity and make it harder for black families to adopt. Many minority families do wish to adopt and can provide loving homes, but often they don't have the money or education of middle-class whites. By the old agency standards, white families were often considered more desirable parents for black children than were black families, so minority-group efforts to adopt were blocked.

The counterargument is that there are not enough minority families seeking to adopt, and if a strict policy against transracial adoptions is pursued, most of these waiting minority children will never find families.

A kind of compromise has been reached: most agencies prefer not to place a child across racial lines unless it can't find a minority family for the child. In practice, Indians and blacks are hardly ever placed with white families; Orientals and Hispanics are quickly placed. This pattern is so neatly in harmony with American racial prejudices that I am hard put to believe it really reflects a liberal concern for preserving identity.

Names. Should you or should you not change the name of a child old enough to recall his first name? I know people who have strong opinions on both sides of this question. The argument against the change is that it strips the child of whatever little identity he has managed to acquire. The argument in favor of changing the name is that it is good to strip away that old identity because the adoption redefines who the child is.

I lean toward giving the child a new name, but I don't feel strongly about the point and do agree that there are cases in which a name change is not a good idea. An older child will probably have an opinion on this matter and should be consulted. Most waiting children who are eventually adopted need to put their past behind them. All the horror and uncertainty they know is to disappear, and this point is emphasized by changing their names. The change can be a very powerful symbol.

Step by Step

Winning over an agency. The problem of waiting-child adoptions often lies with agency workers. Their training and background have prepared them for traditional infant adoptions, but the agencies must now offer untraditional adoptions if they are to survive. Many workers are unprepared for the changes; they can be positively hostile to them. The first task of applicants, therefore, is often to win their workers over to the idea that they can and should adopt a waiting child.

Parent organizations know the agencies that are most sympathetic to waiting-child adoptions. Some agencies are very skilled and understanding. The small city of York, Pennsylvania, for example, is the home of Tressler Lutheran Services. It serves the largely rural population of central Pennsylvania and has been the most influential and innovative of American agencies. There is also a group of agencies, known as Family Builders, which specialize in recruiting families for the adoption of waiting children (see the list "Agencies for Waiting Children" at the end of this chapter). The influence of these agencies extends well beyond their clientele, because they inspire other workers to try. As one Pennsylvania worker said to me, "It's hard to say a child is unadoptable when you keep going to meetings where Tressler people tell how they are placing similar children."

At the same time, there are many adoption agencies that simply cannot bring themselves to place many of the waiting children. They look at what seems to be a typical middle-class couple who want to adopt a disabled child and they say, "These people must be nuts." Modern psychology has so diminished our sense of human potential that the urgings of love, patience, and tolerance are often dismissed as neurotic.

The agency may never say that it won't work with you. Applicants can be left hanging for years. One sign of trouble is endless interviewing. The agency should be able to complete its study in four or five interviews. If it keeps wanting more, something is wrong. Ask point-blank what is going on. These interviews are not a test of your patience; they simply constitute bureaucratic indecisiveness. Push the worker to a decision. It is better to risk hearing "No" today than to wait four years to hear it.

If six months have passed since your application and you still have not met a waiting child, ask why not. The agency will have a good, rational explanation. Don't accept it; the explanation is an excuse. With all the waiting children in this country, it is time for a little imagination. Reasonable explanations for failure are not good enough. If eight months have gone by, step out of the channels and contact an adoption exchange directly (see chapter 9).

Meeting a child. It is always an exciting time when you first meet a child you may adopt. Agencies often like to arrange these meetings on the sly, in order to avoid raising the child's hopes. There is a lot of peeking through two-way mirrors and gazing across crowded rooms. Usually, however, the child knows what is happening. If the meeting results in an adoption, it will become as important a part of the family legend as the first meeting of husband and wife. If it leads nowhere, it will still be remembered with an unusual intensity. I have heard many families describe meetings that did not end in adoption, and the emotion and regret in their voices is as real as for a remembered miscarriage.

A recurring theme in the stories of older-child adoptions is that the child reached out for help, often in the first meeting. Some of these moments are dramatic:

• At age nine, Cyril was living in an orphanage. He had never known a stable home or family love. When Belinda, the single woman who eventually adopted him, came to meet Cyril, they tossed a football back and forth until Cyril suddenly held the ball and said, "I like you." "I like you too," Belinda replied. Cyril then led her to the orphanage chapel and pointed at a statue saying, "That's the Virgin Mary. She was Jesus' mother. You're going to be my mother." Belinda had brought a Polaroid camera and Cyril took a picture of her standing next to the statue.

• "I don't like you," said twelve-year-old Tomaso in a defiant tone as he climbed into a prospective father's lap and hugged him.

• Elizabeth was diagnosed as severely language-disordered. She seemed bright, but, at age four, had never been heard to speak. When one couple was brought to meet her, they all played for a while and Elizabeth suddenly asked, "Are you going to 'dopt me?"

Stories like these multiply quickly when one talks about waiting-child adoptions. In every case they involve a great risk on the child's part. The children have been hurt so much in the past, and here they are inviting rejection once again. This moment of risk taking and reaching for help is important to the adoption. Without it, the adoption is just one more case of the adult world knowing what's best for the child and going ahead, willy-nilly.

Most states do require the child's consent to adoption after a certain age, although in some instances the requirement can be waived by a judge. The chart on pp. 76–79 summarizes state laws about this issue. A few states also have laws that could interfere with the adoption of an older child by a young adult. They require that there be a minimum age difference between parent and child. Those laws are also summarized in the chart.

Placement. One woman with many years' experience working in waiting-child adoptions told me she would like to see the adoption be simultaneous with the child's arrival in the new home, because it would force the family to acknowledge a commitment right from the beginning. I understand her point, but placements do not work that way. When a waiting child enters the home, there is a lot of testing of the waters.

Typically, there is a honeymoon period that might last as long as six months before any problems appear. The honeymoon stage frequently sees a great blossoming of what had been severely stunted development. Perhaps the most common story I have heard in talks with adoptive parents has been that upon arrival in the family the new child was grossly underdeveloped but began to improve almost at once.

Stunted development can be of any type—physical, emotional, social, cultural, or intellectual. With younger children, physical recovery is often astounding. Children start to grow as soon as they come into the family. I know of one infant, not expected to live, who was diagnosed as suffering from "failure to thrive" before being adopted at age one month. He was brought home and doubled his weight during his first month with his new parents. By the time he was eight and a half months old, he had the physical development of a baby twelve months old.

Another case was that of a seventeen-month-old Korean girl, whose weight at the time of arrival in her adoptive home was seventeen pounds. She was not yet walking or talking and was suffering from malnutrition severe enough to have turned her hair red and given her a protruding belly (both symptoms of a protein deficiency called kwashiorkor). By her second birthday, she was running and talking as

The Law and the Older Child

State	Age of Consent					Minimum Parent-Child Age Difference	
	10	12	14	None	Can Be Waived	10	15 years
Alabama			✓				
Alaska			✓				
Arizona		✓					
Arkansas	✓						
California		✓				✓	
Colorado			✓				
Connecticut			✓				
Delaware			✓		✓		
District of Columbia			✓				
Florida		✓					
Georgia			✓			SPO* ✓	
Hawaii	✓						
Idaho		✓					✓
Illinois			✓				
Indiana			✓				

*SPO = single parent only

76

| State | Age of Consent | | | | | Minimum Parent-Child Age Difference | |
	10	12	14	None	Can Be Waived	10	15 years
Iowa			✓				
Kansas			✓		✓		
Kentucky		✓			✓		
Louisiana				✓			
Maine			✓				
Maryland	✓						
Massachusetts		✓					
Michigan			✓				
Minnesota			✓				
Mississippi			✓				
Missouri			✓				
Montana		✓				✓	
Nebraska			✓				
Nevada			✓			✓	
New Hampshire		✓					
New Jersey	✓					✓	
New Mexico		✓					

State	Age of Consent					Minimum Parent-Child Age Difference	
	10	12	14	None	Can Be Waived	10	15 years
New York			✓		✓		
North Carolina		✓					
North Dakota	✓				✓	✓	
Ohio		✓			✓		
Oklahoma		✓					
Oregon			✓				
Pennsylvania		✓					
Rhode Island			✓				
South Carolina				✓			
South Dakota		✓				✓	
Tennessee			✓				
Texas			✓				
Utah		✓				✓	
Vermont			✓				
Virginia			✓				
Washington			✓				
West Virginia		✓					✓

State	Age of Consent					Minimum Parent-Child Age Difference	
	10	12	14	None	Can Be Waived	10	15 years
Wisconsin				✓			
Wyoming			✓				

well as other children her age and had ceased to show any signs of malnutrition.

With older children, there is often a comparable intellectual growth. Typical is the case of the nine-year-old who entered his new home reading only at the first-grade level but who a month and a half later had reached the third-grade level.

Of course, no one who adopts a child should count on such a blossoming. I also know of cases where what was thought perhaps to be stunted development was found to be real retardation.

At around the time the adoption is to be brought to court, there is a tendency for the placement to go sour. This is the point when the child, fearing rejection, rejects the new family first. Often the child's behavior seems psychotic and dangerous. Some parents may be tempted to dismiss this eruption with the observation "It's just a phase."

Yes, it may pass; it probably will, once the child feels he is a member of the family. But remember, you cannot expect him ever again to be on perfect behavior, as he was during the honeymoon period.

Support. The adoption of almost any waiting child calls for a lot of support from agency workers, from friends in adoptive-parent associations, and, in some cases, from specialized groups. The final list in this chapter names some foundations concerned with severe health problems. A helpful book for parents of severely disabled children is: *The Special Child Handbook* by Jean and Bernard McNamara (New York: American Elsevier, Hawthorn Books, 1977). It assumes that the parents of the child are the biological parents, but it still has a lot of practical information.

The adoption decree. The final decree completing the adoption often comes as a profound relief to both the child and the parents, but it is usually slow in coming. Agencies are hesitant to seal the commitment, so they stall, asking for more and more information—a typical delaying tactic favored by all hesitant bureaucracies. For the child who has waited so long, this continued uncertainty is terribly distressing. It also interferes with the family commitment. One mother, whose adoption decree was still not final a year after the arrival of her daughter, said, "Whenever something happens, it brings me to my senses and I realize we are not a true family. True families don't have to ask permission to take their child on a vacation." Because of these ambiguities and accompanying anxieties, you should press for the final decree as soon as you are sure you want it.

Agencies for Waiting Children

Although many agencies place waiting children in adoptive homes, some are more convinced of the desirability of such placements than others. Some are also more open to the individual qualities and eccentricities of adoptive families than are others. Perhaps the most experienced and open of all are the agencies of the Family Builders group, which began in Michigan during the late 1960s and spread across the country during the seventies. They place only waiting children whom other agencies are unable to give homes. They charge no fee. The members of the network are:

CALIFORNIA

Family Builders by Adoption
P.O. Box 9202
North Berkeley Station
Berkeley, Calif. 94709
(415) 531-5913

COLORADO

Family Builders by Adoption
5800 Cody Court
Arvada, Colo. 80004
(303) 425-1667

DISTRICT OF COLUMBIA

Peirce-Warwick Adoption Service
5229 Connecticut Avenue, N.W.
Washington, D.C. 20015
(202) 966-2531

FLORIDA

Project CAN, Family Service Centers
2960 Roosevelt Boulevard
Clearwater, Fla. 33520
(813) 531-0481

ILLINOIS

Lutheran Child and Family Services
7620 Madison Street
P.O. Box 186
River Forest, Ill. 60305
(312) 771-7180

KANSAS

Spaulding Midwest
1855 North Hillside
Wichita, Kans. 67214
(316) 686-9171

MASSACHUSETTS

Project IMPACT
25 West Street
Boston, Mass. 02111
(617) 451-1472

MICHIGAN

Spaulding for Children
3660 Waltrous Road
Chelsea, Mich. 48118
(313) 475-8693

NEW JERSEY

Spaulding for Children
36 Prospect Street
Westfield, N.J. 07090
(201) 233-2282

NEW YORK

New York Spaulding for Children
22 West Twenty-seventh Street, 10th Floor
New York, N.Y. 10001
(212) 696-9560

Permanent Families for Children
Child Welfare League of America
67 Irving Place
New York, N.Y. 10003
(212) 254-7410

OHIO

Spaulding for Children—Beech Brook
3737 Lander Road
Cleveland, Ohio 44124
(216) 464-4445

PENNSYLVANIA

Women's Christian Alliance
1610–1616 North Broad Street
Philadelphia, Pa. 19121
(215) 236-9911

SOUTH CAROLINA

Children Unlimited
P.O. Box 11463
Columbia, S.C. 29211
(803) 799-8311

TEXAS

Spaulding Southwest
4219 Richmond Avenue, Suite 100
Houston, Tex. 77027
(713) 850-9707

WASHINGTON

Medina Children's Service—TASC
123 Sixteenth Avenue, P.O. Box 22638
Seattle, Wash. 98122
(206) 324-9470

Child Health Foundations

ASTHMA: *Asthmatic Children's Foundation,* P.O. Box 568, Spring Valley Road, Ossining, N.Y. 10562

AUTISM: *National Society of Autistic Children,* 1234 Massachusetts Avenue, N.W., Suite 1017, Washington, D.C. 20005

BLINDNESS: *American Council of the Blind,* 1211 Connecticut Avenue, N.W., Suite 506, Washington, D.C. 20036

American Foundation for the Blind, 15 West Sixteenth Street, New York, N.Y. 10011

CEREBRAL PALSY: *United Cerebral Palsy Association,* 66 East Thirty-fourth Street, New York, N.Y. 10016

DEAFNESS: *Alexander Graham Bell Association for the Deaf,* 3417 Volta Place, N.W., Washington, D.C. 20007

National Association of the Deaf, 814 Thayer Avenue, Silver Spring, Md. 20910

DOWN'S SYNDROME: *Down's Syndrome Congress,* P.O. Box 90547, Lakeview, Wash. 98491

EPILEPSY: *Epilepsy Foundation of America,* 4351 Garden City Drive, Suite 406, Landover, Md. 20755

HEMOPHILIA: *National Hemophilia Foundation,* 25 West Thirty-fourth Street, Suite 1204, New York, N.Y. 10018

JUVENILE DIABETES: *Juvenile Diabetes Foundation,* 23 East Twenty-sixth Street, New York, N.Y. 10010

MENTAL RETARDATION: *National Association for Retarded Citizens,* P.O. Box 6109, Arlington, Tex. 76011

SPINA BIFIDA: *Spina Bifida Association of America,* 343 South Dearborn, Room 317, Chicago, Ill. 60604

PART II
Finding a Child

6

Adoptive-Parent
Associations

The rise of adoptive-parent organizations has been the most encouraging and important recent development for families hoping to adopt. In response to the tidal wave that smashed the old adoption system, hundreds of local groups have been formed. (See the "Directory of Parent Associations" in the Appendix for a list of such associations.) By now there is a national coordinating organization as well: the North American Council on Adoptable Children (NACAC).

These groups do not add up to a new system for adopting, but they have proven useful in many ways, especially as sources for information, counseling, and encouragement. The very localism of the groups is a benefit in making sense of the specific situation at hand. In a field as chaotic and confused as adoption, the broad overview often becomes too general and families need to find local guides who know the trails in their district. Agency workers seldom know much more than their own routine. Public officials usually don't know a thing beyond official procedure, and they often have to look up even that much. It is the parent groups that have daily experience with a whole variety of adoptions and know which routes are currently meeting with success.

By now, so many different organizations have appeared that a number of types are recognizable. All of them offer sympathy and information, but they can have two basic differences in approach. People belonging to one set see themselves as advocates for children. These organizations try to recruit adoptive parents and focus on adoptions of waiting children. These groups are particularly valuable as places for getting to know parents who have already adopted waiting children. For example, you may find yourself attracted to the thought of adopting a waiting child but still have questions about your ability to cope with the challenge. Through parent organizations, you can meet and talk with people who have already gone through such adoptions.

The members of a second group consider themselves advocates for the parents who want to adopt. Because the majority of adoptive parents set out with the idea of adopting newborn infants, these organizations are especially strong at providing information and contacts for infant adoptions. They know the names of local contacts for international adoptions, the licensed workers who can provide the necessary studies, and the details about local agencies—which ones will do what.

In practice, each type of group provides some of the services of the other. Child-recruitment groups provide information for families looking for healthy newborns; parent-oriented groups promote the adoption of waiting children. Yet the underlying difference is real and usually can be sensed by members. People lucky enough to live in an area with several organizations will likely find they are more comfortable with one group's attitude than another's.

There are also a number of specialized types of parent associations. The most important of them assist in international adoptions, which often require a lot of do-it-yourself labor. Parents have banded together to provide necessary information, and quite a few of these groups have become successful enough to form branch chapters. Without these organizations, independent adoptions of foreign children would be almost impossible. Agency-based organizations have also sprouted. These groups are common for foster parents; in the case of adoptive parents, such associations usually concentrate on some special aspect of the agency's adoption program. One East Coast agency, for example, includes a large Korean adoption program, and families who have adopted Korean children through the agency have formed an association. The mere existence of agency-based groups provides strong evidence for the importance of the counseling and support services these associations offer. Most agencies oppose the creation of groups outside their immediate control, but the parents have proceeded to form organizations anyway.

A third specialty group is the pure support groups. At their best, these are small gatherings of people who know and like one another and who have similar adoption experiences to share. The parents might all have adopted infants, or all have adopted small children from

India, or the parents themselves might all be single people who adopted older children. These groups are usually small enough to seat everyone around a dinner table. Often they are offshoots of a larger association, and they remain important parts of an adoptive family's life long after involvement with the larger organization has ended.

Services

The size, wealth, and quality of leadership of parent organizations vary so much that it is impossible to say what services are typical of them all. The "president" of one group reported to me that the major function of her association was an annual barbecue. Many organizations exist chiefly as phone networks of sympathetic voices; others are quite elaborate and formal. Only the largest will have all of the following services:

Orientation. A good example of the orientation service at its best was a panel discussion I once attended on infant adoptions. Almost one hundred people were in the audience. The panel's speakers had all recently adopted infants, some privately, others internationally, and one couple through an agency. There were also a few professionals who worked with different aspects of adoption. Getting speakers with such varied knowledge and experience into one room was quite a feat. By the end of the program, everybody in the room (including those on the panel) had learned some new ways people in their area could seek out and adopt an infant.

There is a certain potluck quality to these orientation sessions. Often their programs are not as immediately useful as the panel discussion I just described; however, all people who regularly attend these meetings are bound to gain a fuller understanding of the situation in their area.

Workshops. Many organizations offer regular services for families hoping to adopt. These workshops may require several sessions. Although it is best to start your search for a child by joining a parent group, most people have been searching for quite some time before they look for help. By then they know many of the problems, but few of the solutions. At the workshops they meet other people with similar stories and learn about a wider range of possibilities.

Workshops are one service in which the pro-child or pro-parent split is often felt. Organizations that see themselves as advocates for waiting children tend to use their workshops to bring particular waiting children to your attention, while other groups put more emphasis on listing names and addresses of people who can be helpful in your search.

A more advanced form of workshop has been developed by Families Adopting Children Everywhere (FACE) in Maryland. It has a six-week, twelve-hour course offered through adult education programs. The course has been a great success and is now offered in a number of Maryland's community colleges. News of the program caused a sensation at a national conference of adoptive-parent associations, and other groups around the country have begun to develop similar courses.

Contacts. The Baker family finally adopted a baby boy, but their description of the long search to find him was a typical story of adoption frustration: they approached every agency in the phone book and were rebuffed. Eventually the Bakers heard about a parent group in their area and contacted it; from the group's workshop they learned of a number of agencies in their area that were not listed in the phone book. They contacted them all, only to be rejected time and again. Finally, however, one of the association's officers was able to call an acquaintance in an agency and persuade her to work with the Bakers.

Such forceful help cannot be expected every time and certainly is unlikely until after you have done a lot of work yourself, but these groups have established extensive and valuable contacts. They know lawyers acquainted with adoption procedures, translators who can help in foreign adoptions, and agency workers who are likely to be sympathetic. When you exhaust your possibilities, a parent association can usually suggest another name or place to try.

At the same time, you can use the association as a prime source to build your own contacts. Introduce yourself to speakers at the group meetings; get a set of cards printed with your name and address and write on them "Hoping to adopt" before handing one to each person you meet. These people may not place children, but from time to time they may hear about an available child or a pregnant woman who plans to give up her baby.

Phone banks. The majority of parent associations are neither rich enough to maintain offices nor populous enough to hold frequent meetings, so a lot of their work is done by phone. Members often joke about the two-hour phone conversations that always seem to start just at dinner time. These calls, often from strangers who are desperate to adopt, mix information, counseling, and support. Because the conversations are long and demanding, the best-organized groups have developed lists of volunteers who are available at specific times. These members are flooded with calls, so it is a courtesy to them if you restrict your inquiry to official hours.

Some of the larger parent groups have developed mail networks instead of phone systems. The best example of this approach is the Latin American Parent Association (LAPA). Families write to this group, describing their situation and adoption hopes and enclosing a self-addressed stamped envelope. The organization replies with information and questions. The back-and-forth correspondence permits families to acquire a large amount of up-to-date information.

Newsletters. The bulletins put out by parent groups are usually of marginal value—they provide dates of forthcoming events, comment, and a few random facts. Some organizations offer a variety of publications, which can be anything from bound books to typescripts describing adoption procedures at one place. *OURS* magazine lists a number of available publications. Another source for books is the NACAC Resource and Membership Office, 3900 Market Street, Suite 247, Riverside, Calif. 92501. Telephone: (714) 788-6423.

Postplacement Support. After a child enters your home, adoptive organizations continue to be of service, providing support, social contacts, and counseling. Some adoption agencies, especially the privately endowed ones, do offer help after placement, although that help almost always comes as individual counseling rather than social support. Other agencies, most notably the public ones, really don't have the time, money, or interest to help counsel a family after an adoption is completed. But this kind of continuing mutual support is a fundamental part of every parent group.

Lobbying. Politics is not usually an issue for families considering adoption, but then comes the awakening. People approach adoption with the assumption that America is a place that loves dogs, kids, and apple pie. The discovery of the government's lack of concern about the chaos in the world of adoption comes as a profound shock. One woman said to me, "Even after five years with the group, I keep catching myself being surprised. I'm always realizing I was just a Pollyanna again." As a result, many parent associations have become involved in local politics, and members testify before state legislatures to press for laws more favorable to adoption and the needs of waiting children. The NACAC association was specifically formed to give parent organizations a voice on the federal level in the creation of national policy.

Placement. Parent groups are not agencies and are not licensed to place children in homes. Yet it does happen, from time to time, that a pregnant woman who wants to give up her baby for adoption calls a parent association. Some respond with "I'm sorry, we can't help you"; others will notify a waiting family and tell them that an independent adoption can be arranged. The situation has to be handled carefully, but I know of a number of lawful adoptions that began in just this way.

Fees. The cost of maintaining the associations is usually met through collecting dues and occasionally by charging for the workshops. In the past government funds have been available to support specific projects, but with severe government cutbacks, there is uncertainty about how much longer these funds will be available. On the whole, parent groups operate on a frayed shoestring and need donations in return for services.

Issues

Professionalism. Agency workers are unhappy about the rise of adoptive-parent associations. Their disapproval is usually stated in terms of professional aims versus amateur enthusiasm; it is a battle the agencies cannot hope to win. Their workers face two important disadvantages:

• *Experience.* Workers may have long histories of placing children in adoptive homes, but very few of them have ever adopted children themselves. When it comes to counseling, few workers can say, "I know exactly how you feel because I went through it too." This bit of empathy in a time of frustration and pain is so welcome that applicants just naturally turn to their contacts at a parent group instead of to their agency workers.

• *Neutrality.* Workers counter the first argument by pointing to their professional expertise, which enables them to judge which placements are most likely to succeed, but of course this judgment is precisely what families are eager to avoid. Simple prudence keeps parents from being too open with their workers about any doubts and fears they may have. After the placement of a child, prudence still dictates that parents not raise too many problems with their workers. A worker might misunderstand and decide the child should be removed from the home. None of these fears applies in the case of parent groups. There a parent can discuss fears, doubts, and anger openly without having to worry that candor may ruin all chances of adoption.

Resistance. Sometimes agencies have become so irritated with a parent group that they take their anger out on an applicant who has come to them via that association. There are many reports about this problem, but it has been hard to find anyone who will actually say that his activities in an association made adoption more difficult. Not surprisingly, no agency workers will admit that they do not like to work with people who are members of a parent group, but a lot of workers do grumble about "amateur meddlers." Caution suggests that although there is no need to hide your involvement with an adoptive organization, it is best not to stress such contact when talking with an agency worker.

Minorities. With a few notable exceptions, parent groups have an almost exclusively white, middle-class membership. Some of the more forthright leaders have expressed their disappointment that they have not been more successful in broadening their membership. It is up to each reader to decide how much or how little help can be had from a local association. Even though some groups can look like gatherings of the Daughters of the American Revolution, they do have valuable information for all adoptive parents.

Rumors. Perhaps the worst thing that can happen to a parent organization is for it to undergo a transformation from an information source into a rumor mill. The adoption maze is filled with hearsay, and inevitably there are people who take misinformation at face value. When frustrated families get together, they may swap rumors instead of reporting helpful information. The best way a group can combat this tendency is to turn adoption workshops and panel discussions into two-way affairs in which searching families report their experiences. Questionnaires have been developed by some parent groups to be used by members after they adopt a child. Through these services, any changes in the local situation can be reported as quickly as possible.

Adoption rumors run toward defeatism, cynicism, and miracle cures. Tales of miracle cures promote frauds. One person becomes convinced that so-and-so is a promising source for a child, and this person generously shares his hunch with others. Soon the fraud is attracting lots of customers.

False hope inevitably turns to despair. A striking example of this problem was revealed in a rumor passed along by several people at one association, a rumor that Korean adoptions had become impossible. In fact, there was a nearby agency that had strong Korean ties and was giving preferential treatment to applicants who said they wanted to adopt Korean children.

Cynicism is often behind both the miracle cure and the defeatist claims. Agencies are accused of blocking adoptions for simple monetary reasons. Bureaucrats are assigned the most callous of motives for the slow grinding of their gears. Of course this cynicism breeds a sense of hopelessness, but it also makes people easy prey for promises of miracle cures. The argument runs as follows: since adoption is deliberately made difficult by greedy agencies, adoption would be easy if only one could find an honorable intermediary.

Like all cynical arguments, this one is difficult to refute. All protests can be dismissed as naive or self-serving; however, greed and a lust for power are not the root of the problems in contemporary adoption. Honorable people do plunge into the adoption maze, but they still find a maze. Agency workers are seldom wicked and many in fact are splendid people. Like the rest of us, though, they suffer from human weaknesses—prejudice, fatigue, and a lack of imagination.

Problems of cynicism and misinformation are by no means universal in parent associations and are easily parried when encountered, but be alert to them. When seeking information at parent groups, steer clear of members who reduce all adoption problems to the connivances of darkly motivated individuals.

Step by Step

Information. Your first priority in approaching a parent association should be to pluck out the information offered through workshops, orientation sessions, and the phone bank. Try to get specific names and facts. What local agencies handle the sort of adoption you are seeking? What contacts are useful in international adoptions? What are the average costs? Are there any important local laws that complicate adoptions? (This last matter is often difficult to determine, because many people have no idea which aspects of adoption are peculiar to the local scene and which are nationwide.)

At this early stage, your primary need is for help in finding your way to the maze entrance. Emphasize that concern in your initial contacts with parent groups. You need to know how to get started.

Counseling. Once you begin the process, a new series of questions and doubts begin to arise:

• My worker is recommending such-and-such type of child. I'm attracted to the idea, but wonder if it is really right for me.

• I am waiting for a particular woman to give birth. Now I learn that the mother is not sure if the father is white or black. I think I want the baby in either case, but wonder if I can really handle a biracial child.

• My agency wants several hundred dollars before starting its study. Is there any reason for me not to pay it?

Take questions like these to your parents group. Other people have already confronted these same worries. Find out who they are and talk to them.

The adoption of waiting children has inspired two contrary schools of thought about counseling. One side stresses the difficulties of a particular adoption, while the other seeks to be encouraging and suggest that "you can do it." I prefer the second approach, although there is no denying that some people have to be hit pretty hard before they wake up to the difficulties of an idea. These people are the ones who, after hearing about all the problems of a particular adoption, say to themselves, "Well, I don't think that would happen to us." You should try to balance whichever approach you get. If all the talk seems to be on the gloomy side, ask if there aren't some pleasures and satisfactions as well. If the talk follows the opposite tack, insist on having the difficulties specified in detail. Don't settle for less than the full picture.

Support. After a while you won't care about facts or advice; you will just want somebody to say the effort is worthwhile and all will turn out well in the end. You will be lucky if you have an old friend who offers this kind of support. Many people discover that their friends are not at all understanding of the ambition to adopt, especially when seeking to adopt a waiting child. In the parent group, however, you will find many people who appreciate your desire, know it can be done, and are rooting for your success.

See the "Directory of Parent Associations" at the end of this book.

7

The Agencies

Agencies are the best-known adoption institutions, and many people start out with the assumption that all legal adoptions must be conducted through them. This assumption is false; many legal adoptions do not use them. Agencies are nonprofit firms with licenses to place children in adoptive homes. They can also conduct confidential inquiries into the backgrounds of applicants.

Books usually identify three types of agencies: public, religious, and private. Public agencies normally charge no fee or quite a small one. The religious-based agencies are maintained by all major faiths and are often willing to place children with families from outside their sponsoring churches. No person considering adoption should avoid a religious agency merely because she is not a member of that particular religion. Private agencies are the least predictable as to quality and integrity, ranging from the extremely helpful to the outright fraudulent. They also have quite a spread in fees.

Open lists versus reserved lists. In practical terms, this public/religious/private distinction is technical and often secondary. The real issue for families is the agency's policy toward its own waiting list. In this matter, agencies can be distinguished as either *open* or *reserved.*

Some agencies place people on their waiting lists after only a minimal amount of screening. Applicants who approach these agencies are almost certain to have a child placed with them eventually, but the wait may be five or six years. Because of the extent of this wait, age becomes a major screening issue. An agency that lists a couple when they are aged thirty-five and thirty-four is not likely to be able to help them before they turn forty-one and forty. Open-list agencies seldom accept people past their mid-thirties for infant adoptions.

Reserved-list agencies do a lot of screening before they accept anyone who is interested in adopting a healthy infant or preschooler. Because agency practices vary so widely, getting on a list is often just a matter of luck. If an agency has an opening on its list, the next applicant may be arbitrarily accepted. I visited one agency that accepted applicants once each year during a two-hour period. If you came through the door during those two hours, you were on the list; if not, you were off. Naturally, the line for applicants begins to form days before that two-hour period arrives. Another agency maintained superelite standards for families and rejected all but the most traditional applicants.

The difference between waiting-list policies leads to many practical concerns for people applying to the various agencies. Throughout this chapter, the distinction between open-list and reserved-list agencies will be the only one I will stress.

Both types of agencies face one set of concrete facts: (1) there are many more people coming in search of infants or preschoolers than there are children available at the agency; (2) it costs an agency time and money to study the background of an applicant; (3) an agency will begin to study people only if it thinks the applicants are likely to receive a child.

From the perspective of families, these points mean that dealing with almost any agency is likely to be a long and frustrating experience. If you work with open-list agencies, years of nearly perfect silence can pass. If you confront reserved-list agencies, it takes such hard work to find someone who will simply accept your application that the struggle often inspires bitterness and resentment.

The difference in waiting-list policies reflects differing attitudes toward untraditional applicants. By and large, reserved-list agencies continue to serve the well-to-do professional and managerial classes. I have talked with a few reserved-list agency directors who would, I'm sure, maintain a reserved waiting list even if it meant that the babies would have to wait for placement. The anger caused by such agency policies adds an unpleasant tone to one's experience in the adoption maze. Whether I spoke about agencies with people on the East Coast, in Texas, or in California, I heard persistent condemnation. The anger was almost a physical thing. Not surprisingly, these areas have mostly reserved-list agencies, which turn away most of the families who approach them. In a state like Wisconsin, which has mainly open-list agencies, I found that people spoke in much more civil tones about adoption agencies. Quite obviously, from a public relations standpoint, agencies do better if they maintain open lists.

The prepared approach. Because of the differences in agency attitudes, it is best to have the fullest possible sense of what an agency is like before you approach it, especially if you are an untraditional applicant. Parent associations should be able to alert you to the policies of the various agencies in your area. The best of them will even have agency contacts who might help you get on the reserved lists. At the very least, when you telephone an agency, you should be prepared to discover that it uses a reserved list, so if you are promptly turned away, you can recognize that the rejection says something about the agency, not about you.

Public agencies, in theory, cannot argue that whole classes of people are unworthy to adopt children. In practice, their responsibility to consider "the best interests of the child" permits them to deny an adoption, but it makes it difficult for them to say point-blank "We don't allow adoptions by people who are   [fill in the prejudice of your choice]   ." Such a remark would leave them open to a lawsuit. Instead, they just let people drift until they give up. Jacobina, in chapter 2, put up with a decade-long runaround because she had gone to a public agency that did not wish to help her, a single black woman, but did not dare turn her away.

Public agencies that would like to keep reserved lists can become fairly blatant in their practices. One adoptive father recalled his introduction to public-agency policy in an orientation session: "At that first meeting they proceeded to break the hope of everyone there. They left us with no doubts that because we were white and Jewish and wanted an under-five-year-old, we would be six times harder to help. If they could have thrown us out of that meeting, they would have." The irony was that after all that discouragement, this couple was accepted almost at once for a study. The agency had managed to scare off so many applicants that its white-family list was getting short.

Waiting children. You can adopt a waiting child only through an agency, but this should not be a problem, since so many children are waiting. Remember, however, the reserved-list policy grew up because of a dislike for some of the kinds of people applying. This attitude also affects waiting-child applications. Many agencies now

place waiting children only because it is either that or go out of business. Regrettably, this practical conversion was not accompanied by
any fundamental change of heart about people. The attitude that leads
an agency to want a reserved waiting list is reflected in a distaste for
many of the families (often working class) who wish to adopt waiting
children. The agency workers may feel real bafflement that anyone
would want to adopt a child who is not a Gerber-label perfect baby.

Cornelia Pesaro's story is typical of the problems some people face:
she and her husband were going through an agency's list of waiting
children and were attracted by the photo of a three-year-old girl
named Nancy, who was listed as borderline retarded. Both Cornelia
and her husband were acquainted with several retarded children, and
they had a clear sense of what they were asking about. Nonetheless,
their agency worker could never imagine why anyone would be interested in a child like Nancy. The Pesaros were well educated. Nancy
would never graduate from high school. The Pesaros still insisted that
they meet Nancy. The agency refused, arguing that first they needed
a lot of counseling on the subject of retarded children. The Pesaros
replied that they knew retarded children, but could not be expected
to make any decision about Nancy until they saw her and got a sense
of her. This circle of agency delay and family pleading might have
lasted forever had not the Pesaros found a newborn baby boy from
quite a different source and adopted him independently. After that
incident, the agency refused even to discuss an adoption of Nancy. A
few months later Cornelia saw Nancy's photograph in a list of children
still waiting to be adopted.

I am not suggesting the situation is hopeless, only arguing that
preparation is necessary. Agencies can provide the quickest route
through the adoption maze. They can do the best job of matching your
needs and gifts with those of individual children. I do know people
who found working with agencies, even with reserved-list agencies,
to be simple and enjoyable. One such person, a lieutenant colonel,
expressed surprise at the thought that anybody might find the adoption process difficult or confusing. (Let's call his family the Colonels.)
Perhaps it was luck, perhaps it was military efficiency, but the Colonels did approach the agency in just the right way. They went for their
first interview in May and received a daughter the next February.
Their story illustrates how neatly it can be done.

First, the Colonels had a clear idea of what sort of child they were
looking for—a girl, preschool age. When they went for their inter-

view, they were unable to say just why they wanted to adopt, but they were quite articulate about why they wanted the child to be a preschool-age girl. They framed their answers in terms of their family's needs and what they had to offer a child.

They had never spoken to anyone at a parent association, but a good friend, also an adoptive parent, was knowledgeable about local adoptions and suggested the agency best able to help them. So the Colonels applied there rather than calling a number chosen at random from the Yellow Pages.

Both husband and wife spoke freely and openly with the agency, keeping the interview reasonably professional and businesslike but without trying to hide things and without ever becoming defensive. They won the agency worker over to their side.

At this point, they did become involved in a parent group, meeting other families who had already adopted. The Colonels found themselves thinking about adoption more clearly and were able to speak openly about questions that they hadn't previously even thought about. In the meantime, the agency worker pushed their cause, and one day it was done: a two-and-a-half-year-old daughter arrived.

Step by Step (Reserved-List Agencies)

Initial phone call. The chaotic spirit of reserved-list agencies is illustrated by the situation in New York City during the summer of 1983. At that time, there were nearly fifty agencies in the city licensed for adoption, but anyone looking in the Yellow Pages found the names of only nine. The rest didn't bother to advertise their existence. In other cities I have also found a number of agencies that were not listed in the Yellow Pages—stark evidence of how challenging it can be just to find your way to the maze entrance. Get a full list of local agencies from your parent association.

Most agencies refer to the first contact—almost always a phone call—with a prospective applicant as the "initial screening." Before telephoning, you should try to learn which agency screenings are least likely to filter you out. If you are hoping to adopt an infant, only a few agencies will be willing to speak further. This preparation may seem like needless delay when a simple phone call would reveal everything, but from the agency's viewpoint, your phone call is not simple. It is a request for a service they cannot expect to provide. The majority of reserved-list agencies have a policy of actively discouraging people who say they want to adopt.

From the information acquired in the course of your preparation, you should develop a short list of agencies in your area that are likely to help you. Tell them you are interested in adoption and are trying to get information. (That's a less threatening goal. They have information; they may not have a child.) Let the agency raise the matter of the type of child you want. If you are hoping for an infant, tell the worker that your thoughts lean in that direction but that right now you are chiefly interested in just getting information about adoption—how it works and what is possible. If you don't want an infant, say so clearly. Again, however, you are calling for information, not a child.

The agency commonly wants to get some information of its own: your name, age, length of marriage, number of children already in your family, type of child you are thinking of adopting. It should also invite you to an orientation meeting, although it may say that in your case the meeting will be waived and that it will get back to you. If the matter is put on this indefinite basis, take the name of the person you are speaking to and fire off a brief note expressing your thanks for the attention and restating your desire for an appointment.

You should also prepare a longer list of local agencies that are likely to screen you out. Call them and say you are asking for information. The point of these calls is not to crash through the screen but to make contact. If they indicate that nothing will follow from your call, send them a letter thanking them for their time and saying that you are sorry they cannot help you right now, but that you hope they will keep you in mind, just in case. Enclose an adoption résumé (see sample) with the letter. It is quite possible that this letter will go into the trash, but most agencies will follow bureaucratic procedure and file it in some dead file.

It does happen that an agency sometimes becomes responsible for an infant and has nowhere to place it. A large Catholic agency with a reserved list, for example, had a child born in its hospital but the mother specified that the baby be placed in a Protestant home. This agency had routinely turned away Protestant applicants and so had no suitable family on its waiting list. It went through its files and found a three-year-old letter from a Protestant couple. That couple was more than delighted by the miracle that had suddenly turned up a child. They had never expected to hear from the agency again.

Adoption Résumé

You should have photocopies of a one-page sheet with the following information. Send this sheet to any agency that does not offer to send you an intake questionnaire. A sample follows.

NAMES:	Oliver and Ann Sutter	
ADDRESS:	1776 Allen Lane	
	Summerville, Ill. 12345	
PHONE:	(312) 555-1212	
BIRTH DATES:	Oliver—May 16, 1950	Ann—October 28, 1948
RELIGION:	Protestant	
ETHNIC BACKGROUND:	Oliver—Canadian	Ann—Italian
OCCUPATION:	Oliver—Salesman	Ann—Biology teacher
TYPE OF CHILD SOUGHT:	Infant or preschooler.	
AREAS OF FLEXIBILITY:	Physical disability all right. Certain emotional disabilities acceptable. Mixed race all right. Either sex.	

Of course, this kind of miracle is so rare that not two readers in ten thousand can expect to find a child this way, but your chances are poor with every contact. If you are looking for an infant or preschooler, you must try as many unlikely sources as possible, knowing that one of them will succeed eventually.

Orientation. You should go to every informational meeting you are invited to. From the applicant's point of view, the purpose of these meetings is to be kept up to date. The agency explains its policy, outlines its costs and procedures, and discusses the children it has waiting.

From the agency's perspective, these meetings are an opportunity to determine which applicants it is most likely to be able to help, so the meeting focuses on adoption through that particular agency. Usually these meetings underscore the difficulty of locating a healthy infant. Many people who come to these meetings are completely unaware of the extent of the changes in adoption. They often have not thought beyond the old idea "Well, if we can't have a baby biologically, let's adopt one." Remember, if you are not limiting your search to a healthy newborn, say so out loud.

Application forms are generally passed out, although some agencies request that you write your own letter of application. Always take the form and apply. At this point neither you nor the agency is committed to working together and neither side is yet able to make a clear judgment about the other.

First interview. This step is sometimes called the "intake interview" or "initial consultation." Whatever you call it, it is the first time you and the agency have an opportunity to look each other over closely and discuss in detail what you want and what the agency can do for you.

Agencies like to say that the quality they are most eager to find in applicants is "flexibility." Like most buzzwords, the term is inexact. Agencies like applicants who are flexible only in the sense that they are interested in more than just a newborn child. A person who is so flexible as to become vague, however, is not favored. A more accurate definition of the qualities preferred in applicants is that they be specific and open. "Specific" means that the applicants know the type of child sought—age range, racial and ethnic range, any disabilities they would consider or refuse to consider. "Open" means that the applicants are willing to state their desires clearly and frankly.

The agency has two questions it wants answered: Will these people accept one of the children we will be able to provide? Will one of the children do all right with this family? If the answers to these questions are yes, the chances of getting on the waiting list are good.

Too many applicants approach this important interview with no thought other than "Oh, please, please, accept us." This attitude becomes especially obsessive if applicants have been turned down before. Qualifying for a study by an agency—any agency—begins to seem like the only real barrier to success.

You will do better if you keep your own interests in mind. Is this agency likely to provide the kind of child you are looking for? Does it look like you will be able to work with this agency? After all, your time is limited too. You may be willing to spend it generously in order to find a child, but you don't want simply to waste it. Eventually you are going to be working with just one agency, so ask yourself: Is this the one I want to work with?

I have heard many people say that they didn't care which agency handled their study, just so long as one did it: "You can always have a copy of the homestudy sent to another agency." I have never known a person to report that this attitude led to success.

The worker. The single most important factor in determining the outcome of your first interview and, later, the agency study is how well you get along with your worker. Many agency workers care about people and act sensitively toward them, but of course there is a wide range in worker abilities. Even within a single agency the talents of the workers vary considerably. For most people, the worker assigned to them determines what they think of a particular agency. In recalling their experiences, people seldom comment on agencies' general policies. Instead they say things like:

"I had a wonderful time with [agency X]. The social worker was so enthusiastic. I remember she called a few weeks after the intake interview and sounded so excited. 'I got it. I get to be your social worker,' she said. I felt she liked us and was on our side."

"I have as little to do with [the agency] as possible. My social worker is probably a very nice person in ordinary life, but she has no sympathy for me or why I want to adopt."

The two people quoted above were speaking about the same agency, though not about the same worker. The first speaker got from application to final court decree in two years. The second was still struggling to have an adoption completed three years after the agency had placed a child with her. During all those years, her agency worker kept raising new questions about procedure, information, and counseling. In these bureaucratic settings, it is up to your worker to decide whether to hasten or prolong the process. Thus, from your viewpoint, the most important question about any worker is whether or not he will become your advocate. Win the worker and you win the agency.

If you have the good fortune to develop a strong relationship with your agency worker, all is well and good. If not, your case is still not lost, but you must set the worker at ease. For many workers the most intimidating aspect of applicants is their chip-on-the-shoulder resentment. A lot of people are angry about having to allow so intimate an inquiry into their search for a family. Agency workers have a chip on the shoulder too, resulting from the impossibility of their task—deciding whether or not you have the skills necessary to be a parent. The workers are often terrified that applicants will see through their facade of expertise, so they put up a stony exterior of cool professionalism. This impersonal exterior, of course, merely increases the frustration and anger of applicants. The workers sense the growing resentment and retreat even deeper behind glazed eyes. Such a cycle is hopeless. It means that the one person on the agency committee who has any real sense of you is terrified. The committee verdict is inevitable: application denied.

To avoid this catastrophe, you must resist any temptation to get your back up and to try to force a decision. That approach cannot work in a bureaucratic setting. Your personal strength simply drives the terrified bureaucrat deeper into his shell. You have to have the courage and the shrewdness to be nonaggressive when you face your worker.

If a discussion goes poorly, the worker may mount a defensive assault on your ego (lest you attack first). You might, for example, report that you were a quiet child in school and did not have too many close friends. Instead of a nod or a noncomittal writing down of the facts, the worker can reply, "That's very unusual." If you panic and spring to your own defense, you lose. You must have the cool to turn this challenge aside. "Oh, is it?" or "I sure hope it's not going to hurt my chances for adoption" are better answers. Adoptive parents must make their workers feel that they recognize the workers' humanity, respect their position, and want to work with them, not challenge them.

Application. With reserved-list agencies, formal application often is a major step. The willingness of an agency to accept your application commonly means a willingness to work with you. Formal application calls for a number of documents—birth certificate, marriage certificate, a copy of the previous year's income tax return, and a health statement. Previous military service, naturalization, or divorces also have to be documented. Sometimes a police clearance is requested. Most agencies still require that applicants who are seeking to adopt an infant provide a doctor's report attesting to their infertility.

All these documents serve to establish that you are who you say you are. They are taken seriously and are unlikely to be a source of problems. When submitting them, draw your worker's attention to any health or financial abnormalities, explain them and why they will not interfere with your ability to raise a family. Add the words "I hope that's not going to be a serious problem with our application." Bureaucrats can waive rules as readily as they can invoke them. They like to be told things and to be asked for favorable consideration. They do not like to be surprised and learn that something was kept from them.

The study. After the first interview, both you and the agency have a better idea of each other. If the agency thinks it is likely to be of help, it will report that it wants to study you. (Their report is usually called a "homestudy" or a "case study.") At this point you have to decide whether or not to allow this particular agency to do the study. If you have applied to another agency and would rather work with it, then this is a time for frankness. Call it; report that another agency has offered to do a study, but that you would prefer to work with the agency being called. Perhaps it will respond favorably, perhaps not, but at least your position will be clear.

It might be tempting to allow a study by every agency that wants to do one, but the agencies will not be amused. If they find out what you are doing, they will drop you—all of them. How might they find out? From your references, perhaps. Agency workers know one another and something might come up in conversation that would tip the game.

For most people, the approach of the study is a little frightening. Agencies often stress that doing a study does not mean they have already decided they can place a child with you. However, it is unusual for a study to result in a negative report, because agencies don't like to take on the expense of a study unless they think it will turn out satisfactorily.

The study can take different forms. The shortest I know of consists of a single two-and-a-half-hour interview. Typically, however, a study involves three interviews. One is a joint session with both husband and wife (plus any children); it is usually held at the family's home. Then interviews are conducted individually with each member of the couple.

Some agencies have begun experimenting, looking for ways to make the study less intimidating and more useful to the applicants. These new studies can be quite imaginative. Some even ask the applicants to write their own study report. The most common of the new forms is the group study. In this method, a number of applicant families get together once a week, usually for five to ten weeks, to discuss specific issues of adoption. These discussions are designed to teach at the same time that they give the agency worker a sense of each person's interests and capacities.

Whatever form they take, homestudies often provoke resentment. Applicants say pregnant women don't have to explain that they are sure they can handle the chores of being a parent, so why should the applicant? Agencies justify the studies on the grounds that they have a responsibility to the children not to put them in unacceptable homes. Their point is sound, but not all questions asked during a study seem to keep to that matter. I know a woman whose worker asked, "Were you trying to have a baby before you decided to adopt?" and, when told yes, went on to ask, "How many times a week did you and your husband have intercourse?" Such questions are an invasion of privacy, and certainly there is no need to answer them. They should be politely parried.

The report. The written study that comes out of these interviews covers the following areas:

• Factual data—This section lists age, religion, occupation, dates and nature of agency contacts, physical details, health, financial situation. This material is chiefly useful in determining whether or not a particular child might be suitable for your family.

• Family data—The main issue here is how strong the marriage is. The study also inquires into how the applicants get along with other members of their family. The agency wants to be sure that any child it places in your home will find a reasonably stable setting. More studies probably fail on this issue than on any other.

• Child data—This section lists the kind of child sought (age range, preferred sex, and so on). There is also a report on other experiences with children. The key danger of this part of the study is that it will define an applicant's interests or abilities too narrowly. Make sure that the worker understands any and all characteristics on which you are flexible.

• Conclusion—This section evaluates your attitude toward adoption and your understanding of children; then it recommends that your application be either accepted or denied.

Most agencies do not like applicants to see copies of their report. There is no good reason for the secrecy beyond the fact that bureaucracies never like outsiders to see documents about themselves. I do know a woman who managed, quite outside the agency's knowledge, to obtain the report. To her surprise and pleasure, the document was filled with favorable comments. Unless your references say unflattering things, there is not much of a way for the interviewer to come up with unfavorable facts. The agencies do not engage in detective work and know only what you, your documents, and your references report.

Agency decision. No honorable agency will conduct a study unless it believes that the conclusion will be favorable; however, agencies do have the power to decide that a child should not be placed in your home. Rejection is rare, but it happens, usually only with strong cause. I know several instances in which the reason for rejection sprang directly from the applicant's mouth. One case involved a white man seeking to adopt a black child. In the course of an interview he voiced a few racial slurs and was deemed unsuitable for his proposed adoption. Another rejection came about because the prospective parents were able to describe discipline only in terms of physical punishment.

Sometimes poor references hurt, although that problem is unusual. In selecting references you should name only people you can rely on to say good things. Before listing people, check with them to let them know you plan to use their names.

On those rare occasions when a study ends in rejection, you have the right to know why. With some public agencies you also have a right of appeal, but that prospect is uncertain and seldom leads to anything fruitful. Sometimes the reason is correctable—perhaps temporary financial difficulties—and you can have the rejection changed to a simple postponement of a final decision. On the whole, however, the best response is to shrug it off; you have met a dead end in the maze. This agency is not going to put you on its list. Success lies elsewhere.

That advice is easy to give, nearly impossible to swallow. Usually people who are rejected develop deeper anger toward agencies. Somehow you are going to have to get past that fury, because when you approach the next agency worker, you had best be smiling.

The most common reason for rejection is the applicant's alienation of the worker. Something put the worker off and the searching family is turned down. The rejection can lead to increased resentment, which provokes still more rejection and frustration. I spoke to one family who were caught literally for years in this cycle of rejection/ more resentment/further rejection. Of course, by the end they were giving the most sarcastic sorts of answers to workers' questions:

QUESTION: Have you got a closet to put the child's clothes in?
ANSWER: What do you think? We're going to throw her things on the floor?
Application denied.
QUESTION: What would you think about this child? (Shown a photo of a six-and-a-half-year-old girl)
ANSWER: Why, she's beautiful. (Suspicious pause) What's wrong with her?
Application denied.

In fact, these people are good and loving parents. They were also determined—it took five years of struggle for them to adopt. They were finally accepted by a reserved-list agency, but only after they had been so completely defeated by the cycle of rejection that they came humbly and hopelessly before one final worker. She responded sympathetically to their case and their application was accepted.

Waiting. Once you have the study behind you, there can be a long, long wait. Do not assume that some invisible process is working off in the distance to locate a child for you. As an absolute minimum you should call the agency every four months, just to reassert your interest. It may respond with the yeah-yeah voice so common to bureaucrats who have no news, but your call is still important. Follow it up each time with a short note confirming your phone call. The agency will toss the note in your file and eventually someone will say, "Gee, these people really seem to care." If you do not insist on a newborn infant and if the agency has books of photos, go through the listings at least once every two months.

Fees. Agencies that charge fees have a variety of payment schedules and quite a range of rates. Some agencies want a fee to be paid upon the filing of an application and even for such initial contacts as the orientation session. I know many perfectly honorable and trustworthy agencies that charge these early fees, but the nibbler charges make me uncomfortable. Because the present adoption scene is so uncertain and requires prospective parents to seek so many contacts, I am disturbed by the growing tendency of agencies to require $20, $30, and even $50 before the first interview. Reserved-list agencies make no reciprocal commitment when such money arrives, and very little money should change hands until an agency indicates that it expects to be able to work with a family.

The total fee is negotiated before the study interviews begin. You should be clear on the agency costs and the payment schedule. Two common schedules are: (1) one-third at the start of the study, one-third on completion of the study, and one-third when the adoption decree is issued; and (2) one-half at the end of the study and one-half at the conclusion of the legal process. Of course, there are many variations on these basic schedules.

The issue of fees has become confused because of the few fraudulent agencies that have appeared. Be cautious of agencies that agree very quickly to do a study and then want a substantial payment in advance. Fees to "keep the files open" are so suspect I would make inquiries with the police. Any agency that refuses to take a personal check is also suspect. One man said to me, "Looking back on it, I feel silly. It was so obvious. Their letter said right out, 'No personal checks. Please send money order or certified check.' But at the time, it just seemed like a good way to get a quick homestudy." Legitimate agencies know that nobody seriously interested in adoption is going to write a phony check.

Placement. "We have a child." It is an exciting day when the agency has somebody it would like you to meet. In the case of older children, the first look may be surreptitious. Other meetings can be more direct. You have the right to say "No." I have known families who, much to their own amazement, even said no to a hard-to-find newborn and still adopted a little later.

Because the wait has been so long, many people become fearful of leaving town on business or for a short vacation, lest the opportunity to receive a child be missed. Agencies are aware of the elementary fact that people cannot shape their whole lives around the uncertainties of placement. If you let your agency know how you can be reached, it will contact you.

Usually agencies will also give you time to get your affairs in order. A common plan, for example, is for the wife to quit her job when the child arrives. This is not always possible on five minutes' notice. By the time an agency is ready to place a child with you, it is usually eager to do whatever is reasonable to ease the process. This is the point where the strengths of bureaucracy are most evident. Having reached a decision, the agency proves flexible and imaginative in implementing it. Thus, the details of placement depend largely on your own circumstances. Some people get through all the steps—notification, viewing, acceptance, and bringing home—in a single day; others can take up to two weeks or even longer.

Step by Step (Open-List Agencies)

The formal steps toward receiving a child from an open-list agency are the same as for a reserved-list one, but they are free from the painful struggle to persuade your worker to take up your cause. Theoretically, you can simply wait patiently for three, five, or however many years are necessary until the agency calls your number. In practice, such patience is ill-advised. Getting on an open waiting list is not a guarantee of ultimate success. No one can predict what your area's adoption picture will be like in a few years. It is also not possible to promise that the study will go well. Nineteen out of twenty open-list-agency studies are completed routinely and without difficulty, but for that twentieth applicant, the bitterness of waiting passively for years only to be rejected in the end is hard to accept. The other chapters in part II on locating a child ought to be consulted, even by families who are on several agency waiting lists.

Initial phone call. The main question with an open-list agency is whether a phone call is sufficient to get you on its list. The agency will screen you during the phone conversation. If you are not immediately ruled out by this screening, it may be that your name will go directly on the waiting list or further contact may be required. Be sure you are clear as to whether or not your call has put you on the waiting list. Also ask for an estimate of the waiting time. The answer will depend on the kind of child you are looking for. As always, if you are interested in adopting a waiting child, make sure the agency understands that that is your ambition. Too often it just assumes the caller wants a newborn. Follow up the call with a note of thanks, restating your interest and pleasure at being on their waiting list. (The worst foul-up is to be told that you will be placed on the waiting list only to learn much later that because of some sort of confusion your name is not in the agency records.) You can use the "Waiting-List Form" to keep a record of agency contacts.

Orientation. Some open-list agencies invite applicants to a group meeting soon after they call; some wait years, until they are ready to begin study. The purpose of an open-list orientation meeting is primarily informational. The sidewise glancing and inspecting so common at reserved-agency meetings can be avoided.

Waiting. Waiting for years is no easy matter. Is anything really happening? Call the agency every six months to make sure it is still operating. Some agencies send out an annual note reassuring you that you are still on their list. If the note asks for a reply, respond at once by phone and then by letter. If the agency does not receive an answer, it will probably remove your name from its list.

Every time you change your address or phone number, you should send the new information to the agency.

Agency contact. Eventually the agency will call to say your name is high enough on its list for it to begin working with you. At this point you should clarify all details about its fees, your desires, and your specific expectations. The agency must now decide whether or not to study you. This question is less frightening than with reserved-list agencies because open-list agencies are not trying arbitrarily to reduce their number of applicants.

Waiting-List Form

Keep a record of your dealings with any agency that says it will place your name on a waiting list.

Agency	Date Notified of Listing	Notified by Phone or Letter?	Name of Person Spoken With	Date of Formal Thanks (in writing)
1.	/ /			/ /
2.	/ /			/ /
3.	/ /			/ /
4.	/ /			/ /
5.	/ /			/ /
6.	/ /			/ /
7.	/ /			/ /
8.	/ /			/ /
9.	/ /			/ /

If one agency decides to study you, should you tell other agencies that have your name on their lists? *Usually not.* Wait until you are sure this study has gone all right. The difficulty with this prudence is that if one open-list agency has reached your name, the other open-list agencies in the area may be about to call as well. Agency workers take it badly if you let more than one agency actually study you. If other agencies begin to call, you will have to tell them that you are working with an agency already.

Application. Formal application with an open-list agency is usually postponed until the agency is ready to begin acting on your case.

The study. The purpose and methods of the agency study and report are the same as with a reserved-list agency.

Fees. Fee schedules are also the same as at reserved-list agencies. You have to be alert to the possibility of fraud with open-list agencies because most take-the-money-and-run agencies suggest that you can get on their waiting lists without difficulty. At the same time, the presence of several open-list agencies in an area tends to reduce the sort of desperate appeal that fraudulent agencies thrive on.

Placement. There is no appreciable difference between placement by an open-list agency and a reserved-list agency's placement.

110

8

International Adoptions

In the fall of 1979 Susan Picasso called her county agency and was placed on its adoption waiting list. The agency phoned back four years later, in the spring of 1983, to say it was ready to begin working to find her an infant. Susan turned them down. Since getting on the county's waiting list, she had twice adopted babies—a boy and a girl—from Latin America.

Speed is not the only reason, but it is certainly the primary one behind the rise of international adoptions. When I listen to people's stories of searches lasting several fruitless years, I shake my head and ask, "Why didn't you adopt from abroad?" The standard answers are that the families didn't know it could be done, they thought it would be too complicated, or they feared it would be too expensive. A fourth reason, racial prejudice, is also sometimes given. The matters of cost and complexity can usually be worked out. Racial prejudice is another question. Except for people with this last concern, international adoptions have become the method of choice for locating an infant. They are more complicated, but they are also quicker. Thanks to the jet plane, families are no longer forced to restrict their searches for adoptive children to the United States.

Of course, there are all kinds of explanations for why a foreign-born baby might be put up for adoption. Just as in the United States, there can be many reasons, but the most common one is the unwanted pregnancy of an unmarried woman. The developing world has not yet seen the radical change in values and opportunities that makes it possible for an unmarried woman to raise her child at home. In many countries it is still a terrible stigma for a single woman to have a baby, and it is a frightful burden for her to try to raise the child. This very traditional reason—the same one that made so many American babies available during the 1960s—is the chief cause for the availability of adoptable infants in foreign countries.

No country can be completely ruled out as a source for an adoptable child. There have even been some recent American adoptions from the People's Republic of China; however, most foreign adoptions concentrate on a few regions: the fringes of east Asia (Korea, the Philippines, Hong Kong); Latin America (especially Colombia); and India. This picture changes regularly. Brazil is becoming increasingly open to international adoptions, while Argentina has pretty well sealed its borders against American adoptions. To keep up with the latest details about international sources, write to the International Concerns Committee for Children (see the list "Sources for Current Information" in chapter 3).

It is also possible for you to have, or to develop, your own connections in a particular country. If you have family ties outside of the United States, you may be able to find a distant cousin who can help you adopt. This link makes it possible to adopt children in countries that are normally closed to American families. For example, Americans cannot usually adopt Polish children, but Polish-Americans sometimes can. It is also good to remember that the United States is not the only place with immigrants. You may have helpful cousins in some third country—for example, there are Armenians in Lebanon and Italians in Ecuador.

The endless river of refugees who haunt American television screens suggest another possible source, but usually the suggestion is false. During your search for a child, you will see many stories broadcast about Central Americans fleeing across a border or Africans getting out of the way of some obscure war, and frequently these news reports will show orphans trapped and suffering in a camp. Many a viewer wonders, "Why not adopt one of those desperate children?" but such adoptions are almost never possible. After the well-publicized confusions of the Vietnamese and Cambodian baby-lifts, refugee organizations are extremely cautious about permitting the adoption of children who may be orphans or may just be displaced. For information about any particular refugee group, write the United Nations High Commissioner for Refugees, United Nations, Room C301, New York, N.Y. 10017. Telephone: (212) 754-7602.

Issues

Rumors. International adoptions have had astonishingly bad press. Foreign publications are full of suspicion-ridden stories about why Americans might want to adopt their country's children. Most commonly, we are accused of seeking slaves. American newspapers have printed equally doubtful accounts of why foreigners might allow their children to be adopted. These reports reflect a worldwide pattern of mistrust of the foreigner. Here are some of the most common tales spread in America.

• *Foreigners see these adoptions as a handy way to get rid of unhealthy children.* Many American newspapers have run stories about international adoptions and their difficulties. These articles often open with an account of a family at the airport waiting eagerly for their infant to arrive from Latin America. Their joy turns to horror as they discover the baby has Down's syndrome. That story turned up in many newspapers, and there is one remarkable detail—these reports all name the same family. Every year thousands of Americans adopt foreign-born children, so by now almost every imaginable incident must have taken place. A journalist is not helping to sort out the adoption maze by suggesting that one horror story is a typical problem. International adoptions, especially Latin American ones, were organized into a reasonably predictable routine during the latter part of the 1970s. Readers need not fear that by adopting from abroad they face an adoption with serious and unforeseen health risks. The portrait of a foreign culture in which parents would calmly toss unhealthy children into some discard heap is a gross caricature.

• *Foreigners give up their babies because they do not love their children.* On the face of it, this rumor is doubtful. Love for one's children has been found in all societies at all times in history. We should not let economic explanations for the value of children in various traditional societies blind us to the fact that the children are also wanted for emotional and personal reasons. It is common to see clear evidence that a child was prized before being surrendered for adoption. A typical case is that of a Korean girl, now called Nan, who was abandoned at an age estimated to be about eighteen months. Nan was simply found in a box outside a Korean orphanage. Somebody set her down, rang the bell, and fled. Nothing is known about her family, why she was abandoned, or where she came from. The one thing we do know about Nan is that when she was found, she was dressed in a new set of clothes. Whoever gave her up first went out and bought a new outfit for the child—an action which argues loudly that Nan was surrendered more in pain than from indifference.

• *The children have been kidnapped from the families of political prisoners.* The Argentine writer Jacobo Timerman says of the murder of whole families by Argentina's government, "Where there was mercy, small children were turned over to grandparents. Or presented to childless families. Or sold to childless families. Or taken to Chile, Paraguay, Brazil and given to childless families." A terrible indictment; however, when you adopt internationally you will find that the biggest nuisance is all the red tape, including documentation of who the child is and how she became available for adoption. The Immigration Service wants copies of such documents before a child can enter the country. I would never recommend a "no questions asked" adoption in the United States and certainly do not recommend one internationally.

Race. A woman with a lot of experience in Latin American adoptions once remarked to me, "The most common question people ask is, 'What do these children look like?' They ask it that way, but of course they are never asking if the children have three eyes." These families are trying to ask discreetly what I once heard a man ask bluntly at a parent's meeting. He stood up and said, "Are these Colombian kids white or what?" The woman he was asking was a very handsome, very brown-skinned native of Colombia. I asked her later what she thought of questions like that, and she replied that at one time she had been taken aback but that by now she was used to them. Indeed she was. She hadn't blinked an eye at the man's question. "Some are white," she said.

Some are, but most are not, and even those who look fully European at birth may surprise you later on. In Latin America olive complexions with unknown mixtures of Indian blood predominate. The head of one American agency that specializes in adoptions from Latin America says he turns away any applicant who insists on "pure European" ancestry. Children from Asia almost never have any European blood.

This racial question is often the biggest one facing families who wonder about international adoptions. Children with Nordic complexions are not to be found along this route.

A second aspect of the racial question is the reaction of friends and relatives. Will other people make life difficult for the child because of his foreign origins? Will they make life difficult for you because you have adopted a foreign child? To some extent the answer depends on the people you know, but I have been pleasantly surprised to find how few social problems result from such adoptions. People living in very conservative, very white communities have told me, "There are several of us here who have adopted Asian children" or "What surprises me is how common it turns out to be." In every interview I have conducted with parents of children adopted from abroad, I have asked about the reaction of others to their multinational families and I found that stories of problems are singularly lacking. Even questions from aggressive strangers on the street seem to be rare.

International families. If you adopt a foreign-born child of another race, your family's identity changes—and changes profoundly. I once overheard a conversation with a man who had adopted two Vietnamese children. He was asked what it was like to raise minority children. "I don't have any minority children," he replied. It was pointed out that he had Vietnamese children, a minority group. "Oh," he answered, "I never think of them as minority children."

The man was kidding himself and not helping his children, who surely have to face and understand their Vietnamese identity, but his questioner also missed the point. It was not just the man's children who belonged to a minority group. This man was part of a minority family; his identity was affected too.

If you adopt a Korean child and, in an effort to be progressive, raise your child to be aware of Korean culture and history but never realize that this culture is now part of your own identity as well, you are evading the major point about families. Families orient their members toward the world, and a change in the family means a change in each member's identity. An international adoption means that a profound reorientation toward some foreign culture has taken place.

Older children. The boom in international adoptions developed because it was, and is, hard to find American babies and toddlers. But there are also many needy older children scattered throughout the world, and they are finding American homes too. The adoption of these older children has provoked a controversy, because many people believe we should adopt America's waiting children first. I have raised the issue with everyone I interviewed who adopted older foreign children. In one or two cases the families had been naively unaware of all the waiting children in America. A few others were

115

drawn to a foreign adoption because children raised in foreign orphanages seemed less emotionally damaged than children who have grown up in the American foster-care system. Most often, though, there was one straightforward and practical explanation—an American adoption took too long. The family grew tired of the agency runaround.

Personally, I have known too many of the world's children to feel that American children are automatically more worthy of help than foreign children; however, there is a more subtle social consideration for favoring the adoption of American children. Children without families are a social danger. It is not just the child who benefits from an adoption. Society gains as well, because a person who might have grown up alienated and alone now has a place in the social system. Therefore, by adopting foreign children instead of American children, the argument goes, you are helping a society other than your own.

In a better world, I would find that social argument quite persuasive; however, at present it is a fantasy for anybody to adopt a child in order to help rescue society. Before adoption can make a significant difference to society, the laws, the judges, and the social workers are going to have to undergo many changes. As it stands now, adopting a child to stabilize society is like picking up litter to end pollution. The thought is nice, but bigger forces are at work. So I come back to family considerations. If you want to adopt an older child and don't mind the extra expense of an international adoption, go right ahead and build your family through international sources.

Step by Step

The most daunting feature of international adoptions is the number of different bureaucracies you have to work with. Families have to comply with the laws of their state government, the federal government, and a foreign government. Even if all the work is done through an agency, there is a lot of extra rigmarole, and many of these adoptions include a good bit of do-it-yourself labor. Nevertheless, it can be done and is done successfully every day. A number of parent associations are specifically devoted to international adoptions and can provide a great deal of information. Groups like OURS, Families Adopting Children Everywhere (FACE), Washington Association of Christian Adoptive Parents (WACAP), Latin American Parents Association (LAPA), and the Open Door Society (all listed in the "Directory of Parent Associations" in the Appendix) have been the most energetic forces behind the great rise in international adoptions. Every region of the country with many foreign adoptions turns out to have an active parent association encouraging them.

Because of the assistance available, international adoptions are usually much faster than domestic ones, despite the extra mountain of red tape. On the other side of all that procedure and travel there is a living child. It is impossible to say flatly how long the process will take, but most take under two years. Four months is rare, but not unknown. A few require two and a half years.

Locating a child. Children in foreign countries are found either through agencies or through private sources. Traditionally Asian children have come through American agencies, while Latin American children have arrived through independent connections, but recently a number of new American agencies have appeared that focus on Latin American adoptions. One of the most debated aspects of foreign adoptions is the role of intermediaries. It is usually cheaper if you do as much as possible on your own, but of course it is a lot less work if you use a go-between.

Agency Adoptions. Only a few U.S. agencies have foreign connections for locating children. If there are no such agencies in your area, you can work with one that accepts applications from throughout America (see the list "U.S.-Based Agencies" at the end of this chapter). That U.S.-based agency will locate a child for you. Usually an agency in your area will be willing to conduct a study of your family and forward its report to the agency handling the adoption itself. In effect you must work with two agencies: one to find the child and one to study you. A book available from the U.S. Government Printing Office, *National Directory of Intercountry Adoption Service Resources,* lists both types of agencies. Working with these agencies is similar to working with a domestic adoption agency.

Independent adoptions (with help). Because most people cannot even imagine how to find a foreign orphanage, a number of adoption "facilitators" have appeared in the United States. They are of two kinds: intermediaries and providers of information. The intermediaries are more expensive. A typical intermediary began doing translation work (official documents have to be translated into the language of the adoptive child's country) and then saw the work expand into a fairly steady business. One translator I visited offered families a twenty-eight-page single-spaced typescript that explained the whole process of finding a child in one particular Central American country. Another translator had become, in effect, the U.S. representative of one South American orphanage. She translated documents, forwarded them to South America, and then notified U.S. families when a baby was available. The legal status of these people is usually undefined. In the federal government's guidelines on international adoptions they are referred to as "independent facilitators" and recognized as useful contributors to the adoption process.

Information sources are the parent groups, such as LAPA and OURS. They will not do the work for you, but they are most helpful in identifying foreign sources for children and explaining how to go about contacting them. Remember, these foreign "sources" are not mysterious fellows on some street corner. They are usually orphanages or welfare agencies, so these adoptions are "private" only in the sense that no U.S. agency is involved. You still work with a foreign agency of some type (public, mission, or private).

Independent adoptions (your own connections). If you have developed your own source for an adoption, you will still have to go through most of the steps listed in this section. You will need a study conducted by a U.S. agency, you will need to have the foreign country grant you custody of the child, and you will have to work with American immigration to bring the child home.

The homestudy. Federal law is decisive on the point of a homestudy: you must be approved by an adoption agency licensed in the United States. The only exception is in the case of a family that has been living abroad and has had the child in their custody for at least two years before entry into the United States.

There is no special reason to worry about this requirement. Even very traditional agencies become flexible when they begin to consider foreign adoptions. It is hard to explain why; perhaps they feel that any Third World child would be fortunate to grow up in America, but agencies do change their tune when they study people for foreign adoptions. During an interview I listened to the director of an exclusive agency go on at enthusiastic length about her elite requirements, when she suddenly stopped and said, more to herself than to me, "But then . . . we don't say that for our international adoptions." She had no explanation for the contradiction, but it is there, and thank heavens for it.

The law states that the study must be conducted by an agency. A free-lance social worker is not good enough; however, some social workers have managed to obtain the proper credentials. In some states there are individual social workers who have been licensed as child-placing agencies and can write proper studies. In other areas there are people classified as "child-placing agents." These are workers who have contractual connections with agencies. They do the work and write the study, but act in the name of a particular agency. The only easy way to find such people is through a parent association.

All studies are dated and expire after one year, so do not have the study done until you have good reason to believe you will locate a child within the coming twelve months.

Waiting. You can put the waiting time to good use, preparing for the exciting moment when you hear a child has become available. Once a child is found, many things have to be done at once, so it is best to be ready. The "International Adoption Planner" may be helpful in preparing for the busy moment when the wait is suddenly over.

Gather the documents you will need to give to the foreign source. Typically these are birth and marriage certificates, and often these documents have to be translated. If there are no translators in your area, you can usually find a person willing and able to do the work at a nearby college.

You can also begin work on the documents you will have to present to American immigration officials. Obtain the forms and fill them out, as much as possible, ahead of time. Also find out about any preadoption requirements in your particular state. You need to know what must be done on the state level before federal authorities will approve the immigration of the child. If you expect to travel to the country to receive the child, find out in advance what the best way is to get there.

Good news. The arrival of the exciting report that a child is waiting is the signal to set many steps into motion. It is a frantic time because every moment of bureaucratic delay means delay in the adoption of a specific child.

Preadoption requirements. Before the child's arrival is approved, states want background information and evidence that the child is legally free for adoption. In some states—Wisconsin is a good example—the requirement for legal proof of the child's availability is so stringent that many waiting foreign children will never meet the legal standards. The purpose of these preadoption requirements is undeniably proper. Foreign-born children are entitled to the same rights

International Adoption Planner

Contacted Sources:

		Dates	
Name & address		Wrote them	Received reply
_____		/ /	/ /
_____		/ /	/ /
_____		/ /	/ /

Documents needed: _____

_____

Date documents assembled: / /   Date translated   / /
Study conducted by _____ Dated   / /
Documents required by state for preadoption _____

_____

I-600 forms from immigration office   requested   / /
                                                       received   / /
Possible travel routes to country _____

_____

_____

Received news that a child is available   Date   / /
Name: _____   Sex: _____
Age: _____   Weight: _____

and protection during the adoption process as native-born children, but when a state insists that an agency of a foreign country comply with state procedure, the good intention becomes arrogance. Not even the fifty states agree on the best procedure.

The preadoptive requirements are in a state of confusion that even by the standards of the adoption maze is dismaying. A federal committee studied the situation in an attempt to develop solid guidelines on international adoptions. Essentially the committee members threw up their hands in despair. Half of the states require prior approval before a child can enter from abroad, but their procedures and the documentation they require vary hopelessly. These also change from time to time, either through legislation or court decisions. You can most easily learn the latest procedure from your parent association or local immigration office.

The states requiring prior approval are Alabama, Arizona, Arkansas, Colorado, Delaware, Florida, Indiana, Iowa, Kentucky, Massachusetts, Minnesota, Missouri, Montana, Ohio, Nebraska, Nevada, New Hampshire, North Carolina, North Dakota, Pennsylvania, South Carolina, South Dakota, Tennessee, Wisconsin, and Wyoming.

Petition to immigrate. An adoptive child is brought into the United States as an "immediate relative who is an orphan," so as soon as you know who you wish to adopt, you must petition for the child to be classified as an immediate relative. These petitions are handled on the I-600 form of the Immigration and Naturalization Service (INS), U.S. Department of Justice. The INS has many district offices to handle these petitions (see the list of immigration offices at the end of this chapter).

The petition will only be approved after the necessary agency study has been done and your state's preadoptive requirements have been met. Approval of this petition requires a fingerprint check by the FBI to see if you have a police record. If they are going to find anything, you should have discussed the matter in advance with the INS.

The law permits such a petition only for children under age fourteen. At least one member of the adopting couple must be a U.S. citizen. In the case of a single parent, the petitioner must be at least twenty-five years old. If you cannot meet all these requirements, you will probably have to get your congressional representative to pass a private bill allowing the child's entry.

If your petition is denied (a very rare event), the INS must tell you why. You have the right to appeal the decision.

Visa. Once the petition is approved, you can obtain a visa from the State Department's Bureau of Consular Affairs. The visa is issued by the consulate in the country where the child lives. It is routinely and usually swiftly issued once INS grants your petition. The visa is never issued before then.

The foreign placement. Every country has its own laws regarding adoption and child custody, but in essence the courts must rule that the rights of the biological parents over the child no longer exist and must then transfer custody to the adopting parents. However, within that basic process there can be many varied and baroque themes. You will need a local lawyer to sort them out for you.

If you are not adopting through a U.S. agency, the foreign orphanage or agency usually will assign you a lawyer. With great reluctance, the U.S. State Department has been dragged into these adoptions, and some embassies in Latin America now provide names of adoption sources and lawyers.

Travel. Often, particularly in Latin American adoptions, adoptive parents go to the country to receive their children. Bogotá, Colombia, has become famous for its cosmopolitan boardinghouses, where Americans, Australians, Scandinavians, and Israelis meet and talk about babies while waiting to complete their adoptions. These waits can be expensive. Most adoptions do not require more than one- or two-week stays, but there may occasionally be a six-week delay waiting for parental rights to a newborn child to be terminated. A few American states insist on imposing a wait of six months, until a final adoption decree is granted by the foreign country.

Whether or not you go to claim the child, the child must travel with an escort. If you meet him at the airport, you will not be allowed to do so until customs have been cleared. These long airport waits are something of a legend in the adoption world. They always seem to be in the middle of the night; the plane is late; the friend who was dragged along has run out of things to say; it takes forever to get through customs; and suddenly there your child is, bleary-eyed and worn out, but at last your child.

Costs. There is no point in publishing cost lists during our inflationary age. They are bound to rise again before this book is printed. International adoptions are more expensive than standard U.S. agency adoptions and are comparable in cost to most legal independent adoptions. They are quite a bit below black market rates.

Some American agencies, in fact, charge more than the cost of a standard international adoption. During the summer of 1983, for example, one Texas agency was placing Hispanic children with families and charging $6,000 to $7,500. At that same time, the Latin American Parents Association (LAPA) listed the price range as $4,000 to $6,500 (all-inclusive) for a Latin American adoption. And a translator-facilitator for a Colombian orphanage was informing her clients that the cost was $5,000 to $6,000.

International adoptions are not cheap, but neither are they unreasonably expensive. The extra expenses come chiefly from the travel and foreign placement costs, but the prices of translation, notarization of documents, petitions, visas, and escort service all add to the swelling bill. You may also be asked to make a donation to the placing orphanage.

Don't be shy about finding out about costs. Agencies should certainly give you a clear accounting. Translators and other facilitators should let you know what you are paying for and should not request the major part of the payment until they tell you that a child has been located.

Arrival. All children should be seen by a pediatrician within eight days of their arrival in the United States. Your pediatrician needs a little humility about this visit, because she has probably never seen a child like yours before. There may be some things that seem alarming but are in fact perfectly normal. In the United States, for example, a baby born weighing just five pounds would go into an incubator; in Calcutta such babies are called "fat." Also, older children can show alarming test results. A Peace Corps doctor once told me that while he had taken blood counts on many normal African children, he had never found a child whose blood count was high enough, by American standards, to avoid the need for hospitalization. These facts help explain why international children seem to thrive when they come to America. They are much stronger than American children would be in the same medical state, and they grow even stronger with American nutrition.

At the same time, this Third World feistiness masks symptoms that, in America, have very noticeable signs. The most important such problem comes from parasites. Almost *all* children from tropical countries arrive with parasites. The problem is temporary, but the condition must be treated. You need to have the child's stool examined by a competent lab, such as the Tropical Disease Center at Tulane University in New Orleans or the Parasite Drug Service in Atlanta. When the lab report indicates the presence of several parasites, some unsophisticated doctors react almost hysterically and naturally this response alarms the parents. The doctors' reaction, however, is unjustified. Many other children have arrived with parasites and been quickly treated.

Language. Suppose you adopt a two-year-old who has never before heard a word of English; how will he get along? In a word, famously. Almost everybody reports that their children understood instructions practically at once and soon began to speak. Children under age five present no problems; they reach the language level of their peers quite quickly. From age six to ten, the speed is still good, although it may be a year before they seem naturally fluent. After age twelve, a child is almost certain to speak with an accent, but can still be expected to speak fluently and well.

U.S. adoption. The U.S. adoption of a foreign child follows the procedure described in chapter 11. Even if the child was fully adopted abroad and you received a final decree of adoption, you should still go through the U.S. process. This second adoption guarantees and protects your child's rights and status as your heir and Social Security beneficiary.

Naturalization. The INS gives your child a "green card" permitting permanent residence in the United States as an alien. Your child does not enter the country as a citizen, and adoption does not automatically confer citizenship on her. Two years after your child has entered the country, you must return to the INS to petition for naturalization. The process is routine, but—just this one last time—there are more forms to fill out.

U.S.-Based Agencies

Although many adoption agencies will assist in foreign adoptions, only a few of them serve the entire United States. The agencies listed below will accept applications from families throughout America. Generally, a local agency is used to conduct the home-study.

Agape Social Services, Box 471, Carrollton, Tex. 75006. (214) 245-8603 (Latin America—hard-to-place children)

Catholic Social Services, 222 North Seventeenth Street, Philadelphia, Pa. 19103. (215) 587-3873 (Korea, Hong Kong, Philippines, Peru)

Children's Home Society of Minnesota, 2230 Como Avenue, St. Paul, Minn. 55108. (612) 646-6393 (Korea, Guatemala, Colombia—hard-to-place children)

Friends of Children of Viet Nam, 600 Gilpin Street, Denver, Colo. 80218. (303) 321-8251 (Korea)

Holt Adoption Program, P.O. Box 2880, Eugene, Oreg. 97402. (503) 687-2202 (Korea, Philippines, Thailand)

International Mission of Hope, 10734 Tancred, Denver, Colo. 80234. (303) 457-4206 (India)

International Social Service, American Branch, 20 West Fortieth Street, New York, N.Y. 10018. (212) 398-9142 (Hong Kong)

Love the Children, 221 West Broad Street, Quakertown, Pa. 18951. (215) 536-4180 (Korea)

Universal Aid for Children, P.O. Box 610246, North Miami, Fl. 33161. (305) 893-1535 (Central America and the Caribbean)

Welcome House, P.O. Box 836, Doylestown, Pa. 18901. (215) 345-0430 (Korea, Hong Kong, India—hard-to-place children)

Immigration Offices

ALASKA
632 West Sixth Avenue, Anchorage, Alaska 99501

ARIZONA
  Federal Building, Phoenix, Ariz. 85025
CALIFORNIA
  300 North Los Angeles Boulevard, Los Angeles, Calif. 90012
  880 Front Street, San Diego, Calif. 92188
  630 Sansome Street, San Francisco, Calif. 94111
COLORADO
  Federal Office Building, Denver, Colo. 80202
CONNECTICUT
  900 Asylum Avenue, Hartford, Conn. 06105
DISTRICT OF COLUMBIA
  1025 Vermont Avenue, N.W., Washington, D.C. 20538
ILLINOIS
  Dirksen Federal Office Building, Chicago, Ill. 60604
INDIANA
  Federal Building, Hammond, Ind. 46320
KENTUCKY
  U.S. Courthouse Building, Louisville, Ky. 40202
LOUISIANA
  New Federal Building, New Orleans, La. 70113
MAINE
  76 Pearl Street, Portland, Maine 04112
MARYLAND
  E. A. Garmatz Federal Building, Baltimore, Md. 21201
MASSACHUSETTS
  JFK Federal Building, Boston, Mass. 02203
MICHIGAN
  Federal Building, Detroit, Mich. 48207
MINNESOTA
  New Post Office Building, St. Paul, Minn. 55101
MISSOURI
  U.S. Courthouse, Kansas City, Mo. 64016
  U.S. Courthouse, St. Louis, Mo. 63101
MONTANA
  Federal Building, Helena, Mont. 59601
NEBRASKA
  New Federal Building, Omaha, Nebr. 68102
NEVADA
  Federal Building, Las Vegas, Nev. 89101
  Federal Building, Reno, Nev. 89509
NEW JERSEY
  Federal Building, Newark, N.J. 07102
NEW YORK
  U.S. Courthouse, Albany, N.Y. 12207

68 Court Street, Buffalo, N.Y. 14202
26 Federal Plaza, New York, N.Y. 10007

OHIO
U.S. Courthouse, Cincinnati, Ohio 45201
Federal Office Building, Cleveland, Ohio 44199

OREGON
U.S. Courthouse, Portland, Oreg. 97205

PENNSYLVANIA
U.S. Courthouse, Philadelphia, Pa. 19106
Federal Building, Pittsburgh, Pa. 15222

RHODE ISLAND
Federal Building, Providence, R.I. 02903

TENNESSEE
Federal Building, Memphis, Tenn. 38103

TEXAS
Federal Building, Dallas, Tex. 75242
U.S. Courthouse, El Paso, Tex. 79984
719 Grimes Avenue, Harlingen, Tex. 78550
Federal Building, Houston, Tex. 77208
Federal Building, San Antonio, Tex. 78206

UTAH
New Federal Building, Salt Lake City, Utah 84138

VERMONT
Federal Building, St. Albans, Vt. 05478

VIRGINIA
970 North Military Highway, Norfolk, Va. 23502

WASHINGTON
815 Airport Way, South, Seattle, Wash. 98134
U.S. Courthouse, Spokane, Wash. 99201

WISCONSIN
Federal Building, Milwaukee, Wis. 53202

9

Adoption Exchanges

The most promising institution in adoption is currently the most limited one. At present, adoption exchanges serve only waiting children and only a small percentage of them. However, these exchanges have great potential and are already an important tool for anyone who is getting a runaround from agencies during the search for a waiting child.

Essentially, an adoption exchange is a skeletal form of adoption agency. It brings children and families together, but does not conduct studies of the families and does not work directly with the children. The services an exchange provides to searching families include: (1) newsletters listing waiting children; (2) photo books identifying and describing many of the waiting children who are free for adoption; (3) books listing families hoping to adopt waiting children; and (4) workers who can refer families for specific adoptions.

State and regional exchanges. The exchange system is stacked up on several levels. At the bottom, there are informal links between cooperating agencies. Most states maintain a formal state-level exchange that, as a minimum, can make referrals for searching families. The following table, "State Adoption-Exchange Services," identifies the states with formal exchanges and lists their services. All people living in states that list searching families should make a point of getting into their exchange's book. Your agency can help, or if you are having a difficult time persuading an agency to work with you, you can call the state adoption office directly about being listed (see the list "State Adoption Offices" in chapter 4).

State Adoption-Exchange Services

State	Does State Provide:		
	Formal Exchange	Photo Books	Family Listings
Alabama	✓	✓	
Alaska	✓		
Arizona	✓		
Arkansas	✓	✓	
California	✓	✓	✓
Colorado	✓	✓	
Connecticut	✓	✓	✓
Delaware			
District of Columbia			
Florida	✓	✓	
Georgia	✓	✓	
Hawaii	✓		
Idaho	✓	✓	
Illinois	✓	✓	
Indiana	✓	✓	✓
Iowa	✓	✓	✓

State	Formal Exchange	Photo Books	Family Listings
Kansas	✓		
Kentucky	✓	✓	
Louisiana	✓		✓
Maine	✓	✓	✓
Maryland	✓	✓	
Massachusetts	✓	✓	✓
Michigan	✓	✓	
Minnesota	✓	✓	
Mississippi	✓	✓	✓
Missouri	✓	✓	✓
Montana			
Nebraska	✓	✓	✓
Nevada			
New Hampshire	✓	✓	✓
New Jersey	✓	✓	✓
New Mexico	✓	✓	✓
New York	✓	✓	
North Carolina	✓	✓	

State	Formal Exchange	Photo Books	Family Listings
North Dakota			
Ohio	✓		
Oklahoma	✓	✓	✓
Oregon			
Pennsylvania	✓	✓	
Rhode Island			
South Carolina	✓	✓	
South Dakota			
Tennessee	✓	✓	✓
Texas	✓	✓	✓
Utah			
Vermont	✓	✓	
Virginia	✓	✓	✓
Washington	✓	✓	
West Virginia	✓	✓	✓
Wisconsin	✓	✓	
Wyoming	✓		

A network of regional exchanges provides information beyond state boundaries (see the list "Regional Adoption Exchanges" at the end of this chapter). All of them publish newsletters that are well worth subscribing to if you are looking for a waiting child. There are also two national exchanges.

Any family that has been working with an agency for eight months and has still not found a waiting child should call a regional exchange. Usually this work with the exchange is done entirely by phone. The primary question the exchange considers is whether you are interested in the kind of children it lists. A rule of thumb is that the higher up in the exchange system you go, the longer the child has been waiting.

Photo books. The most powerful and dramatic tools of the adoption exchanges are the photo listings of waiting children. Many agencies and parent groups have copies of the photo books. The easiest way for an agency worker to describe the waiting children is by presenting a book filled with photos and thumbnail descriptions. About half of the states maintain photo books, and some agencies also have books of their own.

It is almost impossible to go through these books without great emotion. ("Those horrible books" is the way I have heard several people describe them.) Page upon page of children in desperate need is spread out before you. One woman who studied the books many times before a child was placed with her remembered, "I used to come home weeping, just devastated. All those children, and at best I could help one or maybe a family pair." Another man told me of the time he showed his mother-in-law some photos, asking, "Which do you favor as a grandchild?" She picked them all.

Others are affected just as deeply by the books, but in quite the opposite way: they flee in terror. It is a perfectly understandable reaction, but it helps neither the applicants nor the children. Those children are not going to be helped by the world's continual refusal to face the dreadful truth that they are in need.

Once you start looking at these books, you need imagination as well as strength. Many of the photos are terrible. Pictures of black children especially tend to be underexposed and set against dark backgrounds. The prose descriptions of the children are often brutal and insensitive. (The Connecticut books are a happy exception to this rule.) Somehow you have to see past the page to the fundamental fact of a real child who needs somebody.

I have never heard people give good reasons for picking the children they found in the books and finally adopted: "Caught my eye." "I don't know. There was something about her." "He wasn't my first choice. I was more interested in a deaf child I saw listed, but I decided to ask about him anyway."

Your first introduction to the books is likely to be wearying and it does not grow much easier, but your reaction to them is very important in the eyes of the agency. From its perspective, the books summarize the kinds of children who are available. If you are not interested in them, agencies and exchanges probably cannot help you.

Regional Adoption Exchanges

NATIONAL

National Adoption Exchange, 1218 Chestnut Street, Suite 204, Philadelphia, Pa. 19107. (215) 925-0200

Council of Adoptive Parents (CAP), 700 Exchange Street, Rochester, N.Y. 14608. (716) 232-5110

EASTERN

Delaware Valley Adoption Resource Exchange (DARE), 1218 Chestnut Street, Suite 204, Philadelphia, Pa. 19107. (215) 925-0200

Three Rivers Adoption Council, 220 Grant Street, Pittsburgh, Pa. 15219. (412) 922-8382

CENTRAL

Child Care Association of Illinois, 300 East Monroe Street, Suite 106, Springfield, Ill. 62704. (217) 528-4409

Rocky Mountain Adoption Exchange, 3705 East Colfax Avenue, Suite 105, Denver, Colo. 80206. (303) 333-0845

WEST COAST

Aid to Adoption of Special Kids (AASK), 3530 Grand Avenue, Oakland, Calif. 94610. (415) 451-1748

Northwest Adoption Exchange, 909 Forty-third N.E., Suite 208, Seattle, Wash. 98105. (206) 632-1480

10
Independent Adoptions

It is difficult to write enthusiastically about independent routes to adoption because they are so unpredictable. A family may search for a short time and meet prompt success or it may struggle for many, many years and encounter only frustration. Yet, I do know a number of people who successfully and legally adopted independently after agencies spurned them. Almost everyone who is interested in adopting an infant should at least keep open the possibility of adopting independently.

It is not practical to insist that adoptions be done through agencies, especially now that so many agency waiting lists are closed and so many pregnant women refuse to work with them. It is no longer acceptable to argue that people should not be free to develop families as they would like or that everyone must make use of social workers.

Despite the many recent changes in adoption, state governments have paid almost no attention to the new conditions. In most states, independent adoptions still float in legal uncertainty, being neither lawful nor unlawful. Adoptions for profit are of course illegal everywhere, and many agencies like to suggest that all independent adoptions are part of the baby-selling racket. These private adoptions are sometimes called "the gray market," a genteel term that acknowledges legality but still implies that the adoption is shady. Professionals are not always so subtle. I have heard many agency workers refer to "illegal adoptions" when they only meant nonagency adoptions, but the fact is that legal and honorable adoptions can be arranged independently.

As is usual in matters where there is no clear law, all that is honorable in independent adoptions has become tainted by the presence of its criminal neighbors, while all that is criminal has gained a faint perfume of tolerability because of its honorable acquaintances. People who enter this foggy region often feel shame, but they seldom know guilt. I have talked to a lot of people who were embarrassed about having adopted independently, but I never spoke with a soul who thought he'd done anything wrong.

Eventually this situation must change. People want to adopt babies. It is fully possible to do so independently while respecting the rights of the child and of the biological parents. Yet the pro-agency argument is serious enough and well-established enough that it ought to be considered by anyone planning to adopt.

I asked William Pierce, the president of the major adoption agency lobby in Washington, D.C., why I should advise readers to adopt through an agency. His reply, in sum, was: If the only concern of a family seeking a baby is that it find a baby, then perhaps an agency is not the only way for them, but there are many infertile couples and few babies. When the interests and rights of the child and biological mother are taken into account, some families are found to be more worthy of raising an available infant than are others. No private intermediary can be expected to weigh all these competing interests.

People—he continued—have no inalienable right to have a baby. It is true that the desire for a child is powerful and thus tempts many operators to exploit and profit from this desire, but that temptation does not mean the proper course is to legalize nonagency adoptions. The children have a right to protection. The women who choose to give birth and surrender their children for adoption have a right to know that their children have gone into good and loving homes. The best thing frustrated families could do would be to help rebuild the adoption system that collapsed during the 1970s.

It was with the nostalgic close of his argument that Mr. Pierce's position revealed a loose thread. He defended a number of agency "standards" he felt should be maintained: the home at the time of adoption should be large enough for a child to grow in; the mother should not work; parents should be able to afford to spend a month's pay (8 percent of their income) on the agency fee; parents should not be overweight; parents should not be older than their late 30s; parents should not have undergone vasectomies or tubal ligations. In short, they should be the traditional adoptive family, adopting for the traditional reason. If you fail to qualify, too bad; you have no inalienable right to raise a baby.

This argument insists on the agency's right to judge applicants in accordance with a preset list of qualifications. In a pluralistic society like ours, that sort of judgment cannot always be fair.

Although it is true that nobody has an inalienable right to a baby, when it comes to something as fundamental as establishing a family, all people have an inalienable right to see that the adoption system does not automatically discriminate against them. We should all have the right to an equal chance.

A final point concerns the biological mothers whose rights Mr. Pierce repeatedly defended. Mothers do not have a duty to surrender their children to adoption agencies. Such an action is one of several choices open to them, and these days many women are deciding they would prefer not to work with agencies.

So what is to be done? There are many points in the pro-agency argument that must be respected. It is true that something must be done to end the chaos of the adoption maze. Tragically, it is also true that the desires of parents are so strong and the situation is so confusing that criminals are able to profit by trampling on the rights of the children and the biological parents.

Fortunately, there is a middle ground. The choice need not be between agency adoptions and profiteers. I have met families who, after a long runaround from agencies, were able to adopt infants independently and at low cost. The chief virtue of the agency route is that it could be so much simpler than the independent one; it is not necessarily more uplifting.

Iowa is the most progressive state on this issue. It has established a law that brings order to independent adoptions and allows the honorable to sort themselves out from the ignoble and the criminal. This approach is based on a system of "certified adoption investigators" who study each adopting family. The study is like a regular agency study and requires several interviews, including a visit to the family's home. The investigator is not allowed to place a child with the adopting family and neither is the biological mother allowed to do so directly. A third party is required. Often this third party is a doctor; sometimes it is a lawyer, occasionally a minister. When the court considers an adoption petition, a statement of costs must be submitted and justified.

Like anything else, the system has its problems. There are no controls on rates charged by investigators, and although expenses must be explained to the court, there is no theoretical limit to what could be charged. Some investigators want quite a bit more than others. I was amused to listen to one investigator express her own concerns about the system. She regretted that beyond periodic re-certification there was so little control over investigators and that the investigators have to make recommendations on their own rather than through a committee. These concerns come down to a worry that the adoptions really are independent and the investigators are not part of some superagency.

The Iowa system guarantees that a serious study of the adopting family will be done without forcing families to be restricted by agency prejudices. It also allows biological mothers who do not wish to work with agencies the freedom to avoid them. The large number of inves-tigators makes it reasonably easy to get a study done. Most impor-tant, the Iowa system lets people know what is and is not allowed.

Step by Step

Surveying the local setting. Before embarking on an independent adop-tion you must find out two things. Are independent adoptions possible in your state? Is there a prescribed way of obtaining them? Usually a parent group knows whether the situation is simply chaotic, flatly illegal, illegal but with large loopholes, or definitely legal. At this time you should seek the assistance of a lawyer, since parent groups sel-dom know the details of the law, even though they have a fair amount of practical acquaintance with the subject. In 1983 the only states where independent adoptions were completely barred were Connect-icut, Delaware, Massachusetts, Michigan, Minnesota, and North Da-kota.

If independent adoptions are simply impossible in your state, you must find a local agency willing to work with you, adopt internationally, or go out of state for an independent placement. A loophole ambiguity in most state laws permits out-of-state residents to adopt a child who is a resident (see the chart "State Adoption Procedures" at the end of chapter 11). Unfortunately, many people have no easy way of locating an out-of-state child, so they end up using the black market. Thus, we find a paradox: states that seek simply to outlaw all inde-pendent adoptions end up promoting the black market.

Locating a baby. The hardest part of an independent adoption is finding an infant. Often instead of finding a newborn baby, you will find a pregnant woman. For an adoptive mother, this is a time of emotions nearly as powerful as those felt during pregnancy. Adoptive mothers sometimes even go into sympathetic labor pains when the biological mothers' time comes.

Essentially you have one task—getting the word out that you are looking for a baby. Begin with your own connections. None of your friends or acquaintances should be unaware of your desire. Women should let their gynecologists know of their interest. Also tell any teachers, other doctors, ministers, and attorneys you know.

Normally, the search for an independent adoption is kept at this level. People usually spread the news of their interest wherever they go and usually it is enough, but it is slow. You never know how long it will take—half a year or five years. Success is random. International adoptions are usually much faster, and sometimes even agency adoptions are quicker.

Families who combine an unusual amount of extroversion and desperation can sometimes summon the gumption to pursue independent sources more aggressively. I hesitate to recommend these steps because, although they are widely discussed in adoption circles, I do not know of many cases where they have actually worked. However, families who cannot get through agency doors and who do not wish to consider international sources may find that they have to work harder at locating independent sources.

Primarily, this extra effort calls for increased imagination in searching for available infants. By now I have heard a lot of stories about different connections that succeeded: a friend whose wife worked in a hospital gift shop; neighbors who moved away and a year later called to say that their new neighbor's unmarried daughter was pregnant; a man at a professional conference who met a colleague whose daughter had been raped and was pregnant; a friend whose niece was said to be on the verge of a nervous breakdown as she tried to steel herself for an abortion; a co-worker whose sister-in-law didn't want to interrupt her career and so, even though she was married, was thinking about giving the baby up for adoption. The only lesson I can derive from this variety of stories is that the potential sources for an adoptable infant are as diverse and unpredictable as the society we inhabit. Wherever there are young women or people who care about young women, there may be someone who knows of an abandoned baby or an unwanted pregnancy.

As suggested earlier, you should have business cards printed with your name, address, and phone number. When you meet people socially and find yourself talking about adoption (and you *will* find your-self talking about it), give them your card and write on the back "Hoping to adopt."

A bolder step is to try to contact likely women directly. A few people have actually found the nerve to stand outside an abortion clinic or counseling office and hand out sheets of paper saying that they want to adopt; however, if you take this most direct route, you should *not* use your name and phone number. For your own protection, you should only deal with the biological mother through a lawyer. Any flyers given out to potential mothers should have either your lawyer's address or an answering service phone number.

It is also possible to advertise your interest in a local newspaper (again using your lawyer's address), but this approach really enrages agencies. Agencies seldom interfere in specific independent adop-tions, but they do often move against advertising.

Protecting your rights. One point that agencies like to stress is that independent adoptions cannot seal the different parties in airtight com-partments. Energetic people can often find out who the biological parents are or who the adoptive parents are. Friends, relatives, and professional acquaintances may reveal the secret. This point is so true that anyone who cannot stand the possibility of the secret becom-ing known should either limit the search to a few professional inter-mediaries (for instance, your gynecologist and minister) or simply forget about adopting independently.

The terrible fear has been that if there is not perfect secrecy, the biological mother may one day reappear and demand "her" child. The chances of being struck by lightning are probably greater, but this fantasy worry is too powerful to be ignored. You cannot live your life in ceaseless doubt about the integrity of the adoption. For your own protection, you must see to it that the rights of the biological mother and father are fully and properly terminated. The fundamental re-quirement of this process is for your lawyer, not you, to work with the woman. The biological mother cannot challenge an adoption unless she can convince a judge that she did not voluntarily surrender her child. Your lawyer knows how to handle these terminations; you do not.

Open adoptions. An alternative—one that flies in the face of tradi-tional agency theory—is to embrace openness as a positive good. It is no longer so automatic and obvious that perpetual secrecy is best. Some people have taken the absence of sworn secrecy so far that the biological and adoptive parents have met and planned the adoption together. The argument in favor of this process is that it transforms all parties into real people rather than leaving them as blank stereotypes, but there are a lot of persistent doubts about it as well. In some parts of the country, notably Pennsylvania, the idea has attracted more support than elsewhere. But never consent to such a step without your lawyer's approval, and if you do meet, do not specifically urge the biological mother to give up her child for adoption.

If a pregnant woman phones. Sometimes word of your search for a child will directly reach a pregnant woman, who will call you and say she is willing to give up her child for adoption. Tell her you are interested and that to protect her rights she should talk to your lawyer. Then give her your lawyer's phone number.

Do not engage in prolonged conversation at this time, not even if you are planning on an open adoption. If the woman says she is thinking about adoption but is still unsure, do not say, "Oh, I hope you decide to give up the baby." Stick with the point that you are interested and she should speak with your lawyer. If you don't yet have a lawyer, take her number and tell her you will have your lawyer call her.

This caution may seem petty and trivial, but the less urging you give the caller, the more obviously voluntary her action will be. If she telephoned you, she is serious.

Finding a lawyer. Adoption is a branch of family law, but if your Yellow Pages lists lawyers by specialty, most of those found under the family-law heading will concentrate only on divorce. Independent adoptions call for lawyers who are knowledgeable and experienced. Lawyers whose adoption work has been limited to routine agency placements may not be experienced enough for an independent adoption. If you have a lawyer, ask him for a recommendation. If you don't have one, your parent association may help. Your local bar association can also provide names, but their referral service seldom discriminates between the skillful and the less able.

If you plan to pursue a particularly aggressive search for a pregnant woman, you must speak with a lawyer first. Tell him that you want to distribute flyers or even advertise and that you need a lawyer to respond once there are some nibbles. You should put the lawyer on retainer at that time.

For less extraordinary searches you can postpone retaining a lawyer until you actually have a specific child in mind. It is best to prepare for that moment, learning in advance the names of several lawyers who might be used, but it saves money if you do not retain one before it is absolutely necessary.

Costs. Although it is true that the least expensive infant adoptions I know about were independent ones, they are usually expensive— comparable to higher-priced international adoptions. The great variable is in the cost of support given to the biological mother.

If a pregnant woman went to an agency, she could expect counseling, medical care, and, if need be, a place to stay while she carried the child. You may provide these services as well. It is perfectly reasonable to want to do everything possible to ensure the healthy development of a baby you plan to adopt, but it is not free. The medical expenses are the same as the costs you would have if a member of your family was having the baby. The other costs (summed up under the phrase "reasonable expenses") are an extra burden. Your legal fee is usually larger than the fee for an agency adoption for the simple reason that your lawyer does more work and is retained for a longer period of time.

You may wonder if all this constitutes buying a child. I think not. It surely is buying a lot of services that lead to a child, and in that sense anybody who pays an adoption agency fee or anybody who encounters expenses in a biological pregnancy and delivery is also paying for a child. The difference between buying a service and buying a commodity may seem subtle, but it is the difference between buying a package tour of London and buying London itself.

One unavoidable market factor is inflation. The price of independent adoptions keeps going up, and surely part of that rise comes from competition among searching families, who bid up the cost. The result, of course, is to make independent adoptions easier for traditional agency clients than for untraditional clients. Most independent adoptions are made by young professionals or administrators with incomes well above average, especially above the average for young married couples. This bitter fact of cost is one of the strongest pro-agency arguments I know.

Waiting. Once you locate a pregnant woman, the period spent waiting for her to give birth is likely to be one of the most anxiety-ridden times of your life. Many people say they like providing medication and board during this time, just so they can feel a part of the process.

The greatest fear is that the woman will change her mind and abort the pregnancy. No matter what your thinking is about abortion, here is a time when people desperately pray that it not happen. There can be no doubt that one of the attractions of helping the woman meet her expenses during this period is that it lets you try to counter the many pressures that she may be under to end her pregnancy.

There probably is no way to set all fears aside, although passage of the sixth month of pregnancy is a powerful indication that the woman has really decided to bring the pregnancy to term. It is better to turn this anxiety into more fruitful energy, doing the normal things prospective parents do—selecting names, making practical plans, and (once the eighth month has come) buying baby clothes.

Placement. Independent placements of infants commonly take place in hospitals. The hospital stay after giving birth must be an appallingly lonely time for the biological mother; it is also a hard time for the baby who is getting only institutional care. The sooner you can start providing family love, the better. The speed of these placements often means that the baby arrives in your care before the biological parents' rights are fully terminated. In agency terminology, this is an "at risk" or "preadoptive" placement. You should learn from your lawyer precisely what the child's status is. The risk of taking a baby home, loving her, and then learning that the mother has changed her mind about giving up the baby is a terrible one, but your baby needs you now. This is the first of many pains you will risk for your child. If you cannot face that risk—and many people cannot—then don't adopt independently.

New threats. The Small family independently adopted a baby who was born prematurely and immediately surrendered by his mother. When I talked with the Smalls, their baby sat quietly on a tabletop, listening to our conversation. He was half a year old. The Smalls were delighted after the years of search to have learned, by the most casual of connections, of the baby's availability. The cost was reasonable too. The attorney's fee had barely been more than the fee for a routine agency adoption. Only the hospital costs for keeping the baby in an incubator and under intensive care had been out of the ordinary. Shortly after I left the Smalls, however, the lawyer submitted an amended and much larger bill. He threatened to take the baby back if they did not pay. Fortunately, the Smalls did not panic. They called a parent association and were directed to a different lawyer, who assured them that their baby was not an item to be repossessed like a too-costly car. Do not allow yourself to be blackmailed by idle threats.

The final decree. After placement, the legal steps for an independent adoption are the same as for any other adoption, but in many states, the process takes longer if the placement was not made by an agency. During this period you will have to have a study done to determine the suitability of the adoption. The basic idea behind this study is the same as that behind the studies discussed in chapter 7, with one exception. Agencies ask themselves whether or not they think they can work with you; independent adoption studies focus more sharply on the question of whether this particular family will be good for this particular child.

Charlatans

No book on how to get rich from money markets would ever insult its readers by including a paragraph on why it is a bad idea to try and short-circuit the system by robbing banks. I apologize for now raising that sort of paragraph here. The fault lies not with declining morality but with a situation that has been allowed to persist in such chaos for so many years that nobody is quite sure where the line between right and wrong procedures can still be drawn.

There are two techniques, widely favored by profiteers, that are often presented to inexperienced parents as simple ways to evade outmoded details of the law. One of these is filing a false statement of adoption expenses. Often this action is described as a simple procedure, one quite irrelevant to the rights of any of the parties involved in the adoption. The term for that little procedure is "perjury." The second technique is to adopt an American infant outside the country, say in Mexico. Mexican adoptions have taken the place of Mexican divorces, which were popular in the years before divorce became easier in the United States. The status of these divorces was always subject to challenge, and the rights of a family built on a Mexican adoption are equally shaky. Lawyers who advise either of these techniques are not clever, skillful, or experienced men of the world. They are charlatans.

PART III
Working with the Law

11

Adoption Law

You have not reached the end of the adoption maze once you have located a child. The courts must approve the adoption. Happily, you are unlikely to find yourself in a difficult legal battle. The landslide majority of adoption cases are routine affairs; usually there aren't even two rival sides. In the ordinary case, there is just your side, the judge, and an agent for the court. The hearing is rather informal and lacks most of the features that make serious dealings with the law seem unpleasant. The rules of evidence are more humane than strict. There is no public gallery of curious strangers gawking at you.

The one critical rule is that in order to ensure the firmness of the adoption, the legal process must be followed to the letter. The law always puts an emphasis on proper procedure, and this tendency is doubly true in the matter of adoption. Adoption is unknown to English common law, the source of most American laws. Indeed, England had no adoption law until 1926, so there is no ancient body of respected customs and principles that was developed over the centuries by judges considering adoption cases. Lacking such a tradition, many judges refuse to grant a jot more than what the written law specifies.

Most American adoption laws were developed during the last half of the nineteenth century as a way of helping neglected and orphaned children. The comparative newness (as judges see it) of adoption laws means that mistakes in procedure can sometimes have consequences that are out of all proportion to the trivial nature of the errors.

Complicating the matter further is the way adoption flies in the face of common-law theories about inheritance. Adoption law agrees that love and care, not heredity, make a family, but common law goes back

145

to feudal theories that put the emphasis on blood ties. Thus, when legal questions about family and property arise, unless the adoption law is specific, there is a body of common law working against you.

Because the law is not as helpful and sympathetic as it should be, it is important to pay attention to its demands. The law is one area where it often takes many pounds of cure to straighten out the mess brought on by overlooking a half-ounce of prevention.

Legal Assistance

It is reasonable to begin with the assumption that your adoption will follow the standard pattern and that it will proceed without serious legal problems. If you are using an agency, you may not even be expected to hire a lawyer. The agency itself is familiar with the routine and usually prepares the necessary forms and documents. In many states you will not need a lawyer at the hearing; however, you should consider adopting without a lawyer only if your case is purely a routine agency adoption. It is important to have legal advice if you hope your adopted child will be able to inherit from your relatives, or if you are adopting independently, or if you want to legalize an informal adoption that took place years ago. You should also see a lawyer if the child you wish to adopt has property of her own. Adopting a child from another state or even moving to another state before the completion of an adoption can raise a host of special problems, which are discussed in the next chapter.

Step by Step

Preliminaries. The legal process has two parts. The first involves ending the biological parents' rights and duties toward the child. This opening phase is often completed before the adoptive parents even see their new child. The second part is the adoption itself. Ordinarily the biological parents have nothing to do with this half of the procedure.

The intermediary in the placement is the one who should obtain all proper documents ending the old relationship. If a child is placed directly with you for adoption, it is your responsibility to see that the proper written consent is obtained. The consent must be for adoption, not simply an agreement to turn the child over to your care. Because the consent is so important, you should retain a lawyer to see that any independent adoptions include a legally satisfactory termination of parental rights.

If you are adopting an older child, his consent to the adoption is also necessary (see the chart "The Law and the Older Child" in chapter 5). In most states children age fourteen and older must agree to the adoption, but this rule varies from state to state. In a few cases, children as young as ten must state their willingness to be adopted.

Petition. From a human point of view, the central moment of adoption comes when the child is placed in your care. The rest is anticlimax. The courts tend to agree that the child's arrival is a key event, and the final adoption often depends on how much time has passed since the child was placed with you. Thus, although such a great event is unlikely to be forgotten, be sure to record the date of your child's placement so that you will have it for future legal reference.

Usually at the time of placement you are asked to sign the appropriate documents that will petition the court for permanent adoption. Most states require that the petition be filed promptly once the child is actually in the home.

The petition notifies the court of the intention to adopt. State laws spell out what it should say. The trend is to have the petition list: (1) the date and place of birth of the child, if known; (2) the name the adopting parents have given the child; (3) the date the child was placed with the new parents and who placed him in their care; (4) name, age, and length of residence of the new parents; (5) marital status of the adopting parents—date and place of marriage if married; (6) a statement that the new parents have the ability to care for the child and that they wish to accept the rights and responsibilities of being the child's parents; (7) a description and estimate of the worth of any property owned by the child; (8) the name of anybody whose consent to the adoption is required but who has not yet given it. There is also a growing trend to call for a full financial statement, listing the expenses involved in seeking the adoption.

The proper court. The general principle is that the petition should be submitted to the court in the area where the adoptive parents live. Many states require that the new parents be residents of the state, and a few laws include specific residency requirements of six months to a year.

Sometimes, however, the petition is filed in the court for the area where the child has been living. Because it is normally less trouble for the child to move directly into her new home than it is for the new parents to move into a hotel, this second method is uncommon, but if circumstances seem to call for it, many states permit it.

Military personnel normally use the court for the area where they are stationed, even though they may maintain a legal domicile elsewhere. A few states require military personnel to have been posted in the state for at least a year before they can adopt.

Different states have placed adoption under the control of different types of courts. Many states still use the probate courts, which were designed to administer estates and consider wills. Their use is a quaint reminder that our adoption laws arose from a Roman process for controlling inheritance. Other states use general courts or the newer family-relations courts, but the type of court does not have much practical importance in shaping the adoption process.

The residence requirement. If you are a newcomer to a state where there is a specific residence requirement, you need not wait to begin your search for a child. The residence law refers only to how long you must have been in the state before you can file an adoption petition.

Preparation for the hearing. Filing a petition for adoption sets the court in motion. The main issue the court must determine is whether or not you have a suitable home for the child. If the adoption was handled by an agency, the agency study is usually sufficient. If the adoption is an independent one, the court will want a report from the state welfare department concerning your ability to provide a good home. The court will direct the welfare department to get in touch with you.

In those rare cases in which somebody outside your family has a legal interest in the case, the court will notify that person about plans to hold a hearing on the adoption.

The hearing. The hearing is a meeting to consider the petition. Unlike most court activities, adoption hearings are confidential. Strangers are not allowed to be present, and once they are completed, the records are sealed. Often the hearing is held in the judge's chambers rather than in the courtroom.

The judge can ask questions, but this is not a cross-examination. The point is to make sure that all is as it appears. Because the judge is not seeking to confirm a list of facts, but, rather, to get a sense of what the home will be like for the child, the rules of evidence are ordinarily relaxed and the adopting parents can speak freely about their thoughts and opinions without having to worry about anyone raising objections.

The majority of hearings are uncontested. Along with the petition is a report either recommending the adoption or stating that no evidence adverse to the adoption has been found.

Waiting period. The hearing usually ends with the issuance of a temporary decree of adoption known as an "interlocutory decree." The details of the decree vary among the states, but in every case the temporary decree gives the new parents legal custody of the child and imposes on them the obligations of parents.

The theoretical justification for the waiting period is that it gives the court time to be sure you really are providing a good home for your child. The state welfare department may call to be sure all is well. Although the adoption is not yet final, the temporary decree has shifted all the legal assumptions over to your side. Up until issuance of the decree you are expected to show that you can provide a good home. After the decree the burden of proof is removed from your shoulders. Anybody who raises questions finds it is up to him to make his point.

Some child psychologists have urged that the waiting period be abolished in order to end all doubt and anxiety. Sometimes the wait is reduced, but the deliberate nature of legal processes does not inspire much hope that it will disappear.

The adoption decree. Typically the waiting period ends six months after the child is placed in the home. The temporary decree is replaced by a final one. The child's name is legally changed, and a new birth certificate is issued in her new name. The records in the case are sealed and normally cannot be inspected.

The most important feature of this decree is that it is final. The law has at last caught up with the reality of the situation. The biological parents now have no legal relationship to the child and have no right to question the adoption. The courts also have withdrawn from the matter and list the adoption case as closed.

Statute of limitations. Because it is important for both parent and child to know that the adoption is fully reliable and cannot be shaken as a result of some error in the legal procedure, more and more states have been passing laws which say that no questions about the adoption can be raised after a certain time—usually one or two years. These laws guarantee that technical questions about an adoption will not somehow lead to its undoing.

Costs. The court costs of the adoption are the responsibility of the adopting family. They are usually waived, however, and in many states the law specifically says that the family is not to be charged for the court's service in the matter of an adoption.

Parental Rights and Responsibilities

Most state adoption laws include sections proclaiming that after the adoption decree has been issued, the new parents take on all the rights and responsibilities of parents whose child was born to them in "lawful wedlock." As every parent knows, there are a lot more responsibilities than rights in raising a child.

Expenses. After the adoption decree, you have the right to have the child live with you. At the same time you have the responsibility of paying for the child's clothing, food, shelter, medical care, and education. In recent years, as a means of encouraging the adoption of waiting children, adoption subsidies have been developed in many states (see chapter 15).

Taxes. Parents have the right to list their children as dependents and claim them as tax deductions. Adoptive parents have the same right. In fact, because the costs and responsibilities normally begin when the child arrives and not just when the final decree is issued, you can claim the child as a dependent from the moment he is placed in your home.

Support income. Sometimes the parents' income varies with the number of children in the family. Social Security and state welfare payments are the most common forms of such income. Adopted children are entitled to the same support payments as biological ones.

As with most laws, this last rule can be overturned if it is stretched too far. A famous New Mexico case involved an eighty-year-old grandfather who adopted his daughter's two children simply as a scheme to increase his Social Security payments. The appeals court frowned on such imaginative financing and voided the adoption.

Parental permission. In most cases, parental permission is not a legal question. Giving or denying permission to go to a particular movie, stay up late, or borrow the keys to the car are obviously outside the court's jurisdiction, but the law does step in when a child is still underage and wants to get married, or become a soldier, or is in need of medical treatment. In these situations, the parent must give consent and you, as the parent of an adopted child, have full legal power to sign or refuse to sign all such consent forms.

The child's property. On rare occasions, the adopted child has some property of her own. You are normally not entitled to control or administer the child's property unless a court appoints you the guardian of the estate. The law is not making a special distinction between biological and adoptive parents; as a rule, the law never allows a parent "guardianship of the estate" without judicial approval. If you plan to adopt a child who owns property, your lawyer should see about having you appointed guardian of the estate at the same time the adoption is authorized.

Difficult Cases

Every so often a legal battle over adoption gets into the news. The cases are rare, but when they do arise, they get heavy publicity. Their combination of human interest and callous bureaucracy gives them a universal newsworthiness. As a result of the publicity, anybody with a memory stretching back over ten or more years may have the impression that there are a number of hard-fought adoptions. Of course, the one million routine adoptions during the same period have gone unnoticed. Adoption fights are rare, but when they do occur, they usually concern the following issues.

Restrictions on placement. An agency or a court may rule that a certain type of child cannot be placed in your home. By now, most of these restrictions, particularly the racial ones, have been declared unconstitutional. In one sensational case from the 1960s a Cleveland judge blocked an adoption sought by a white husband and his Japanese wife. The judge ruled, "The good Lord created five races and if He intended to have only one, He would have done so. It was never intended that the races should be mixed." By now, fortunately, adoption law is shaped more by the U.S. Constitution than by what fallible judges declare to be the will of God.

Agency policies of discrimination, however, can be so fixed that they might as well be law. If an agency refuses to put a child in your home, or if the state welfare department refuses to approve a particular adoption, you may find that you have little recourse. A lawyer is likely to advise that nothing can be done, although sometimes he may be able to recommend further action, if you are willing to pay the costs of a prolonged legal struggle. If a particular child is at issue, a lawyer should be able to tell you whether a suit is possible or not. If the question is more general—a matter of an agency forbidding you to adopt anyone at all—a lawyer can tell you whether or not an independent adoption is likely to be possible.

The one legal restriction on placement that still survives in many states concerns religion. The rule is usually that, *whenever possible,* the child should be adopted by parents who share her religion. In the case of an older child who has been raised in a particular faith, the law is reasonable, but it is difficult to speak seriously of a newborn infant's religion. The law does prevent religions from recruiting new members by adopting them, but it also discriminates against religious minorities and nonbelievers by sharply reducing the numbers of children available to them for adoption. One loophole is in the legal phrase "whenever possible." Some states are less strict than others about how great an effort must be made to match religions.

Withdrawal of consent. The most troublesome adoption cases involve a mother who has changed her mind about giving up the child for adoption or who never consented in the first place. Because this question is so complicated, it is discussed fully in chapter 13.

Inheritance. One of the ironies of the entire adoption process is that it was given legal form in order to permit inheritances outside the bloodline, but inheritance is still one of the murkiest areas of the law. The values of feudal England and the Roman Republic have not mixed easily.

Today, in all the states and in Washington, D.C., adopted children inherit from their adoptive parents. That is the universal rule. You needn't worry about it. You do not have to do anything special about it. The law is settled. Clarity soon fades, however, once we move away from that central point. In a few states, parents may not inherit from their adopted child. In a few states an adopted child can inherit from his biological parents.

The confusion becomes important in cases of inheritance from relatives. If you expect to inherit from a parent, an uncle, or some other member of the family, it is a good idea to talk to a lawyer about the status of the child you wish to adopt. In some states the law specifically says that in all matters of inheritance, adopted children are to be treated as biological children. But other states are not so specific, and judges often give what they call a strict construction to the adoption law. That is, if the law does not spell out a point in undeniable detail, they turn back to the common law and its superstition about blood.

Thus the will of an adoptive grandparent may state, "I leave x amount of money to be divided equally among all of my grandchildren." A judge steeped in common law can rule that the bequest refers only to the bloodline and can deny your adopted child his fair share.

Raise the question of inheritance with your adoption lawyer. The issue is so caught up in questions of interpretation, state borders, and local precedent that no book can sort the matter out for you.

Informal adoptions. Historically, the most common form of adoption has been the simple one of giving a home to a needy child. Usually a relative, neighbor, or friend of the family who is aware of a child's plight steps in and gives the child a family. Such adoptions continue today and are as valid psychologically as any others, but legally they are subject to question. In law these informal adoptions are known as "equitable adoptions." They become legal problems when questions of inheritance, Social Security benefits, and insurance claims arise. Once again, it is time to approach a lawyer.

All such questions can be avoided if the adoption is formalized. Formal adoptions can still be arranged, even if the informal adoption is years old. They are even possible if the adopted child has grown to adulthood. Because legalizing the situation overcomes so many difficulties, informal adoptions ought to be formalized.

Appeals. The judge is only a judge, not a king or a dictator. If he rules against you in any adoption matter, you have the right to appeal. Usually the appeal must be filed promptly.

State Variations

The step-by-step procedure outlined in this chapter is the standard one for the country, but of course each state passes its own laws and the laws are not all uniform. The waiting period has inspired the largest number of local innovations. Every possible variation on it seems to have been passed as law somewhere. A number of states have introduced systems requiring a slightly shorter wait for parents who adopt through agencies than for parents in independent adoptions.

The following chart lists the major procedural variations. It includes the specific kinds of information outlined below:

Court—These symbols tell which court handles adoptions: C = chancery court; F = family court; G = court of general jurisdiction; J = juvenile court; P = probate court.

Residence—"Required" means petitioners must be residents, but no specific time has been defined. "None" means there is no requirement.

Waiting period—Unless it says otherwise, the time specified is the minimum time allowed between placement and issuance of the final decree.

Note—An * means that in the notes following the chart there is a further comment on the state's law.

State Adoption Procedures

State	Court	Residence	Waiting Period	Note
Alabama	P	none	9 months	*
Alaska	G	none	court's discretion	*
Arizona	J	required	6 months after petition	
Arkansas	P	none	6 months after hearing	*
California	G	county required	6 months (agency shorter)	
Colorado	J	none	6 months to one year after hearing	
Connecticut	P	none	90 days after petition filed	*
Delaware	F	required	6 months to one year	
District of Columbia	G	required or agency	6 months after hearing	
Florida	G	none	90 days before petition filed	
Georgia	G	required	60 to 90 days after petition filed	*
Hawaii	F	none	court's discretion	*
Idaho	G	required	court's discretion	
Illinois	G	6 months	6 months after hearing	
Indiana	P	required	court's discretion	
Iowa	G	none	5 months	
Kansas	P	none	court's discretion	

155

State	Court	Residence	Waiting Period	Note
Kentucky	G	one year	none after petition	*
Louisiana	F/J	none	30 to 60 days	*
Maine	P	none	court's discretion 6 months to one year	
Maryland	G	none	up to one year after hearing	
Massachusetts	P	none	6 months	
Michigan	P	none	up to one year after hearing	
Minnesota	J	one year (waivable)	3 months	
Mississippi	C	90 days	none after hearing	
Missouri	J	none	9 months after petition filed	
Montana	G	required	court's discretion	
Nebraska	G	none	6 months	
Nevada	G	see below	court's discretion	*
New Hampshire	P	6 months	6 months to one year	*
New Jersey	J	none	see below	*
New Mexico	G	required	see below	*
New York	F/G	none	6 months	*
North Carolina	F	6 months	up to one year after hearing	*

State	Court	Residence	Waiting Period	Note
North Dakota	G	required	see below	*
Ohio	P	none	see below	*
Oklahoma	G	required	6 months after hearing	
Oregon	G	none	2 months	
Pennsylvania	G	none	up to 6 months	*
Rhode Island	F	required	court's discretion	*
South Carolina	F	none	up to 6 months after hearing	
South Dakota	P	none	see below	*
Tennessee	G	one year	one year after petition filed	
Texas	G/F	none	see below	*
Utah	G	required	6 months	
Vermont	P	none	6 months	*
Virginia	G	required	75 days to six months	*
Washington	G	none	none	
West Virginia	G	required	court's discretion	*
Wisconsin	P	required	see below	*
Wyoming	G	required	6 months	

Alabama: The petition is filed three months after the placement; final decree is granted six months after the hearing.

Alaska: The hearing ends in issuance of the final decree rather than a temporary one.

Arkansas: The adoption can be challenged if new parents are divorced or separated within two years of issuance of the adoption decree.

Connecticut: If the child is unrelated, she must be in the home for over a year before a petition can be filed.

Georgia: Single people petitioning to adopt must be at least twenty-five years old.

Hawaii: Statute of limitations does not apply to fraud cases.

Kentucky: If a child was not placed in the home by an agency, the new parents must wait three months before petitioning the court for adoption. The presence of only one adopting parent is required at the hearing. Biological parents have the right to object to the race or religion of adopting parents.

Louisiana: The petition is filed six months after the placement.

Nevada: If two or more children are to be adopted, petitioners must have lived in the state for six months. The petition is filed after the child has been in the home for thirty days. The hearing leads to the issuance of a final rather than a temporary decree.

New Hampshire: The six-month residence requirement can apply to either the petitioner or the child.

New Jersey: If any adverse matters are to be presented at the hearing, adopting parents must be notified at least five days before. If the child was placed by an agency, the final decree is issued right after the hearing. In the case of independent adoptions, the final decree comes six to nine months after the hearing.

New Mexico: The waiting period for an agency adoption is six months after placement of the child in the home. For an independent adoption it is six months after the court has been notified of the placement.

New York: The waiting period uses the system described under New Mexico. The statute of limitations is vaguely worded, although in general the final decree cannot be questioned once it is issued.

North Carolina: The waiting period is one year after placement by an agency, or in the case of independent adoptions, one year after issuance of the temporary decree. The statute of limitations is vaguely worded, but for most purposes the final decree cannot be questioned after it is issued.

North Dakota: The waiting period is the same as the one described under New Mexico.

Ohio: The waiting period is the same as the one described under New Mexico.

Pennsylvania: The court requires an investigation of the suitability of the home and notification of the placement before the petition is filed.

Rhode Island: The petition is filed six months after the placement.

South Dakota: The petition cannot be filed until six months after the placement. After the hearing there is no temporary decree, only a final one.

Texas: See the procedure described for South Dakota.

Vermont: The hearing is held at the end of the waiting period. The court then issues a final decree.

Virginia: The petition is filed six months after the placement.

West Virginia: The waiting period is not specifically defined, but the hearing leads to a final adoption decree rather than a temporary one. The statute of limitations is vaguely worded and permits the biological father to question the adoption if he acts promptly after learning of it.

Wisconsin: See the procedure described for South Dakota.

12

Interstate Adoptions

The law grows more complicated and grinds to an even slower pace when a child from one state is adopted by a family in another state. The chief problems involve differences about who can place a child in an adoptive home; differences about when the child can be placed; differences in the rules for ending the rights of the child's biological parents; and differences in agency standards.

One near-universal result of these problems is an increase in the waiting period before the adoption is completed. Every state insists that the child spend some time with the adopting family before it will grant an adoption decree. Commonly, however, a state will not count any time spent when the family lived in some other state. For example, if a family lives in New York, the waiting period is about six months. If during the waiting period the family moves across the state line into New Jersey, there will be another wait of at least six months before the adoption can be settled. A process that should have taken only half a year takes twice as long. Besides the delay, there is the nuisance of confronting a lot more red tape.

Because these interstate issues make matters so complicated, families who plan to adopt independently find that everything becomes a lot easier if the biological mother gives birth in the state of the adopting family. If you are waiting for an out-of-state woman to give birth, you will save yourself a lot of effort by bringing her to your state. If the woman lives in a state where independent adoptions are illegal, this travel is essential.

There is a trend toward some order in interstate adoptions. Most states have now agreed to the Interstate Compact on the Placement of Children (see pages 162–64). This document has clarified the question of who is responsible for the child and has developed a specific procedure for bringing a child into a new state for adoption.

Points of Difference Among States

Bringing a child into a state. One source of difficulty in interstate adoptions is painfully blunt. The guiding concern in most states switches from the interests of the child to the interests of the local taxpayers. States want to be assured that they are not going to have to pay for the upkeep of an out-of-state child if, for some reason, the adoption is not completed. Therefore, although few states have laws regulating the way an adoptable child is removed from the state, many have laws designed to restrict the arrival of independent children.

At the turn of the century, states began passing laws imposing legal barriers to interstate adoptions, and although these laws have since been modified, they have rarely been repealed outright. Michigan, for example, led the way in making interstate adoptions difficult and still makes such adoptions particularly troublesome. Before a child can be placed in an adoptive home there, permission to bring him into Michigan must be granted. Families who move there while in the midst of an adoption and do not first get state permission to bring their new child with them can find themselves in technical violation of the law. Although they are unlikely to have their child taken from them, a family in this predicament may need to endure a foolish amount of extra legal work before they can overcome the technicality and get on with their adoption.

Agency placements from out of state. Some states do not permit an adoption agency in another state to place a child directly in a local home. This rule serves as a protection for local agencies. New Jersey, for example, is bordered by two giant states and has sought to reduce the competition its own agencies face from agencies in neighboring New York and Pennsylvania. Unless the out-of-state agency has obtained a New Jersey license, the placements have to be listed as independent, and the New Jersey courts will treat them as independent adoptions. In effect, this rule prolongs the adoption process by about half a year.

Who can place a child in a new home. There is always legal trouble if a child comes from an independent source to a state that allows only agency adoptions. There is no easy solution to this problem, and often the new parents do not bring the matter to the courts until several years after the placement. By that time, the adoption exists in fact if not in law, and a lawyer may be able to obtain court sanction of the adoption by pleading the need to relieve a hardship case. This sort of evasion is a poor solution, though, because it leaves a question mark dangling for years over the adoption.

When a child can be placed. Technical rules about the custody of a child awaiting adoption are normally of no great concern to the adopting parents. They are more of an issue for whoever places the child with the family. However, the procedure becomes a serious issue if there are conflicts between the two states involved in an interstate adoption.

The worst sort of conflict is over the question of who is legally responsible for the child during the waiting period before adoption. In all states the child's guardian is the intermediary between the biological parent and the adopting parent. In some states that guardianship continues and can only be ended by the adoption itself. In other states the guardianship must be given to the adopting family before placement is made. These two methods directly contradict each other and make adoptions between differing states more difficult.

Rights of biological parents. Every state has its own rules about how and when the rights of the biological parents are ended. A perfectly legal and valid process in one state may not be proper procedure in another. Even when a law says specifically that it will accept procedures "valid under the laws of another state," judges are reluctant to insist on the validity of a procedure that is very different from the local one.

Agency standards. Some agencies are more liberal and less reliant on stereotypes than others. A child may be placed in the home of a family in a state where the adoption would be perfectly acceptable, but then the family may move to a new state where the local welfare agency has serious doubts about the family's suitability. States are seldom so insistent on their local standards that they remove a child from a home, but the waiting period can be considerably prolonged.

Costs. As a normal rule, the adopting family pays all the extra costs of interstate adoptions. Sometimes, however, one or more agencies in the various states can be persuaded to help pay part of the expenses. This solution is usually available only in hardship situations and even then is considered a special privilege.

Solutions to
Interstate Differences

The quick solution. Often the easiest and fastest way of avoiding all these tangles is to adopt the child in her state. Instead of bringing the child straight to their home, the adoptive parents first go to the child's state and apply for adoption there. The chief difficulties of this approach are cost and residence requirements. The expense of everybody's transportation and hotel accommodations can be prohibitive. If the state requires the adopting parents to be residents, an out-of-state adoption is probably impossible.

A further complication is inheritance. Some courts are especially suspicious of out-of-state adoptions and can question inheritance rights under this condition. It is a good idea to get advice from a local lawyer about your child's inheritance position. He may advise you that your will and insurance policies should specify that adopted children are to receive their share of inherited property.

The Interstate Compact. The Interstate Compact on the Placement of Children is an attempt to resolve these many problems. The compact works like a treaty among the states in which all signers agree to abide by the same rules and procedures on interstate adoptions. It is administered by the American Public Welfare Association, 1125 Fifteenth Street, N.W., Washington, D.C. 20005.

The compact has ended a number of confusions. First, the question of the risk to local taxpayers has been resolved by insisting that until the adoption is final, the state where the child came from is responsible for the child.

Procedural questions about guardianship and the rights of biological parents are settled before the placement is made. The idea behind this rule is to clear up all problems as quickly and neatly as possible before they are raised by a judge.

The compact does not overcome the problem of a state that allows only agency placements. If one state permits only agency placements, the compact requires that a child brought in from another state must also come via an agency. The issue of agency versus independent adoption has even been made a bit more difficult by the compact. The compact forbids an independent source in an agency-only state to place a child in a home in a state that normally permits independent placements.

Another matter that has not been overcome by this compact is time. The waiting period is still dragged out.

The compact's principle. Under the Interstate Compact the receiving state is expected to grant permission to bring the child into its territory as long as the adoption does "not appear to be contrary to the interests of the child." This principle has been designed to overcome the problem of different standards defining "the best interests of the child."

Compact signers. By the summer of 1983 the compact had become law in forty-six states: Alabama, Alaska, Arizona, Arkansas, California, Colorado, Connecticut, Delaware, Florida, Georgia, Idaho, Illinois, Indiana, Iowa, Kansas, Kentucky, Louisiana, Maine, Maryland, Massachusetts, Minnesota, Mississippi, Missouri, Montana, Nebraska, New Hampshire, New Mexico, New York, North Carolina, North Dakota, Ohio, Oklahoma, Oregon, Pennsylvania, Rhode Island, South Carolina, South Dakota, Tennessee, Texas, Utah, Vermont, Virginia, Washington, West Virginia, Wisconsin, Wyoming.

Step by Step

Interstate Compact procedure. The Interstate Compact procedure applies only if both states involved in the adoption have agreed to the compact. If both your state and the state where the child is coming from have enacted the compact, then you *must* use this procedure.

First, the person or agency who wishes to place the child in your home must notify the proper authority in your state that it intends to place a child with you. (The list "State Adoption Offices" in chapter 4 names these authorities.) Upon receiving this notice, your state may ask for further information. It is at this time that the legal questions of guardianship, rights of biological parents, and so forth should be cleared up.

Only after your state has given permission can the placement actually be made. The adoption process then continues according to the laws of the state where the child has been placed.

Moving during the adoption process. A ruling of the administering secretariat spelled out how the compact is to be used when a family moves from one state to another after a child has been placed with them but before the final decree is granted. (This procedure assumes that both states have agreed to the compact.)

If an agency made the placement, it is responsible for bringing the situation to the attention of the authority in the state where you plan to move. In an independent adoption it is usually impossible to ask whoever was responsible for the placement suddenly to take on the duties and responsibilities of the compact. The welfare department of the state where the placement was made or the court where the adoption petition was filed should be the one to notify the proper authority of your new state about the pending move.

13

Legal Quagmires

The Old Testament's most famous court case concerned child custody. Two harlots appeared before King Solomon, each claiming a single baby as her own. Solomon ordered that the child be split in two, but when the real mother protested, she was granted custody of the baby.

American courts regularly face cases in which two or more parties fight over the custody of a child. Most concern divorces, but a growing number involve adoptions. The main differences between contemporary cases and the biblical one are that present-day judges rarely have Solomon's divine wisdom and never have his summary power to settle an issue in so swift and decisive a manner.

The appallingly slow exercise of justice in cases that will determine the lives of growing children could be illustrated by any number of horror stories. A typical one concerns a boy identified in the courts only by his initials, JSR. He was born late in 1967 to a woman who developed multiple sclerosis shortly before giving birth and became a paraplegic. In this tragic situation the mother tried at once to give up her child in favor of adoption, but for unknown reasons the Washington, D.C., welfare department would not allow her to do so. Instead JSR had to live in several foster homes. When he was four years old, he was finally placed in a home in preparation for adoption, but then the biological mother refused to abandon her rights to the child.

In cases like this it is possible for the welfare department to seek a court order forcibly terminating the rights of the biological mother. A year and a half after he was placed with his new family, the matter of JSR's adoption came to trial. By then he was five and a half. The court ruled that because a stable relationship with the adopting family was developing, it would be contrary to JSR's best interests to be returned to the mother he had not seen since birth. The adoption was allowed.

The biological mother appealed, and in 1977 the appeals court upheld the lower court's ruling and permitted the adoption to proceed. Six years passed from placement for adoption to settlement of the case. Imagine the trauma for the child if the appeals court had ruled that ten-year-old JSR had to be returned to the woman who had given him up all those years before. Even so, the outcome was more lucky than lawful. Another court might easily have ruled that the "best interests of the child" standard was too vague or that it is unconstitutional to deprive the biological mother of her child without first finding that she is unfit. This kind of slowness and uncertainty, which forces children to wait years before determining their family status, is far too common.

The following glossary defines some legal terms and precedents frequently encountered in adoption proceedings.

Glossary of Adoption Legalese

de facto—a situation that exists in reality even if it is not based on law. A de facto family is composed of parents and child who consider themselves a family and have the emotional ties of a family but no legal document recognizing their relationship.

guardian ad litem—a court-appointed representative who seeks to determine the child's best interest in a custody case.

Meyer v. Nebraska—a 1923 Supreme Court decision that the Constitution's Fourteenth Amendment protects the individual's right to establish a family.

parens patriae—the notion that the state is the protector of its people. This doctrine implies that when the state intervenes in a matter, it is responsible for the welfare of all those who are caught up in the action and unable to fend for themselves. In a custody dispute the children are ensnared victims and thus deserve the court's protection.

standing—the legal right to bring a matter to the attention of a court.

Stanley v. Illinois—a 1972 Supreme Court decision that the rights of the biological father are as fully protected as those of the biological mother.

Extraordinary attacks on an adoption. There can also be custody fights between families and adoption agencies. One New York case involved a family that applied to an agency for adoption, underwent the full investigation of its fitness, was found to be suitable, and had a child placed in the home. While the adoption was moving toward legal completion, the mother gave her new child one severe spanking. The agency learned of it and seized the child. The adopting parents obtained a writ of habeas corpus and got the child back, but the agency appealed the case. The court ruled that the agency had overreacted and that the child could stay with his new parents. The parents were to receive counseling about the limits of child discipline, and the adoption process would be suspended for six months while the counseling was going on. So the result of the agency's intervention was merely to delay rather than ruin the adoption.

Another case, this time with a less happy ending, concerned a woman living in Maryland who applied for an adoption. She was divorced but managed to hide this fact from the adoption agency, and eventually she received a child to adopt. Before the adoption was completed, the agency learned that the mother was divorced, and so they opposed the adoption. The biological mother had flatly stated she wanted her child to be placed with a married couple. The court's decision was that the dishonesty of the applicant and the wish of the biological mother made the adoption impossible. The petition to adopt was denied and the child was returned to the agency.

What to do. Fortunately, even though their numbers seem to be growing, cases like these really are extraordinary, composing only a fraction of all adoptions. But when they do arise, such cases must be taken seriously. As a practical matter, you should hire your own lawyer at once.

If a biological parent raises a question about a child who was placed in your home by an agency, the agency may bring its own lawyers into the case. It might seem as though the agency is entirely on your side and you can rely on their lawyers, but you should still have your own legal counsel because the agency's interests may not coincide perfectly with either yours or the child's. Agency lawyers often have a broader interest than the stakes in your particular case. Quite understandably, their fundamental concern is with the continued ability of children to be adopted through agencies. Because the agency's lawyers may be focusing on the larger picture while you are intimately caught up in the details of the case at hand, you should be represented by someone whose position coincides 100 percent with your own.

Types of cases. The enormity of the legal bog depends on the number of conflicting legal principles it raises. These principles are usually not too numerous if the problem is between the adoption agency and the adopting parents, but the complications spread like mushrooms if the case arises from objections voiced by biological parents.

Biological parents changed their minds. In routine cases, the adoption process begins when the biological parents voluntarily surrender all their rights to the child. Every once in a while a parent changes her mind and asks for the child back. Rare as they are, these cases are often given heavy publicity and sometimes frighten families with adopted children. They seem to suggest that the biological mother can change her mind whenever she wants. This false impression comes from imprecise reporting. News stories seldom go into the details of the adoption procedure and do not make it clear that a final decree had not been granted. Parents of adopted children need not be frightened by such cases once they have received final adoption decrees. In a few states the biological parent can never change her mind after signing the consent form. In some states consent cannot be withdrawn after the temporary adoption decree has been given. In no state does a parent have the right to withdraw consent after the final decree.

Almost all states require that if a biological parent withdraws consent, there must be a court hearing on the matter. The old tendency of rulings was to allow biological mothers to withdraw consent pretty much at will. The current trend is the reverse. Courts recognize that moving back and forth between homes is profoundly disturbing to a child, even a very young one. Psychologically speaking, a child's true parents are the people who care for him. Biological relations are irrelevant. The courts are slowly coming to realize this fact, and withdrawal of consent is not as easy as it once was.

Biological parents who have never agreed to adoption. The really ugly cases, the ones with tangles as thick as a briar patch, are those in which children have been removed from families despite the objections of the biological parents. Family integrity is so fundamental a concept to almost every society that the power of a state to break up a family almost always carries disturbing implications. Adoptive parents also find the idea troubling, since the whole point of adoption is to ensure the new family that its integrity is rock firm.

Nevertheless, it has long been felt that there are times when the state should have the authority to step in. The oldest such American law came shortly after the Pilgrims arrived, when in 1648, the Mas-

trine is of little help in guiding judges. More important are past cases. Some states accept the notion that the child's best interests are usually met by staying with the biological family, some states lean the other way, and some spin like a wheel of fortune, making the outcome almost impossible to predict.

Because the best-interests doctrine has proven so hollow in actual practice, there is some movement toward finding an alternative phrase. Some reformers advocate making decisions on the basis of "the least detrimental alternative." This phrase is certainly more cynical in tone, but has not yet shown itself any more helpful in practice.

The child's position. A more serious reform than changing clichés has been to try to see that the child's interests really are made clear to the court. During the 1970s this movement gained great strength and is now a regular feature of most extraordinary adoption cases. Because judges have neither the time nor the ability to look after the child personally and determine his best interests, somebody is appointed to perform that task. Unfortunately, at this point the reform movement has split in two, arguing over who should be appointed. The older idea was that a social worker should investigate the case and report to the judge on the child's best interests. A newer idea is that the appointment should go to a lawyer. The likely outcome is for both professions to be used together to help assess the child's interests.

The record of this reform is spotty. It has certainly given fuller employment to child psychologists and family lawyers, but the help provided to the children is less clear. Precedent and prejudice are still dominant in court decisions, yet there does seem to be an increased chance that the relevant facts of a child's plight will be brought to the attention of an alert judge. So, although the child's position in these prolonged legal struggles is far from enviable, it probably is better than before.

Your chances. Generally speaking, states take any of three different approaches to disputed adoptions. One is to lean heavily in favor of the biological parents. States with this attitude begin with a strong presumption that the child is best served by being returned to the original parent. These states do not recognize claims made by the new parents waiting for final adoption, even if the child has been with them for years. Furthermore, in these states unfitness is difficult to establish because past misconduct is not accepted as proof of present unfitness. In one spectacular Mississippi case, the biological father shot the would-be adoptive father four times, but the judge ruled that this conduct plus the fact that the biological father had previously been quite indifferent to the welfare of his children did not prove that, in the future, the father would be morally or otherwise unfit as a parent. Adoption was denied. Abandonment is also hard to prove, because occasional birthday cards or even an inquiry with the welfare agency can be enough for a judge to deny the charge. States following this pattern are Alaska, Arkansas, Connecticut, Florida, Georgia, Idaho, Indiana, Iowa, Kansas, Kentucky, Louisiana, Minnesota, Mississippi, Missouri, Montana, Nebraska, Oklahoma, Pennsylvania, South Dakota, Virginia, and West Virginia.

The opposite extreme is found in states that insist the biological parents must have very pressing reasons before they can sever the ties a child has established with his new parents. In these states, the court focuses on the rights of the child rather than on the rights of the biological parent and begins with a presumption that children's best interests lie in the stability of established psychological bonds. States following this pattern are Alabama, California, Illinois, Maryland, Michigan, New Jersey, North Dakota, Ohio, and Oregon.

Between these two poles are states that seek to settle each case on its own merits. Their rulings are the least predictable and depend a great deal on the particular judge. Often, as in Vermont, a trend toward favoring the stability of the child's environment is counterbalanced by a strong pro-biological-parent precedent that must be overcome. These states seek to weigh all factors concerning the original parents, the child, and the attachment to the new parents. States in this group are Arizona, Colorado, Hawaii, Massachusetts, New York, North Carolina, South Carolina, Tennessee, Texas, Vermont, Washington, and Wisconsin.

Appeals. Both sides can appeal a decision, but the losing side must deliver the child to the winning party's custody during the appeal.

Constitutional Rights

One reason these cases can last for years and their outcomes can be hard to predict is that so many fundamental rights are in conflict. The Constitution recognizes a number of rights that in theory ought not be denied but that seem to work against one another in hard-fought adoption cases. In these cases one part of one clause in the Fourteenth Amendment comes up time and again: the clause that says no state shall "deprive any person of life, liberty, or property, without due process of law; nor deny to any person within its jurisdiction the equal protection of the laws." Although these words are quite properly praised in every high-school civics class, they contain an Arabia's worth of fuel for legal argument.

Liberty. There is no question in any court that the right to raise a family is a fundamental liberty guaranteed by the Constitution, but we find an immediate problem in cases that involve both a biological family and a psychological one. In such disputes the integrity of one family must fall in order to preserve the integrity of the other.

The psychological (or de facto) family is created after a child is brought into a home with the intention of being adopted. In such cases the child and the parents begin to think like family members. Eventually (and often "eventually" comes very quickly) emotional bonds are formed between parents and child which are so strong that breaking them is as traumatic as breaking up a biological family. Until recently courts did not take the idea of a de facto family seriously, but the trend has been growing to acknowledge its reality. It received a strong boost from a unanimous Supreme Court ruling known as *Quilloin* v. *Walcott.* In that case the Court permitted an adoption and gave as one of its reasons, "This is not . . . a case in which the proposed adoption would place the child with a new set of parents with whom the child had never before lived. Rather, the result of the adoption in this case is to give full recognition to a family unit already in existence." This 1978 opinion gave great heart to supporters of de facto families.

Due process. Because the liberty of two separate families is at stake, the question becomes which family's liberty can only be interrupted after due process. If it is the biological family, then the burden is on the other side to show that termination of rights is justified. If, however, it is the de facto family, then the burden switches to the biological family to show that the established family should be broken up.

The presumption has been that the biological family is favored, but this idea grew out of the discredited common-law theory that children are the property of the biological parents. Present thinking sees a family as being built on personal rights rather than property rights, and this shift has created a trend toward favoring the child's de facto family.

Equal protection. A decision that one side's liberty is protected by the need for due process means that the other side has an uphill battle on their hands. This difficulty often strikes its victims as being unfair and contrary to the guarantee that they will be protected equally by the laws. Protest against the situation is more common than victory, but it sometimes happens that a judge is persuaded and reverses the demands of due process.

PART IV
Foster Homes

14

Foster Care Explored

Your state's foster-care program is still another means through which you can bring children into your family. In theory, the difference between foster care and adoption is simple and easy to define. Adoption is permanent; foster care is temporary. Children enter foster care because of some problem that prevents them from staying at home, but they expect to return eventually and they are not available for adoption.

The home problem varies; it might be that the mother is unmarried and an alcoholic but is receiving medical treatment. Her child is placed in a foster home during the treatment period. If indeed she does recover and becomes able to resume the duties of a mother, the child will be returned to her.

Often, of course, the problem does not have so bright an outlook. The father may be a bully who beats the child. The mother may suffer from mental illness that makes her unpredictable; sometimes she acts responsibly, but at other times she neglects the child for days on end. In such cases, the future is far more clouded. Public agencies may try to help the parents, but no one expects them to improve very rapidly. Still, they are the child's biological parents and they may improve over time, so the child becomes a foster child with an uncertain future.

Occasionally the child has come from a background of utter horror and there is no chance of a return home, but because of legal delays the child is not yet available for adoption. Again, foster care is the temporary solution.

Different states have different methods for formally distinguishing between the types of foster care. The types of foster care listed below are the most common foster-care categories. It looks like a neat and orderly list, but the reality is that a child's category can change or be unclear from the start. Typically the situation begins ambiguously and only gradually takes on a coherent shape.

Types of Foster Care

Emergency—A sudden problem has arisen. The child is placed in a foster home for no longer than thirty days.

Limited—The arrangement is temporary, but the length of time is uncertain. The biological family is being helped to prepare for the child's return.

Preadoptive—The child will be adopted as soon as the biological parents' rights are terminated.

Permanent—Special problems prevent adoption. These days agencies should usually be working to free the child for adoption.

Specialized—Children are disabled, seriously ill, part of a family group, or unmarried teenagers with babies of their own.

The cases that lead to foster care are many, but in every instance there is a barrier that prevents the child from simply being given over to a family for permanent adoption, so some more temporary solution is needed. Foster care is supposed to be a short-term answer to a problem while a more lasting solution is developed. This idea is what chiefly distinguishes it from adoption.

Behind this simple difference lies a world of implications. The rewards of foster care are focused in a special way. The roles of the placement agency and of the biological parents shift radically. The rights of foster parents are not the same as the rights of adoptive parents, and even the reaction of friends and neighbors to the arrangement can be different from what it would be if you had adopted.

New trends. During the 1970s foster-care programs and the moral values that support them underwent a radical change. Before that decade the chief complaint about foster care was that the vagueness of the word "temporary" had allowed everyone to become lazy. It is difficult for agencies to resolve most of the home problems that lead children into the foster-care program; it is easy to let the matter slide. It is painful for judges to rule finally and forever that parents are unfit and can never have their children back; it becomes convenient to let the matter slide. It is humiliating for a biological parent to say, "I will never be in a position to raise my child," and to abandon all parental claims. So all too often the children did slide into a bottomless bog where they were trapped for years.

The persistent uncertainty facing the children is the scandal of foster care, and during the 1970s it became generally accepted that children are poorly served if they live on temporary status for a long time. It is disturbing for well-adjusted adults to be placed on "standby" for a few hours at an airport while an airplane seat is hunted up. Imagine growing up on standby, never knowing if you are to live with a family for only a short time more or until you have come of age.

Because of this continuing problem, there has been a great upheaval in the nature of foster care. The paramount need now seen is to stabilize the child's position quickly. Across the country the trend has been to try to clarify the child's status as soon as possible; however, in the legal world even lightning travels by mule and "as soon as possible" still means a long time. Too many children continue to grow up in foster care. They may eventually be released for adoption, but the process is still so slow that many are approaching adolescence before their biological parents' rights are finally ended. By then it is hard to find homes for them. The children are too old and have been too traumatized to be adopted quickly.

The attractions. There are a number of reasons why a person might apply to become a foster parent rather than seek to adopt. First of all is the fact that many people love children and want to help them. (This reason is the one agencies prefer.) Over the years a family might see many foster children come to live for a while and then leave. This stream of children who find help at a desperately troubled time in their lives is its own reward. The children are all individuals with their own stories, identities, and needs. The opportunity to work personally and intimately with children attracts a number of people to the foster-care system.

Another important appeal of foster care is financial. Foster parents are always given money to help raise their foster children. Usually this money is not enough to make foster care a profitable activity, but it can considerably reduce the expense involved in having a child in the home. Thus, people who would like children but cannot afford to raise them often turn to foster care. (The financial aspects of foster care are discussed more fully in the next chapter.)

One reason for becoming a foster parent is a direct result of the new thinking about foster care. It has recently become possible to enroll with many foster-care agencies on a "preadoption" or "at risk" basis. Children are placed in such homes with the idea that the placements will eventually lead to adoption. This approach should not be taken lightly—after all, a living person is coming into your home— but it does offer a way for both child and adult to get to know each other before they make a permanent commitment to become a family. Preadoptive foster care might be compared with courtships of the old-fashioned type. They were a time of testing to see if the basis of an enduring relationship could be established. It was understood that matters might not work out, but the courtships were not begun casually and their object was known from the start.

There can also be special reasons that make foster care preferable to adoption. A typical example involves the relatives of the child. The biological parents may be alive but unable to care for a child, and want to surrender their duties to a cousin, brother, aunt, or in-law. In a case like this, adoption can provoke many confusions and tensions within the family, but a completely informal arrangement leaves the relatives' position dangerously ambiguous and unprotected. Foster care formalizes the relatives' role (and brings in expense money) but does not confuse the kinship ties. It is usually preferable to adoption.

A mistaken attraction. Do not become foster parents in the expectation of making much money. The pay is bad. If you have several foster children in your home at once, you can come out ahead, but you will have earned every dime of it. There is no disgrace in finding that the foster-care money appeals to you and no reason to blush over the idea that money is one of your motives in applying to an agency. The agencies will not think any less of you because of your monetary interest, but if money is your only reason for thinking about foster care, stop. You are letting yourself in for very hard work, very long hours, and (if you don't love children) darn few rewards. You may end up spending the profits on baby-sitters just to get a break.

The satisfactions. The primary rewards of raising biological or adopted children tend to be expressed in the context of the long term. Children are "a comfort in one's old age," they grow up to make you proud, or they continue the family line. Of course, there are many short-term pleasures too, but there are also many sacrifices and hardships. In foster care, the short term is probably all you have. The short-term difficulties have to be justified by the short-term rewards.

Inevitably the satisfactions have to come from love. The child is a nuisance today and will be nowhere in sight when your old age comes around, but you can accept the situation because of your affection and concern for that individual child's welfare. When departure time comes, you must be satisfied that you got as much as you gave. The future is uncertain and no longer your responsibility, but the past can be accepted without regrets.

Foster parents sometimes react to the temporary nature of the arrangement by holding love back. It is a natural and understandable way to try to protect oneself from the pain of eventual separation, but this holding back cheats the children, who need love, and cheats the parents, who will find that without love their foster work brings few of the satisfactions it should.

These satisfactions are not for everybody. Americans traditionally believe that they should sow today and reap tomorrow. We do not often gather the fruits at the same time we labor, but for those with the right attitude and with enough courage to love, foster care is extraordinarily rewarding.

The children. For all its differences, foster care begins with the same fact as adoption: a child is in need. Something has happened to interfere with the traditional situation in which biological parents are responsible for their children. Children in need of foster care, however, are in much more ambiguous situations than are children available for adoption.

A foster child is filled with many questions. Should I let go of the past or not? Am I to blame for what is happening? Am I being kidnapped or what? Dare I trust these foster parents?

Another fact of foster care is that no child enters the program for simple reasons. The most common reason for placing a child in a foster home is that the biological parents have abused or neglected the child. The situation has become so serious that the child cannot stay at home, although there may be hope that the relationship can be salvaged. Another problem may be that the parents are going through a period of great difficulty—divorce, illness, financial collapse—and are unable to take care of the child. Usually, though, some form of neglect or mistreatment has accompanied this sudden problem, for families do not customarily relinquish their children to institutional care unless they are in a state of extraordinary breakdown.

The problems that caused the removal of the child from the biological family are not forgotten. If adults have meant only violence to the child, you cannot expect to be trusted right away. If court action was necessary in removing the child from the family, the child may well believe she was weighed in the balance and found lacking. Fears retained from life at home may lead to nightmares, bed-wetting, asthma, or demands for constant reassurance. Being a foster parent calls for extra duties and sensitivities unlikely to be a part of ordinary parent-hood. It is up to the foster parents to provide the children with a sense of security, a knowledge of the reality of love, and a confidence in their own self-worth so that the trauma of going into foster care is transformed into a memory of growth.

The agency. In adoption, the agency places a child in your home and then disappears from the scene. In foster care, the agency is a con-tinuing presence. Foster parents, in fact, should feel that they are part of the agency. (There is no such thing as the independent place-ment of foster children.) Parents are encouraged to turn to the social worker for advice.

Working with an agency is not always appealing to people. Biological parents commonly dislike the idea of going to outside sources for advice on child rearing, since such action can seem to reflect on the parents' own suitability for their role. Foster parents may feel the same way. It may also seem risky to turn to the agency for help. A foster parent might wonder, "What if the social worker decides that I'm having too much trouble and takes the child back?" Although this fear may seem reasonable, it is misguided. The experience of social workers has been that the foster parents who call with many ques-tions and complaints do stick it out, while the foster parents who try to go it alone are the ones who throw in the towel after a few months and give up the foster child.

Once a child is placed in your home, your chief contact with the agency will be through the worker assigned to the child's case. When you have questions involving the foster child, the caseworker is the person to ask. Other duties of the caseworker include maintaining all official records concerning the child's status, working with the child's biological parents, and, most important, developing a permanent plan for the child.

This plan is particularly important now that there is so much em-phasis on avoiding the aimless drifting of children. The purpose of the plan is to clarify the child's future as quickly as possible. As a foster parent, you have the right to participate in the formulation of this plan.

Essentially there are two plans for a foster child. The preferred one is to return the child to the biological parents. If this first plan is not possible, the alternative goal is to release the child for adoption. Adoption may be by the foster parents or by some other family, but these days the foster parents normally are given the first chance to adopt.

Because of the pressure to develop a plan quickly, the agency's presence tends to be more noticeable than it was formerly. An important factor in determining whether foster care is for you is how well you can work with the agency. If you can see it as a useful supporting institution, as a source of information and advice, then you will probably do all right. If the agency seems to be merely a nuisance to be tolerated in order to have a child placed in your home, foster care may not be for you.

The biological parents. The original parents have no role in the life of a typical adopted child. Usually they are unknown; in every case they have no legal right to intervene. In foster care, the situation is much different. Because the hope is to return the children to their permanent care, the biological parents are actively encouraged to maintain contact with their children. Biological parents have visiting rights.

The relation between foster child and biological parents is a major and unique characteristic of foster care. It is common for foster parents to feel anger toward and contempt for the biological parents. After all, it was the parents' problem that led to their child's original entry into the foster-care program. This anger is likely to grow if the child seems to suffer from the visits of a biological parent. You will naturally want to shield the child from the pain and upset that accompanies a visit with a disturbed and immature or irresponsible parent. Foster parents must accept the fact that official doctrine in every agency is that it is good for biological parents and children to maintain contact. If the child returns weeping or angry after such visits, the agency will still want contact to be maintained. This position will change only if the agency decides to try to free the child for adoption.

Foster parents must also appreciate the divided loyalties of the foster child. The biological parents occupy a special and private place in the child's soul. As a foster parent, you must be diplomatic enough to understand that your foster child will probably never trust you enough to accept criticism of the biological parents. Such criticism will always be taken personally. Part of your task as a foster parent is to preserve the child's self-respect; criticism or snide remarks about the parents, no matter how justifiable, will stunt the child's sense of personal worth.

The foster child also has a right to confidentiality concerning biological parents. As a foster parent, you have the right to learn the details of your foster child's past. Your neighbors have no such right. There is, however, a strong urge to talk about such things, because the behavior of the biological parents is often so surprising. They may have a history unlike anything you have previously encountered outside a gothic novel. Out of respect for the privacy of your foster child, you must be able to keep such stories to yourself.

Taken as a whole, the role of the biological parents is one of the most unusual features of foster care. Adoptive parents do not face anything like it. The need for confidentiality, diplomacy, and toleration in this matter is a special challenge found only in foster care.

Friends and relatives. After all this talk about how the situation of foster children differs from that of adopted and biological children, this next point may seem surprising, but foster parents must resist the words and actions of friends who imply that there is a serious difference between foster children and other children.

Remember the root of all the differences I have discussed: the placement of the child is temporary. Although this difference has many implications for the child, the agency, and the biological parents, it has none that matter to your acquaintances. Sometimes neighbors might suggest that a foster child has only a second-class position in the family or a friend might question your own authority in the matter of dealing with the child, arguing, "He's only there for a while." You have to have the courage to stand up to these challenges and to insist otherwise. For however long the placement does last, the child is a part of your family and your authority is not to be questioned by outsiders. In this matter you are just like every other parent.

Your rights. Recently there has been an active effort to increase the rights and powers of foster parents. A number of foster parent associations have been formed, most of them attached to particular agencies. You should ask about the existence of such a group at the agency's orientation meeting.

These associations serve two purposes. They allow foster parents to learn from one another's experience, and they provide the power that comes from having a common voice. Some of this power has been used to improve the legal status of foster parents, and a lot of it has been used directly for the benefit of the children.

An example of the kinds of things foster parents can do for the children was demonstrated in New York City. Somehow the practice developed there of bringing babies to foster homes and then removing all their clothing except for the diapers they were wearing at the moment. It was the foster parents who protested this stripping of the children and who finally got a halt to it after the issue was raised at a foster-parent association meeting.

Because of foster-parent associations, foster parents are now given the first opportunity to adopt their foster children, and they have the right to be included in the development of a long-term plan for the children in their care. Yet there is no avoiding the fundamental truth that foster parents have neither the legal responsibilities nor the recognized rights of adoptive parents. There are, however, ways to have some rights transferred to you if the child is a permanent member of your family and adoption is not possible. These are discussed in chapter 15.

Step by Step

The steps for foster care are similar to those for an agency adoption, with some noteworthy differences. First, foster children can only be placed in homes that are licensed to care for foster children, and the standards for licensing are set by law. These are generally tougher than the legal standards used to qualify adoptive parents. The other important difference concerns finances. Once a child is placed in your home you will begin to receive money for that child's care, so you don't have to be as well-to-do to bring a foster child into your home. Commonly, foster parents have had smaller incomes than adoptive parents.

Application. In most states, the majority of foster children are placed by public (state or county) agencies. In a few states (New York is the major example), private agencies are responsible for placing most foster children in homes. A third possibility (Texas provides an example) is for both private and public agencies to have foster-care services. If the matter is purely a public one, the issue of where to apply is resolved. You can't shop around for another city hall.

If you have a choice, look over several agencies. They certainly intend to scrutinize you. Because you will have a much longer term relationship with the agency than you would if you were applying for an adoption, it is particularly important for you to have an agency that is congenial to your tastes and that will be able to serve you after placement. The most important person in your relationship with the agency will be the caseworker, but unfortunately you will almost never meet any caseworkers before a child actually arrives in your home. The people who handle your application are usually not the same people you will be working with once you become a foster parent. Thus, you have to go on secondary clues, predicting the quality of the caseworker on the basis of the agency employees you do meet. If you know people who are already foster parents with a particular agency, ask them about the caseworkers they have known.

Two important characteristics of caseworkers vary from agency to agency. The first is job stability; some agencies seem to have a much higher turnover in personnel than others. This is important because there is likely to be an administrative review of the situation in your home whenever the caseworker changes. These reviews are often times of anxiety in foster homes, since they underline the uncertainty of the child's future and the dependence of everybody on the agency. It is in your interests for agency personnel to be as stable as possible.

A second variable is the legal knowledge of the caseworkers. Schools of social work commonly fail to give their graduates solid grounding in the many laws and regulatory procedures they are going to confront. Even if the caseworkers did leave school with a good understanding of the legal machinery, they may not have kept up to date on changes in the law. Foster care is subject to federal, state, county, and city laws, all of which often change. Many agencies leave all the regulatory matters to their lawyers while the caseworkers remain unaware of new developments. This tendency can lead to missed financial and adoptive opportunities. The best agencies are the ones that make a point of bringing legal changes to the attention of their caseworkers and make sure that they understand the ramifications of the new laws.

When you first phone an agency, you should be as clear in your mind as possible about your intentions. What sorts of children are you interested in? Do you have age, sex, or racial preferences?

The agency you call will probably have some questions for you. Do you meet the state's legal requirements? Are you looking for the sort of child the agency works with? Do you match the religious and racial background of the children?

If you and the agency find each other mutually acceptable, you will be invited to an orientation meeting. At this session the agency should explain its policies, the rates of payment, and the legal and documentary requirements you must meet. You should ask about a foster-parent association. Is there one connected with the agency? How active is it? The easiest way to get a sense of the agency is to meet with members of the foster-parent association, but you may find that the agency does not encourage this course. At the end of the orientation session, you should be given an application.

If in your initial phone call the agency indicates that it cannot help you, find out why. If there is a legal impediment, you may be permanently blocked. More likely, however, the problem is less severe. Perhaps the agency does not receive many of the kinds of children you could best care for. Ask the person on the phone to suggest a more suitable agency.

The study. The foster-care study of the family has a different focus from the adoption investigation. First is the question of whether or not the applicant can really accept a child with problems. The answer depends on the emotional strength of the applicant's own family.

A second issue is how well you can get along with all the extra matters stemming from the temporary arrangement of foster care. Will you be able to work with the agency and get along with the biological parents? Are you able to give of yourself fully when the rewards are short-term? Will you be able to accept the fact when the time has come for the child to leave?

A historical peculiarity of the foster-care study is that it emphasizes the foster mother and downplays the role of the foster father. Agencies like to think they are getting away from this tradition, but it remains true. Thus it is particularly valuable for the mother to show that she has a strong character and thinks of children as individuals. The chart below lists ten typical questions in an interview. If you cannot answer at least some of the questions in the preferred way, perhaps you should rethink your desire to apply.

Training. As part of the preparation for the arrival of a child, some agencies include training in how to be a foster parent. This constitutes a major new trend in foster care. Training is also becoming available to foster parents after their applications have been approved. Indeed, pressure from foster-parent groups is one reason for this growing emphasis. Recent social changes in the availability of drugs and in sexual customs have led many foster parents to feel the need for insight into what is happening and how they can respond to these changes. Agencies have begun to provide their foster parents with sessions on specific subjects (such as sexuality, drugs, and learning problems) and on general child development.

Ten Typical Foster-Parent
Interview Questions and Answers

Questions	Answers	
	Preferred	Disturbing
For both applicants		
1. How old are you?	At least thirty-four.	
2. How did you become interested in being a foster parent?	Want to help children.	Think a child could help you.
3. Who makes the chief decisions in the family—concerning money, moving, etc?	Joint responsibility.	
4. How many children were in your family when you were growing up?	The more the better.	
For the mother		
5. Have you ever had children other than your own stay overnight with you and without their parents?	Yes, at least once, for four or more days.	
6. Do you have other children in the family? If yes, what pleases you most about each? If no, what pleases you about the children you do know?	Evidence that you think of each child as an individual, unlike the others.	Evidence that you stress your own expectations about how children ought to be.
7. Were you the youngest child in your family?	No.	
For the father		
8. Have you changed your ideas about discipline because of experience with children?	Yes, with a specific example.	
9. Have differences with your wife about children's behavior led you to new ideas?	Yes, indeed.	
10. How would you feel about working closely with a social worker?	Like the idea a lot.	

The federal government's Department of Health and Human Services has developed a course explaining the demands and peculiarities of foster parenting. In several states there is a movement to make such courses mandatory before children can be placed in a home.

Certification. Legally, you must be licensed if you are to house a foster child. This is a formality. If the agency investigation concludes that you are suitable, the license is automatic. Technically, the need for a license means that the agency cannot ignore the state's basic laws concerning the condition of homes where children are placed.

Placement. Children are placed in homes on an emergency or standard basis. In many jurisdictions, emergency placement is becoming the more common form. The name "emergency" means what it sounds like: the child's situation is sudden and pressing. An emergency placement begins with a phone call to the prospective home. The child's condition and background are briefly outlined. Then comes the question: will you accept this child? Yes or no? If the answer is yes, the child will be in your home in a matter of hours.

A standard placement is less hectic. It is preceded by your being given as much information as possible about the child. You may, for example, see the child's "life book." This book is like a family album; it contains photos of the child and the home he has lived in. It serves as a way of providing the child with a personal history that can survive even though life has been so unstable. During this preparation period, the child is also told something about you.

Whether it is a standard or an emergency placement, the central question remains: Will you accept this child? In the course of preplacement interviews you should have indicated the sorts of children—age, sex, religion, race—you would prefer to care for. You should also have gotten a sense of what you can and cannot do. Now that the process has moved to a specific situation you may feel that, heavens, you don't know. How can you say? You have only instinct to go on, and if instinct says yes, all you can do is plunge in.

You are allowed to answer "No" without jeopardizing your chances of having some other child placed with you. All agency workers I have spoken with agreed that they prefer to hear "No" from parents who think that the child in question is not what they had in mind or can handle.

The child's arrival is an exciting moment of introductions. Be sure that in the fuss of the moment, however, you do not miss out on getting certain vital facts in writing: (1) the child's name in full, including any nicknames; (2) the name and phone numbers of the child's caseworker, including both office and after-hours numbers; (3) any identifying numbers assigned to the child, such as a Medicaid number; (4) the name and phone number of the child's doctor. You should get this last information even if you plan to use a doctor of your own. Your doctor may want to consult with the previous doctor.

Nobody wants to be held to a timetable on a matter with so many variables, but typically the time between application and placement of a child in the home is half a year.

Payment. Support payments for the care of a foster child begin at the time of placement. Many states provide an initial clothing allowance to give immediate extra assistance, since the child is not likely to arrive with many possessions. In addition to the support payments from the state (or sometimes from the county), you may be able to receive federal assistance; however, recent changes in the federal budget have made continuation of this aid uncertain. Adding to the confusion is the usually weak understanding of caseworkers about federal programs. The primary focus of federal aid to foster children has been on nutrition (through the Department of Agriculture) and health (through the Department of Health and Human Services). If your foster child does not eat well at school or needs special medical care, raise the issue with your caseworker. There may be a federal project that can help.

The size of the state payment is fixed by law, and there is little point in trying to fight it. Your foster-parent association may be able to lobby for an increase, but you should assume from the start that the pay rule is established and will be adjusted only slightly during your career as a foster parent.

Medical and other costs. The basic foster-care payment covers the cost of room, meals, and clothing. These expenses will always remain, but of course they are not the only costs of child rearing. The most important extra expense is medical care. The state almost always pays the child's medical bills. The exceptions are patent medicines and orthodontal work (that is, braces on the teeth), which are usually not covered. These are state medical programs, so medical expenses that arise while the child is outside the state are usually your own. A few states, such as Louisiana, do not cover all medical costs.

It is a good idea to have your foster child examined by a pediatrician within two weeks of placement in your home. The wish to provide such care offers you a good opportunity during the preplacement interviews to find out precisely what your state laws say about medical costs.

The state does pay for prescribed medication; however, policies of individual pharmacists on this matter vary. Some do not want to be paid by the state. Talk to your neighborhood pharmacist when your foster child arrives and learn what the policy and procedure concerning payment is. It is best to know these things before an emergency arises.

There can also be extra needs like summer camp, special tutors in difficult school subjects, music lessons, ballet, hobbies—in short, all those activities that keep a growing child interested and interesting. Some states pay for these things, others don't. In almost every case the expense must be approved in advance.

One final issue concerns taxes. There are three clear points: (1) your foster-care payment is *not* taxable income; (2) your foster child cannot be listed as a dependent; and (3) expenses incurred beyond the state payments are not deductible.

The cost of child rearing. The structure of your state's payment policy may have important implications for the age and sex of the children you are able to accept. I suggest you discuss these matters during your preplacement interviews to find out exactly what you can and cannot afford.

During the 1970s a Philadelphia group studied the costs of foster children to families and found several important points. Not surprisingly, the cost of child care increases with age. The big jump occurs when children enter school. Most but not all states take this increase into account and provide larger support payments for older children. If you live in a state that does not alter the rates according to age or changes them only marginally, you should take this into account when you consider the ages of children you can accept. Because of the extra expense of their clothing, it costs more to raise girls between ages six and twelve than it does to care for boys of the same age group. Teenage boys, however, cost more to raise than teenage girls. The boys are growing more interested in what they wear and the extra expense in girls' clothing is no longer so great. Also, teenage boys cost more to feed. At age thirteen the expense of supporting a boy jumps ahead of the cost of raising a girl. No state takes this development into account, and some states pay more for raising foster teenage girls than teenage boys.

191

The following chart contains a state-by-state summary of assistance in foster care. It focuses on matters that will help you decide what age children you can afford. This decision depends on state aid, the costs in your region, your own income, and what you think children ought to have.

Foster-Care Payments
State by State

State	Increase Pay for Older Child?	Initial Extra Payments?	Other Extra Payments?
Alabama	No	No	Yes
Alaska	Yes	Yes	Yes
Arizona	Yes	Yes	Yes
Arkansas	Yes	Yes	Yes
California	Yes	Yes	Yes
Colorado	Yes	Yes	Yes
Connecticut	Yes	Yes	Yes
Delaware	Yes	Yes	Yes
District of Columbia	Yes	Yes	Yes
Florida	Yes	Yes	Yes
Georgia	Yes	Yes	Yes
Hawaii	Yes	Yes	Yes
Idaho	Yes	Yes	Yes

State	Increase Pay for Older Child?	Initial Extra Payments?	Other Extra Payments?
Illinois	Yes	Yes	Yes
Indiana	Varies by county	Varies by county	Varies by county
Iowa	Yes	Yes	Yes
Kansas	Yes	Yes	Yes
Kentucky	Yes	Yes	Yes
Louisiana	Yes	No	Yes
Maine	No	Yes	Yes
Maryland	Yes	Yes	Yes
Massachusetts	Yes	Yes	Yes
Michigan	Yes	Yes	Yes
Minnesota	Yes	Yes	Yes
Mississippi	Yes	Yes	Yes
Missouri	Yes	Yes	Yes
Montana	Yes	Yes	No
Nebraska	No	Yes	Yes
Nevada	Yes	Yes	Yes
New Hampshire	Yes	Yes	Yes

State	Increase Pay for Older Child?	Initial Extra Payments?	Other Extra Payments?
New Jersey	Yes	Yes	Yes
New Mexico	Yes	Yes	Yes
New York	Yes	Yes	Yes
North Carolina	No	Yes	Yes
North Dakota	Yes	Yes	Yes
Ohio	Yes	Varies by county	Yes
Oklahoma	Yes	No	Yes
Oregon	Yes	Yes	Yes
Pennsylvania	Yes	Varies by county	Varies by county
Rhode Island	Yes	Yes	Yes
South Carolina	Yes	Yes	Yes
South Dakota	Yes	Yes	Yes
Tennessee	Yes	Yes	Yes
Texas	Yes	No	No
Utah	Yes	Yes	Yes
Vermont	Yes	Yes	Yes
Virginia	Yes	Yes	Yes

State	Increase Pay for Older Child?	Initial Extra Payments?	Other Extra Payments?
Washington	Yes	Yes	Yes
West Virginia	No	Yes	Yes
Wisconsin	Yes	Yes	No
Wyoming	Yes	Yes	Yes

15

Adopting Your Foster Child

Studies have found that most children who have been in a foster home for two years act as though they think that the home is their permanent one. If they do leave, the change comes as a shock. As they grow older, however, children come to realize that their position is not secure, and this sense of uncertainty becomes troubling. To provide stability and certainty in their lives, more and more foster children are being freed for adoption.

These days the feeling among professionals is that children who have been in a particular foster home for a couple of years ought to be adopted. This is a case of the professionals catching up with the rest of society. Foster parents have long felt they ought to be able to adopt. During the 1960s a common type of human interest story in newspapers concerned parents who had suddenly been told their foster child was being removed to be adopted by some other family. That kind of story is more rare, though not unknown, today, as social workers have come to see that stability is of major importance after all. These days foster parents have the first opportunity to adopt children in their care.

The primary barrier to adoption concerns the rights of the biological parents. After all, taking a child from a parent is no small act. It cuts very close to the core of society, and judges do not do it easily. Because of this impediment, adoption is not always possible, even if there is little likelihood of the child's return to his biological parents. Foster parents, however, are not reduced to impotence in such circumstances, and there are steps you can take to solidify your situation.

First, foster parents should know what the plan for their child is. Is the child's return to the biological parents considered a serious possibility? If not, are the barriers to adoption likely to be overcome? If the barriers do seem insurmountable, what other ideas does the plan suggest?

Legal guardianship. One possibility is having the foster parents named as the child's legal guardians. The advantages of this move are both psychological and legal. It gives everybody a much stronger sense that the question of the future is settled. The child stays with you. It also increases your official status. Foster children are wards of the court, and foster parents have a difficult time getting a judge to consider their interests. Guardians, however, have the right and responsibility to speak for the child. They can take the child out of state without first seeking permission; they can give or withhold consent to the child's marriage, medical treatment, and military service. The disadvantage is financial. Foster-care payments cannot always be made to legally appointed guardians.

The procedure for becoming a guardian is to retain a lawyer who will petition the court for your appointment as guardian. You may be able to work with the agency lawyers in this matter, but I recommend you use your own lawyer if you can afford it.

If even guardianship is impossible, another solution is to sign a formalized long-term agreement to provide foster care. This approach is a last resort, since it is much less binding and has no legal standing in court. It is a written agreement signed by the foster parents, a representative of the agency, and one or both biological parents. In this document all parties agree that the child shall remain in the foster home until grown and that no party to the agreement will try to change the arrangement except under the most extraordinary circumstances. Although the document is not legally binding, it should not be scorned if it is the best thing available. It makes clear that all parties are committed to the present situation, and it does increase the sense of the foster relationship's stability.

The adoption process. The most secure arrangement is legal adoption. The stability adoption offers is considered so important to the child that foster parents who turn down the opportunity to adopt may see the child removed and placed with a family that will adopt.

The procedure for adopting a foster child is the same as that for a regular agency adoption. The foster family has to undergo a new study for consideration of its suitability as an adoptive family. Once

197

the agency approves the adoption, the routine is precisely like that of any other agency adoption.

On rare occasions it can be decided that even though the foster-family relationship is fine, adoption is wrong. The most common reasons for this are: (1) age (agencies allow foster parents to be older than adoptive parents); (2) the father (foster care focuses on the foster mother, while adoption studies inquire more deeply into the father's attitudes); and (3) objections from the child. This last impediment can arise when the child feels a special loyalty to the biological parents. In one case, for example, a foster child who refused to be adopted had a schizophrenic mother. She moved in and out of mental institutions and clearly would never be able to function as a supportive and responsible mother. The boy understood this fact, but he also felt that his mother did what she could and that he would be betraying her if he agreed to a formal adoption. Instead, the parties settled for guardianship and the child grew to manhood in his foster home.

Subsidy. Adoption means an end to foster-care payments, and this financial fact has been a great barrier to adoption. Many states have developed adoption-subsidy programs as a way of overcoming this problem.

Step by Step

Tell your foster child's caseworker that you are interested in adopting with a subsidy. It is at this point that the question of eligibility (discussed below) is decided.

The size of the subsidy must then be negotiated. In most cases, the state has work sheets for calculating a proper subsidy.

When the adoption petition is first presented to the court, it must state that a subsidy is also being sought. This step is important and must be done correctly. The justification for subsidies is that they permit the adoption of children who would otherwise never be adopted. If you first indicate to the court that you are willing to adopt without a subsidy, the court may refuse to consider a later subsidy request.

The legal procedures vary in different states. Sometimes—for example, in Missouri—state courts want to know about plans to seek a subsidy even before a petition for adoption is filed. Be sure your caseworker explains clearly what is expected of you.

The adoption decree includes the awarding of a subsidy. Parents who are denied a subsidy have the right to appeal.

Eligibility. The foster-care agency must rule that the child in question has "special needs" to qualify for an adoption subsidy. That is to say the state must determine that because of some specific difficulty, such as age, race, or physical disability, the child is unlikely to be adopted without financial assistance. In the case of foster parents trying to adopt a child who has lived with them for eighteen months or more, stability for the child becomes a special need, and the critical question concerns the type of aid the child has been receiving during foster care.

Subsidy amount. The basic idea is that the amount of subsidy granted should be about what would be paid if the child were still in foster care. You cannot be paid more than you would receive as a foster parent, but you can be granted a one-time extra payment to cover the cost of the adoption. Children receiving this assistance are eligible for Medicaid.

Effect of a subsidy request on adoption. Hamlet's list of the sea of troubles that afflict mankind includes a reference to "the law's delay." As usual, Hamlet was right. The experience in states with adoption subsidies has been that seeking a subsidy seriously slows down the approval of an adoption and prolongs the child's drift in limbo.

Your rights. Parents seeking adoption assistance have two important rights: first, to a fair hearing, and, second, to privacy. If you are denied benefits, you must be notified of the decision in writing. The notice must be mailed at least ten days before the decision takes effect. You may request an appeal during that ten-day period.

Your privacy is also protected. Access to any information you supply when applying for the aid is restricted. It is specifically forbidden for outsiders to be provided with names and addresses of subsidy applicants and beneficiaries.

Perhaps it should be stressed that adoption subsidies in no way reduce or alter the fact of adoption. Parents remain the legal parents of their adopted children, with all the rights and responsibilities that relationship entails. The only aspect of foster care that persists is the support payments.

PART V
Final Issues

16

After Placement

Shortly after giving birth, a biological mother sometimes goes into a postpartum depression, a lethargy and sense of disappointment when personal dreams and fantasies about a child are transformed into a real and separate individual. Adoptive mothers sometimes enter exactly the same state. "It passes," one mother recalled. "I asked myself how I could feel this way after all the work and time spent [in finding a baby]," a second mother remarked, "but then I reminded myself I'm only human." I suspect that fathers sometimes experience the same feeling, though they would call it some other name.

Adoptive and biological parents alike cover the full range of human emotions in responding to the arrival of a child. The excitement, uncertainty, and extent of the change in one's life is the same . . . well, perhaps the uncertainty is not quite the same. Biological parenthood is less sure, for it is based on the principle of what you see is what you get. Adoptive parents have a chance to consider the child before agreeing to accept her into their home. Agency babies are always examined by a pediatrician and are given a thorough study before being approved for placement as normal, healthy infants. Yet even so, the children are not commodities to arrive with warranties and, as is true for children of biological parents, the adopted children must be accepted for better or for worse.

For all the similarities of their situations, adoptive families have a different origin from that of biological ones, and this has its consequences. The immediately notable distinction is the inevitability of a waiting period between placement in the home and final court-approved adoption. This delay brings its own difficulties and questions, ones unlike anything a biological parent must face.

Pregnancy. The most common source of doubt, as far as infant adoptions are concerned, is pregnancy. After years of unsuccessful attempts to become pregnant and then a further struggle to adopt, many couples find they are going to have babies after all. It is a frequently heard story.

If you become pregnant while waiting for an agency to place an infant with you, the agency will drop you from its waiting list, like it or not. No refunds are given on the adoption expenses you have already incurred. If a baby is placed with you and you then discover that you are pregnant, agencies tend to take the news in good humor. I have never heard of an agency trying to block adoption in these circumstances and, indeed, any such action would be more than appalling.

Help. The arrival of a child can be a great shock to the family, especially to the mother, who finds her whole life dominated by the demands of this tiny creature. I have seen a lot of mothers scramble to try to restore some sort of normality and balance to their lives, but no one supposes that biological parents are thinking of giving up the child. When these same contradictions turn up in adoptive parents, however, people often fail to understand them. Even the parents may not think they are proper and feel ashamed to ask for help.

Even if parents are willing to accept help, they may be hesitant about turning to their agency. Is the agency worker smart enough to appreciate the human paradoxes, or will she think that a call for help is really a plea to take the child back? Often the worker understands perfectly. A smart and experienced worker once told me, "It's the ones who complain a lot that make it. Families who call for help and grumble find out what to do and do it." It is up to you to decide whether your worker is this sensitive or is more rigid in her thinking.

Parent associations can also come to your rescue. The largest ones have programs to help families after the placement of children, but even if your association is not so developed, it surely has members who know all about what you are going through and can talk to you. This is a good time to try to form a small network of your own (emphasis on the word "small")—three, four, or five people like yourself who have adopted children in the same age range. A lot of help comes just from being able to talk about things and hear, "I know. I know." These networks, by the way, are not just for hard-to-place adoptions. Parents who have adopted healthy newborns need them just as much.

Changing your mind. The most striking special aspect of adoption is the ability of the parents to change their minds. This power is more controversial than you might think, because it can encourage families to delay their commitments to children. Nonetheless, the power is real and well recognized. In an agency adoption, up until the granting of the final decree, all you have to do after changing your mind is to call the agency.

If a child has been placed in your home by someone other than an agency, you may feel that you have no one to turn to. The biological mother is long gone; the independent intermediary is of little help. You should contact your local public welfare agency. It can place the child. Do not find a private placement on your own. Such self-reliance can lead to endless legal paperwork while the courts try to sort out parental rights and approve the adoption. If you have a particular family you would prefer to have the child join, you will have to obtain a lawyer to ensure that your duties and obligations to the child are fully terminated. Some of the most spectacular red-tape nooses have been tied by people who tried to skip this rule.

Although giving up any child is traumatic, the most painful and guilt-provoking splits are those involving older children, who know what is happening and can say good-bye with question marks in their eyes. The two most common reasons for giving up an older child are (1) ferocious resistance on the part of a child already in the family and (2) a fear of rejection on the part of the newcomer that is so great that his behavior begins to border on the psychotic.

These problems are so overwhelming and so painful as they build to the breaking point that almost no family can get through them alone. People who insist on trying to resolve such crises by themselves often say later that the worst part was the sense of being totally isolated, of having no idea what to do and no sense that anyone had ever had such problems before. You simply must get help from your parent association or your agency.

17

Genetics

"Who is this child that has come into our home to stay?" Not many adoptive parents can get through their lives without asking themselves that question. The child has so many qualities of her own. Where did such individuality come from? Parents don't always realize that biological families also wonder wherever their children might have gotten certain ideas, tendencies, and physical characteristics. "He didn't get it from my side of the family" is a famous cry of the immature spouse, and in that pathetic shout of the ego we see clearly the evasiveness of the concern. What does it matter where something came from? The child is as she is; *that* is the issue to be addressed. The rest is buck passing.

No one can find his "true identity" by looking to some genetic or historical fact, but of course people everywhere are tempted to embrace fantasy identities. Adoptive families are no more subject to this temptation than anyone else, but in adoptive homes, where children's genetic backgrounds really are unknown, it may be easier to rationalize these buck-passing temptations. After all, genes are real.

The contemporary world is full of talk about genetics and genetic diseases, so we cannot expect either adoptive parents or their children never to wonder about such things. The parents have some control over their adopted children's environment but none at all over their genetic background. When difficulties arise in child rearing, as inevitably they must, adoptive parents often find themselves wondering whether "it might be something hereditary."

I hold that all these worries are fundamentally misguided. The healthiest and most realistic way to think about questions of responsibility and identity is to consider the situation as it exists, not as biological might-have-beens. However, because it is so natural to wonder and to fantasize about the subject and because there is so much disconnected information concerning heredity, the issue cannot be summarily dismissed in the name of good sense.

Predictability. Sometimes a child is known to be genetically "at risk." That is to say, it is possible she will inherit a genetic disease. The report is a confusing piece of information because it sounds bad, but at the same time it seems to offer hope. Heredity works as a great lottery in which each parent contributes half of the child's genes. Sometimes a gene is certain to be passed on, but usually there is doubt about exactly what will happen. Some people are tempted to seize on this doubt and look on the bright side. These people tell themselves, "One chance in two of danger means an equally good chance that everything will be all right." That argument sets up a family for heartbreak. If you are given the opportunity for an "at-risk" adoption, you should base your decision on whether you would want to adopt the child if the risk became a certainty.

For example, a family told that they may adopt a child who is "at risk" for a genetic disease called Huntington's chorea should make their decision as though they had been told the baby would get this disease. Otherwise the family will spend too much time trying to weigh the odds and hoping they come up winners. You can make a more sound decision and set your family on a more sturdy foundation if you forget the odds and ask yourself what it would be like to raise a child with Huntington's chorea.

Genetic disease. Hereditary diseases are more like handicaps than ordinary diseases. They are plain facts of someone's life, posing a challenge that has to be met. Genes themselves always work by regulating the body's metabolism, or chemical activity. Often defects in genetic regulation can be overcome if they are detected early enough.

An example of what present-day genetics can accomplish is provided by the disease phenylketonuria (PKU), which leads to mental retardation in children. At one time PKU was a total mystery, but now its chemistry is so well understood that many children can be saved from retardation by being put on a special diet during the first years of life. A test has been developed for children considered at risk. If this screening discovers the presence of PKU, the diet is prescribed. Because of this practice, children are able to avoid a fate that once seemed inevitable.

Many genetic diseases operate in this way. The gene does not doom the carrier to a particular problem, but it does mean that if the carrier encounters a certain environment, there is a great increase in the risk. For example, a certain genetic disease seems to dispose smokers toward contracting emphysema. The obvious solution for these people is not to smoke.

It used to be said that genes are destiny, but their role is now understood to be more like that of a country's geography than like a person's fate. The mountains, rivers, and deserts of a land are certainly important influences on a country's history, but it is still up to the inhabitants to respond to that geography. A person's genes are his geography; his life includes what he makes of that terrain but is not determined by it.

Genetic responsibility. All parents, biological or adoptive, have the same responsibility toward their children's genetic situations. If any genetic handicaps are known, the parents have to help their children adapt to these conditions. Worries about larger questions of responsibility, about whose "fault" a particular problem might be, are a waste of time. Adoptive parents often find they can respond more openly and lovingly to their children's genetic problems than biological parents can, precisely because they feel no responsibility for the child's genes. An adoptive parent, for example, can keep a PKU infant on his diet and take pride in the fact that such care is being given, while a biological parent might feel guilt or shame in the fact that her child requires so careful a diet. In these cases, a complete absence of responsibility frees the parent from having to think about anything except the child as she really is.

It is best, however, not to feel too smug about one's own genes. Modern genetics has shown that heredity depends on the luck of the draw. Any one of us could have a child with genetic characteristics quite unlike those of the biological relatives we know. (For an example, see the chart on the next page.) In the past, when people thought about heredity in terms of the prescientific notions of blood, families sometimes argued against adoption on the grounds that "you don't know what you're getting." Modern genetics has made the surprising discovery that the hereditary makeup of one's biological child is nearly as mysterious as that of an adoptive child.

Where'd You Get Those Eyes?

An old saw of prescientific notions about bloodlines acknowledged that characteristics sometimes "skipped a generation." In reality, genetic traits can skip many generations. This chart shows the odds of an imaginary reader carrying a gene for blue eyes if his great-great-grandfather had blue eyes but everyone since then has had dark eyes.

Family Tree	Eye Color	Odds of Carrying a Gene for Blue Eyes
great-great-grandfather born 1850–died 1920	blue	certain
great-grandfather 1875–1945	dark	certain
grandfather 1900–1970	dark	1 chance in 2
father 1925–	dark	1 chance in 4
reader 1950–	dark	1 chance in 8

The chances of the imaginary reader carrying his great-great-grandfather's blue-eye genes are as good as his chances of tossing a coin and getting heads three times in a row. Because his great-great-grandfather lived so long ago, the blue eyes in the family might have been quite forgotten, yet the gene survives.

──────

Hereditary immorality. Another old argument against adoption said that adopted children were born because their mothers were immoral and that therefore immorality was in the children's blood. This superstition has worried more adoptive parents than we, in this scientific age, care to admit. Many adoptive families have insisted that their children were legitimate but were orphaned through tragic circumstances. I noticed in conducting interviews with agency directors that the more traditional the agency, the more insistent the agency director was that not all the infants they placed were illegitimate. However, let's face it, most adoptive infants—be they from agencies, foreign sources, or independent connections—are born to unmarried women.

Is there anything to the old saw about vice being in the child's blood? My own belief is that it is nonsense, a piece of folklore invented to make the feudal treatment of illegitimate children seem less outrageous and unjust. There is not one bit of genetic evidence to support it, yet so little is known about heredity and human behavior that the old story cannot be disproved either.

Modern genetics shows, though, that even if there turned out to be a hereditary basis for sexual morality, we could not predict the morals of a child on the basis of the parents. We know from experience that promiscuous parents can raise a puritanical child and that puritanical parents can raise a promiscuous child. The chart above shows how something as ordinary as eye color cannot be guaranteed. We may carry the genes for an eye color that has been unknown to the family for generations. The same would be true for genetic morality. Each of us has sixteen great-great-grandparents. If just one of them had been sexually immoral, we might carry that genetic trait.

Modern genetics thus attacks the old bloodline arguments against adoption in two ways. It confirms that we cannot prejudge the adopted child on the basis of her ancestry and that we cannot be too smug about our own genes. The risks and promises are as broad as all humanity.

Incest. A common fantasy fear of adopted children is that they might grow up and marry someone who turns out to be a brother or sister. Unlikely as this is, it is not quite impossible. If it did happen, however, it would hardly matter. Inbreeding is a genetic danger only if it persists over many generations or if a family carries some very unusual genetic disease. If an adopted brother happened to meet his sister in college and the two fell in love, the genetic risk to any of their children would be minimal. Incest is banned in all societies for social, not biological, reasons. After all, our scientific understanding of heredity is extremely recent and is still unknown to most cultures in the world. The traditional taboos have to do with the needs of extended families rather than any worries about genetics.

18

The Adoptive Family

The old attitude toward adoptive families was summed up in one question friends often asked: "Are you going to tell your child he is adopted?" When the issues about adoption are put this way, there can be no correct answer.

It is wrong to imagine that adoption is so unusual that perhaps it is best kept a secret. It is equally wrong to suppose that adoption is so simple a matter that it can be summed up in a short, plain statement. Yet many adoptive parents accepted the suggestion that perhaps total secrecy was best and that it was not necessary ever to tell their child about her origins. "I never think of her as adopted," one mother said, in justifying lying to a teenage daughter who asked point-blank whether she had been adopted.

It is unfair to condemn the woman out of hand. What this heart-torn mother was pleading was that even though her family was not built along the stereotyped conventions, it was still her family, and her daughter was her own true daughter.

Tragically, when this woman adopted, her agency made no effort to help her realize how common adoption was. She never had any dealings with a parent association, so she didn't meet many other people who had also adopted. Even after raising an adoptive daughter, this woman thought that "real" families are the products of biology. For that mother to say truthfully "Yes, you are adopted" would have been, to her, the equivalent of saying falsely, "No, you are not really my daughter." In order to insist on the deeper truth that the adoption didn't affect the strength of the family bond, the mother told a surface lie.

How can families get around that dilemma?

Obviously, it is best to tell the whole truth: yes, you are adopted and, yes, you are really my child. Yet, there are still many adoptive parents who have never realized that love and history are what build families. Of course, such parents will have a hard time telling their children the whole truth. Instead they feel a need to select a partial truth.

Initially, many parents chose to stress the part about family membership, and so they lied about the adoption. Naturally it was impossible to keep such a thing secret forever, and when the lie was discovered, it often came as a great shock to the children, by then perhaps adolescents or young adults.

Much to their shame, adoption professionals did not respond to this problem by correcting the deeper attitudes that would lead a person to think a child should not be told of his adoption. Instead, the professionals simply took the issue literally and argued that parents should be truthful. By this advice they meant only that the children should be told the surface truth that they are adopted. The other, equal truth about family membership got second place.

Many parents dutifully followed this advice and of course the results were as catastrophic as lies had been for an earlier generation. Although these parents told the literal truth, they also told a deep lie, implying that somehow the family and the bonds between its members were phony. It came as a great surprise to adoption professionals when a new generation of adoptive children came of age and were filled with an obsession to learn who they "really" were.

One of those children was Betty Jean Lifton, who in 1975 published a bitter book entitled *Twice Born: Memoirs of an Adopted Daughter.* The author had been adopted at age two and a half, and when she was grown, she managed to locate her biological mother. Early in the book there is a strange scene in which the author first learns she was adopted. She was a little girl of seven, sick in bed, when her mother came in and told her of the adoption. Her mother concluded, "Now, I am telling you this as a secret. You must never tell anyone, especially your father. It would break his heart. I promised him never to tell you. He wants you to think he is your real daddy." It is hard to imagine a more disastrous way to build an adoptive family.

I can just hear the experts defending themselves, "That is not what we meant at all. That is not it, at all." They certainly never urged families to swear the child to secrecy or to imply that Daddy isn't really Daddy. But by urging parents to tell the child the truth and tell it at an early age, experts made scenes such as the nightmare of revelation described by Mrs. Lifton inevitable.

The fact of adoption is not some simple little $2 + 2 = 4$ proposition that can be summed up in a few well-chosen words. No matter how sensitive and articulate Betty Jean Lifton's mother might have been, there was nothing for her to tell that could have made clear sense to her little girl.

What does the news of adoption mean to a child who cannot possibly understand what the alternative—biological parenthood—is all about? Sexuality, genetics, family trees—none of these things are yet clear to a child. Seven-year-olds are likely to grasp only that they are somehow different, somehow not "really" who they seem to be. Indeed, this sense of difference was all Mrs. Lifton did get. She recalls, "From that day the child is defined, becomes aware of herself as something apart from other people." Even years later, as a married adult, Mrs. Lifton is still stuck in that little girl's surprised and bewildered sense of indefinable difference.

The whole controversy about truth in adoption is now back with us. A generation ago the issue was whether to tell "the truth." Today the issue is how much of "the truth" we should tell. The argument is filled with emotion and can quickly turn any gathering of adoptive families into a shouting match. I have not seen much evidence that this latest form of the argument is treated any more wisely than it was back when the issue was to tell or not to tell. The conflict is still being fought between those who advocate telling the literal truth and those who insist on the deeper reality of the adoptive family.

On one side are adoptive parents who feel profoundly resentful of the suggestion that biological parents are in any way bound up in the child's identity. Americans tend to laugh at the pretensions of some ordinary fellow who just discovered his great-grandfather was a duke. Why should we take seriously the claims of a person to have an identity based on some ancestor she never knew? Yet adoptive families are now being told that biological identity is very important.

On the other side are those who insist that, after all, the truth is the truth and should not be suppressed. They too have much to support them. Americans have not been impressed by theories that say facts ought to be abandoned in favor of mythology. We are particularly unhappy with the idea that private information—facts about ourselves—should be denied us in favor of some nice story. If a person says, "I want to learn something about myself," it seems terribly wrong to decree that it can never be learned.

Because the search for facts and personal history seems only reasonable, many parents at the time of adoption assemble as much information as they can possibly obtain about their child's biological parents. They plan to squirrel away this material for the day the child is old enough and interested enough to know about it. I am sympathetic to this idea; however, I think parents are kidding themselves if they believe that by itself this policy will let them build their families on "the truth."

I have insisted throughout this book that families are subjective institutions, living in the mind. They give people a sense of how they are connected to society. A series of objective facts cannot get to the truth about such a personal thing. Obviously it is profoundly disorienting and undesirable to have a child discover at age sixteen that his parents have lied all these years. Just as obviously, it is no good telling a child of seven something that confuses and bewilders her forever after. Both experiences run exactly counter to what a family is supposed to accomplish. I do not believe it will prove less confusing to tell a child that he is adopted and that his biological parents are so-and-so and so-and-so.

I come back to my earlier positions: parents must find a way to raise their children in the whole truth. Children should know both that they were adopted into their families and that they are full members of these families. This kind of complex truth is learned more by living than by telling.

First facts. Adopted children should never be able to remember a time when they didn't know they were adopted, although, of course, what adoption means can only be understood slowly. Exactly the same situation holds true for biologically based families. Children cannot fully understand their origins until they know the details of sexual reproduction, but they know things like the name of the hospital where they were born and a detail or two about the birth—perhaps the mother quit her job shortly before giving birth or the grandparents came to town for the occasion, that sort of thing. Adoptive children can know similar kinds of details—the name of the agency or intermediary that placed them as well as other bits and pieces. If they were adopted internationally, they should know the name of the country where they were born.

These details are likely to be rather hazy in a child's mind, but they have a powerful message. They allow a child to get a grip on the remarkable fact that her family predates her own existence, that her parents were already doing something when she came into the family. The alternative vision is the famous saying of the slave child Topsy in *Uncle Tom's Cabin:* "I just grew." Those words are a perfect expression of total and baffling alienation from all society.

Most of the facts of adoption simply emerge naturally in speech. If you talk frequently with your child, you will find yourself occasionally starting to say something about the time he was placed in your home or the period when you were struggling to adopt. Don't stop yourself from telling the story simply and truthfully. Biological parents feel no doubts when telling similar stories about the time their child was born or on the way.

If you keep your child's birth certificate displayed somewhere, say in a scrapbook, the adoption decree should be there too.

Differentness. All adoptive children must come to terms with the fact that their family is only one possible form a family can take. Most children do not learn that there are many kinds of families. The few living in a true nuclear family grow up thinking their Ozzie-and-Harriet life is the way every child lives. The many children growing up in one form or another of extended family often never even notice that their experience is quite unlike the general cliché. Adopted children, however, cannot escape the fact that there is something different about the adoptive family.

One good way I have seen parents handle this issue is through parent associations. Through them, children play with other adopted kids and take the fact of adoption for granted. Yet this solution is only a beginning. It allows the children to appreciate the important fact that adoption is not a unique situation, but they must still come to terms with their minority status. Children learn early on that adoption is different:

Thad Simon was adopted shortly after birth. His sister, two years younger, was adopted from South America when she was half a year old, and many of Thad's other playmates were also adopted. When he was five, Thad's mother, who had been thought infertile, gave birth to a baby girl. Thad was astonished to learn that no court action was necessary to bring his new sister into the family.

Ellen Caudel adopted a boy from Colombia and then became quite active in an adoptive-parent group. Ellen's son, Henry, knew lots of children adopted from Latin America, and Ellen used to joke that

215

Henry was going to grow up thinking everybody was adopted. Sure enough, when he was in the second grade, Henry came home one day and reported in amazement, "You know, I'm the only one in my class who is adopted."

It is both hopeless and wrong to try and keep a child from learning that adoption is unusual. What parents can do is help their children realize that there are many different kinds of families but that whatever form they take, they are still families.

Books. Publishing houses issue a steady dribble of books explaining adoption to adoptive children, but I have a hard time recommending any of them. First, the very existence of the books suggests to a child that adoption is a puzzle that calls for explanation. Second, a book can only give a stereotyped explanation of adoption. Waiting children, international adoptions, older children, adoptions by families who already have children, single-parent adoptions, nonagency adoptions—all these fit only clumsily into such works.

I am also alarmed by the nonfamily orientation of most of these books. Often in explaining the adoption, books stress categorically that on one side are the parents and their wishes, while, on the other side, stands you, the adopted child. Instead of concentrating on the unity of the family, which is the essence of adoption, the books emphasize the pieces.

This emphasis is most notable in a popular myth recounted in many books for adopted children. The story depicts parents eager for a child, searching high and low for just the right one, until they find *you*, exactly the child they wanted. Except in the case of waiting children selected from photo books, this neat little tale is plainly untrue. Adopted children are not selected after looking through rows of waiting babies. A child is found and offered to the parents who may say "No" but usually say "Yes."

Along with the distortion of facts, this myth puts extraordinary emphasis on a preestablished identity of the child outside the family. For newborns, this initial identity can only be vague and general. Questions of individuality and family relationships are among the most complex in the whole realm of human affairs. It certainly is undesirable to reduce the whole subject to a personal myth which locates the child's identity entirely outside the family that raised her.

The more complicated ideas that adoptive families are based on the mutual need of the parents and child or that all members of the family gain much of their identity from each other hardly ever make their way into books for adopted children. The reason for such simplicity is clear. The truth is too complicated for a seven-year-old to grasp and cannot be summed up in a small book.

Documents. A rather tricky problem in the search for the whole truth is raised by all the amended documents. Adoptions did not originally include a change in birth certificates. In past generations, people sometimes only discovered they were adopted when they were grown and were drafted or applied for a marriage license and were required to produce a birth certificate. Then, to their amazement, they found that their parents had to refer them to an adoption agency. The amended birth certificate was developed as a solution to this problem, but this solution has produced problems of its own. The amended birth certificate hides all information about what came before the adoption, thus making it difficult to learn what the old records could reveal about one's own past history.

One of the hot contemporary issues of adoption is the adoptee's eventual access to records. The present trend is toward allowing an adoptee to see his original birth certificate and other information indicating the identity of his biological parents. In some states, adoptive parents can, at the time of adoption, request that the original birth certificate not be sealed away. Sometimes the actual place of birth must be shown on the new birth certificate, while some states actually require that a change be made. These state laws are summarized in the following chart. Federal law permits an adoptee to see all material filed with the Immigration Service in an international adoption.

State Laws on Adoption Records

State	Must It Be Sealed?	Available to Adoptee?	Can Show Place of Birth?	Other Data Available to Adoptee?
		Birth Certificate		
		Old	*New*	
Alabama	No	OD	Yes	OD
Alaska	Yes	No	No	No
Arizona	Yes	COO	Yes	COO
Arkansas	Yes	No	Yes	COO
California	Yes	COO	Yes	OD
Colorado	Yes	COO	Yes	Yes
Connecticut	Yes	COO	Yes	COO
Delaware	Yes	COO	No	Yes
District of Columbia	Yes	COO	Yes	No
Florida	Yes	COO	Yes	COO
Georgia	Yes	COO	Yes	COO
Hawaii	Yes	COO	Yes	Yes
Idaho	Yes	COO	Yes	Yes
Illinois	Yes	No	Yes	No
Indiana	Yes	COO	No	COO

COO = court order only; OD = on demand

Birth Certificate

State	Must It Be Sealed?	*Old* Available to Adoptee?	*New* Can Show Place of Birth?	Other Data Available to Adoptee?
Iowa	Yes	COO	Yes	Yes
Kansas	No	OD	Required	OD
Kentucky	Yes	COO	No	COO
Louisiana	No	COO	No	No
Maine	Yes	COO	No	COO
Maryland	Yes	COO	Yes	Yes
Massachusetts	Yes	COO	Yes	Yes
Michigan	Yes	COO	Yes	Yes
Minnesota	Yes	COO	Yes	Yes
Mississippi	Yes	COO	Required	COO
Missouri	Yes	COO	Yes	COO
Montana	Yes	COO	Yes	Yes
Nebraska	Yes	COO	Yes	Yes
Nevada	Yes	COO	No	Yes
New Hampshire	Yes	COO	Yes	COO
New Jersey	Yes	COO	No	Yes

| | Birth Certificate | | | |
| | *Old* | *New* | | |
State	Must It Be Sealed?	Available to Adoptee?	Can Show Place of Birth?	Other Data Available to Adoptee?
New Mexico	Yes	COO	No	No
New York	Yes	COO	No	COO
North Carolina	Yes	COO	Yes	Yes
North Dakota	Yes	No	No	Yes
Ohio	Yes	No	Yes	COO
Oklahoma	Yes	COO	Yes	Yes
Oregon	No	COO	No	No
Pennsylvania	Yes	COO	No	Yes
Rhode Island	Yes	No	No	No
South Carolina	Yes	COO	Yes	Yes
South Dakota	Yes	No	No	Yes
Tennessee	Yes	COO	Required	Yes
Texas	Yes	COO	Yes	COO
Utah	Yes	COO	No	Yes
Vermont	Yes	COO	No	No
Virginia	Yes	COO	Yes	Yes

| State | Birth Certificate | | | |
	Must It Be Sealed?	*Old* Available to Adoptee?	*New* Can Show Place of Birth?	Other Data Available to Adoptee?
Washington	Yes	COO	No	Yes
West Virginia	Yes	COO	Yes	No
Wisconsin	Yes	COO	Yes	Yes
Wyoming	Yes	COO	No	No

Appendix:
Directory of Parent Associations

Keeping up with parent associations is a constant challenge. Most of them have no formal offices and simply operate out of the homes of their members. Of course, members move or reduce their activity, so any published directory must slowly slip out of date. The North American Council on Adoptable Children (NACAC) publishes an annual directory of member organizations, but most parent associations do not belong to NACAC. The adoption resource centers try to maintain full listings of groups in their regions.

ALABAMA

BIRMINGHAM—*Alabama Association of Afro-American Adoption Advocates,* 4516 43rd Avenue North, Birmingham, Ala. 35217

—*Alabama Friends of Adoption,* 701 Rockbridge Road, Birmingham, Ala. 35216

DOTHAN—*Wiregrass Adoption Association,* P.O. Box 6203, Dothan, Ala. 36302

FAIRHOPE—*Advocates for Global Adoption, Parenting Education,* Route 1, Box 266-A, Fairhope, Ala. 36532

FORT PAYNE—*DeKalb County Family for Adoption,* 507 Seventh Street, N.W., Fort Payne, Ala. 35967

ALASKA

ANCHORAGE—*Anchorage Adoptive Parents Association,* 3451 Kachemak Circle, Anchorage, Alaska 99504

—*Anchorage WACAP,* 458 Atlantis, Anchorage, Alaska 99502

FAIRBANKS—*Fairbanks WACAP,* Star Route, Box 70865, Fairbanks, Alaska 99701

—*Golden Heart Adoption Referral Service,* P.O. Box 2022, Fairbanks, Alaska 99707

—*Interior Adoptive Parents,* Star Route 50199, Fairbanks, Alaska 99707

HOMER—*Homer WACAP,* SRA Box 29-A, Homer, Alaska 99603

JUNEAU—*Juneau Adoptive Parent Support Group,* 56780 Thane Rd., Juneau, Alaska 99801

—*Juneau WACAP,* 426 North Riverside Drive, Juneau, Alaska 99801

KETICHIKAN—*Ketichikan WACAP,* 3289 Tongass, Ketchikan, Alaska 99901

PALMER—*Palmer WACAP,* Star Route D, Box 9975, Palmer, Alaska 99645

—*Valley Adoptive Parents Association of Alaska,* P.O. Box 1541, Palmer, Alaska 99645

SITKA—*Sitka Parent Group,* P.O. Box 1220, Sitka, Alaska 99835

—*Sitka WACAP,* P.O. Box 1622, Sitka, Alaska 99835

SOLDOTNA—*Kenai Peninsula Adoptive Parents,* P.O. Box 1356, Soldotna, Alaska 99669

VALDEZ—*Valdez WACAP,* Box 1352, Valdez, Alaska 99686

WASILLA—*Wasilla WACAP,* P.O. Box 363, Wasilla, Alaska 99687

ARIZONA

PHOENIX—*Black Child Advocates,* P.O. Box 39615, Phoenix, Ariz. 85069

—*Hispanic Children's Family Support Group,* 1819 West Elm Street, Phoenix, Ariz. 85015

SCOTTSDALE—*Open Door Society of Arizona,* P.O. Box 3403, Scottsdale, Ariz. 85257

TUCSON—*Arizona Families for Children,* P.O. Box 17951, Tucson, Ariz. 85731

—*Tucson Open Door Society,* 9421 East Creek Street, Tucson, Ariz. 85730

ARKANSAS

LITTLE ROCK—*Black Parent Support Group,* 1512 Izard, Little Rock, Ark. 72202

CALIFORNIA

FRESNO—*League of Mexican-American Women,* P.O. Box 686, Fresno, Calif. 93712

LA MESA—*San Diego Children's Coalition,* 4475 Dale Avenue, #115, La Mesa, Calif. 92041

LOS ANGELES—*Black Linkage for Adoptive Children (BLAC)*, P.O. Box 8414, Los Angeles, Calif. 90008

—*Open Door Society of Los Angeles*, 1214 South Gramercy Place, Los Angeles, Calif. 90019

—*Ward Parent Adoptive Group*, 1177 West 25th Street, Los Angeles, Calif. 90007

NORTH HOLLYWOOD—*Adoptaides*, 12307 Addison Street, North Hollywood, Calif. 91607

OAKLAND—*Advocates for Black Children*, 2822 55th Avenue, Oakland, Calif. 94605

—*Aid to the Adoption of Special Kids (AASK)*, 3530 Grand Avenue, Oakland, Calif. 94610

—*Bay Area Black Adoptive Parent Council*, P.O. Box 10495, Oakland, Calif. 94610

OXNARD—*Black Adoptive Parents and Advocates (BAPA)*, 1131 South Cadiz Court, Oxnard, Calif. 93033

PACOIMA—*Ward Parent Adoptive Group*, 10920 Jamie Avenue, Pacoima, Calif. 91331

PROJECT CITY—*United Native Indian Tribe*, P.O. Box 806, Project City, Calif. 96079

REDDING—*United Native Indian Tribes Adoptive Parent Group*, 3148 Cascade Boulevard, Redding, Calif. 96003

RIVERSIDE—*Concilio Hispanic Parents Support Group (CHPSG)*, P.O. Box 1503, Riverside, Calif. 92501

SAN BERNARDINO—*Association for the Adoption of Black Children (AABC)*, P.O. Box 6643, San Bernardino, Calif. 92412

SAN DIEGO—*Tayari Adoptive Parents*, 884 Bannekar Drive, San Diego, Calif. 92077

SAN FRANCISCO—*Open Arms Adoption Project*, P.O. Box 15254, San Francisco, Calif. 94115

SAN JOSE—*Families Adopting Inter-Racially*, 4008 Haines Avenue, San Jose, Calif. 95136

SANTA ROSA—*Sonoma County OURS*, 1215 Santa Ana Drive, Santa Rosa, Calif. 95404

SEASIDE—*JAMAA*, P.O. Box 552, Seaside, Calif. 93955

SIMI VALLEY—*Open Door Society of Ventura County*, 1936 Arcane Street, Simi Valley, Calif. 93065

TURLOCK—*Families Created by Adoption*, 1071 South Minaret, Turlock, Calif. 95380

VISALIA—*Padres por Los Ninos*, 3832 Feemster, Visalia, Calif. 93277

COLORADO

BOULDER—*Black Homes for Black Children,* 4517 Driftwood Place, Boulder, Colo. 80301

DENVER—*Denver Minority Parents for Adoption,* 3144 Gaylord, Denver, Colo. 80205

FORT COLLINS—*Adoption Awareness Group,* 3100 Longhorn Court, Fort Collins, Colo. 80526

GRAND JUNCTION—*Colorado Parents for All Children,* 2821 Hall, Grand Junction, Colo. 81501

LITTLETON—*Denver OURS,* 6776 South Bellaire, Littleton, Colo. 80122

MONUMENT—*Colorado Parents for All Children,* 18020 Granite Circle, Monument, Colo. 80132

NORTHGLENN—*Adams County Adoptive Parents Association,* 1640 West 106 Avenue, Northglenn, Colo. 80234

WHEATRIDGE—*Colorado Parents for All Children,* 9625 West Thirty-fifth, Wheatridge, Colo. 80033

CONNECTICUT

GROTON—*Friends of the Adoptive Child,* P.O. Box 1269, Groton, Conn. 06340

HARTFORD—*Open Door Society of Connecticut,* P.O. Box 478, Hartford, Conn. 06101

NEW FAIRFIELD—*Connecticut Latin American Parents Association (LAPA), Connecticut Chapter,* P.O. Box 8938, New Fairfield, Conn. 06810

VERNON—*Manchester Adoptive Parents,* 143 Trout Stream, Vernon, Conn. 06033

WEST SIMSBURY—*Granby Adoptive Parents,* 182 West Mountain Road, West Simsbury, Conn. 06340

WINDSOR—*Concerned Persons for Black Adoption,* 742 Kennedy Road, Windsor, Conn. 06905

DELAWARE

CAMDEN—*Kent–Sussex Minority Adoption Group,* 12 S. West Street, Camden, Del. 19934

HOCKESSIN—*Adoptive Parent Group,* 23 Arthur Drive, R.D. 1, Hockessin, Del. 19707

NEWARK—*Delaware Coalition for Children,* 8 Eberly Drive, Newark, Del. 19707

DISTRICT OF COLUMBIA

Concerned Citizens for Black Adoptions, P.O. Box 24040, Washington, D.C. 20024

Council on Adoptable Children of Metropolitan D.C., 604 Aspen Street, N.W., Washington, D.C. 20012

FLORIDA

CLEARWATER—*Suncoast Council on Adoptable Children (COAC),* 1356 Hillcrest Avenue South, Clearwater, Fla. 33516

—*Suncoast OURS,* 2991 Burnice Drive, Clearwater, Fla. 33516

NEWBERRY—*North Florida COAC,* Route 2, Box 24, Newberry, Fla. 32669

PLANTATION—*Lifeline for Children,* P.O. Box 17184, Plantation, Fla. 33318

TITUSVILLE—*Florida Holt Parents,* P.O. Box 1121, Titusville, Fla. 32780

WINTER PARK—*COAC of Mid-Florida,* P.O. Box 1263, Winter Park, Fla. 32790

GEORGIA

ATLANTA—*Georgia Adoptive Parents,* 1041 Oakdale Road, N.E., Atlanta, Ga. 30307

CONYERS—*Newton-Rockdale Adoptive Parents,* 156 Glenn Road, Conyers, Ga. 30208

DOUGLASVILLE—*Georgia Adoptive Parents of Douglas County,* 6199 John West Road, Douglasville, Ga. 30134

LAWRENCEVILLE—*Adoptive Parents Organization,* P.O. Box 164, Lawrenceville, Ga. 30245

MACON—*Macon Adoptive Parents Association,* 2140 Ingleside, Apartment K-7, Macon, Ga. 31204

OAKWOOD—*Gainesville Adoptive Parents,* Route 1, Box 487, Oakwood, Ga. 30566

HAWAII

KANEOHE—*Adoptive Parents League of Hawaii,* P.O. Box 1426, Kaneohe, Hawaii 96744

IDAHO

BOISE—*Family Advocates Program,* P.O. Box 7848, Boise, Idaho 83707

—*Forever Families,* P.O. Box 7824, Boise, Idaho 83707

—*Idaho Foster Parents Association,* 3407 Lassen, Boise, Idaho 83705

CALDWELL—*Adoptive Families of Idaho,* P.O. Box 183, Caldwell, Idaho 83605

LEWISTON—*North Idaho Adoptive Families,* 2012 Powers Drive, Lewiston, Idaho 83501

McCALL—*Southern Idaho Parents for Children,* Route 1, Box 116A, McCall, Idaho 83638

POCATELLO—*Families Through Adoption,* 554 Garfield, Pocatello, Idaho 83201

POST FALLS—*North Idaho Adoptive Families,* P.O. Box 729, Post Falls, Idaho 83854

SANDPOINT—*North Idaho Adoptive Families,* Route 3, Box 465 A, Sandpoint, Idaho 83864

ILLINOIS

CHAMPAIGN—*Adoption Triangle,* c/o Children's Home and Aid of Illinois, Suite 423, 113 North Neill Street, Champaign, Ill. 61820

CHICAGO—*Illinois Parents for Minority Adoptions,* 7930 South Colfax Avenue, Chicago, Ill. 60617

COUNTRY CLUB HILLS—*South Suburban Chicago OURS,* 4501 West 177 Street, Country Club Hills, Ill. 60477

DOWNERS GROVE—*West Suburban Chicago OURS,* 1410 Golden Bell Court, Downers Grove, Ill. 60515

MOLINE—*Greater Quad City OURS,* 2929 Twenty-seventh Avenue A, Moline, Ill. 61265

OAK PARK—*Illinois Council on Adoptable Children,* P.O. Box 71, Oak Park, Ill. 60303

WEST CHICAGO—*The Children's Advocate,* 142 Wood Street, West Chicago, Ill. 60185

—*Parents of Adopted Children Together,* 1N740 Route 59, West Chicago, Ill. 60185

INDIANA

BLOOMINGTON—*Bloomington Association for the Rights of Children (ARC),* 929 Eastside Drive, Bloomington, Ind. 47401

FAIRMOUNT—*Marion ARC,* 592 East Fairmount Street, Fairmount, Ind. 46928

FORT WAYNE—*Fort Wayne ARC,* 1015 West Wildwood, Fort Wayne, Ind. 46807

—*Fort Wayne Adoptive Support Group,* 4606 Tamarack Street, Fort Wayne, Ind. 46815

GAS CITY—*ARC/OURS,* 227 West South First Street, Gas City, Ind. 46933

GOSHEN—*Rainbow Families of OURS,* P.O. Box 390, Goshen, Ind. 46526

INDIANAPOLIS—*Black Adoption Committee,* P.O. Box 1221, Indianapolis, Ind. 46202

—*Indianapolis ARC,* 7109 Lockerbie Drive, Indianapolis, Ind. 46224

—*OURS of Indianapolis,* 5728 Somers Drive, Indianapolis, Ind. 46203

LAFAYETTE—*ARC,* 1021 Holly Drive, Lafayette, Ind. 47905

LAPORTE—*La Porte County Adoptive and Foster Parent Association,* 0516 East 400 S., Laporte, Ind. 46350

NOTRE DAME—*ARC* in Indiana, P.O. Box 509, Notre Dame, Ind. 46551

SOUTH BEND—*ARC,* 921 Adams, South Bend, Ind. 46628

TERRE HAUTE—*Family Education Association,* 2931 Ohio Boulevard, Terre Haute, Ind. 47803

WESTFIELD—*Indianapolis Council on Adoptable Children (COAC),* 16101 Little Eagle Creek Avenue, Westfield, Ind. 46074

IOWA

AMES—*Council on Adoptable Children (COAC),* 254 Village Drive, Ames, Iowa 50010

ANKENY—*Iowans for International Adoptions,* 213 S.W. Flynn Drive, Ankeny, Iowa 50021

BURLINGTON—*Friends of Holtap,* 1219 Caroline, Burlington, Iowa 52601

CEDAR RAPIDS—*Families for Asian Children,* 4403 First Avenue, S.E., Cedar Rapids, Iowa 52402

—*International Adoptive Parents,* 2925 Beaver Avenue, S.E., Cedar Rapids, Iowa 52403

—*OURS,* 6826 Kiowa Tract, N.E., Cedar Rapids, Iowa 52401

CLINTON—*OURS,* 600 Argyle Court, Clinton, Iowa 52732

DAVENPORT—*Council on Adoptable Children (COAC),* 2518 West 43rd, Davenport, Iowa 52806

—*Quad-Cities Conference on Black Families,* 1708 East Eleventh Street, Davenport, Iowa 52802

DUBUQUE—*Open Door Society, Tri-State,* 489 South Grandview, Dubuque, Iowa 52001

HORNICK—*6 Plus,* R.R. 2, Hornick, Iowa 51026

INDIANOLA—*Iowans for International Adoptions,* 403 North K, Indianola, Iowa 50125

IOWA CITY—*Open Door Society of Cedar Rapids,* Route 4, Iowa City, Iowa 52240

MUSCATINE—*OURS,* 913 Newell, Muscatine, Iowa 52761

NEW MARKET—*For Love of Children (FLOC),* c/o Kelley, Route 1, New Market, Iowa 51646

OXFORD—*Families for Asian Children,* R.R. 1, Box 53-A1, Oxford, Iowa 52322

PROLE—*Parents by Choice,* R.R. 1, Prole, Iowa 50229

SPENCER—*Iowa Foster Parents Association,* c/o Tolle, Route 1, Spencer, Iowa 51301

KANSAS

ABILENE—*Council on Adoptable Children (COAC) of Kansas,* Route 5, Abilene, Kans. 67410

—*Kansas State Association of Foster Parents,* c/o Atkinson, Route #3, Abilene, Kans. 67410

CLAY CENTER—*Kansas Adopted Kids International (KAKI),* 728 Washington, Clay Center, Kans. 67432

HOISINGTON—*KAKI,* Route 2, Hoisington, Kans. 67544

KANSAS CITY—*Parents Organized to Support Black Adoptive Children,* 7138 Lafayette Avenue, Kansas City, Kans. 66109

LAWRENCE—*Adoptive and Interracial Living,* 1653 Indiana Street, Lawrence, Kans. 66044

—*Minority Foster & Adoptive Parents Advocacy Council,* 1521 East 28 Terrace, Lawrence, Kans. 66044

MISSION—*Parents by Choice,* 6100 West Fifty-eighth Street, Mission, Kans. 66202

OVERLAND PARK—*Parents Organized to Support Black Adoptive Children,* 10866 Bradshaw, Overland Park, Kans. 66210

TOPEKA—*Adoptive Mothers' Club,* 1206 High Street, Topeka, Kans. 66604

—*Topeka Adoptive Family Group,* 3636 Powell Street, Topeka, Kans. 66604

ULYSSES—*Adoptive Parents Association,* Box 424, Ulysses, Kans. 67880

WICHITA—*Council on Adoptable Children of Kansas (COAC),* 644 North Bluff, Wichita, Kans. 67208

KENTUCKY

EARLINGTON—*OURS in Kentucky,* P.O. Box 46, Earlington, Ky. 42410

LEXINGTON—*Black Citizens for Adoption,* 450 Ohio Street, Lexington, Ky. 40508

LOUISVILLE—*Kentuckiana Families for Children,* 2700 Brownsboro Road, Louisville, Ky. 40206

LOUISIANA

RIVER RIDGE—*Adoptive Couples Together,* 9500 Abel Lane, River Ridge, La. 70123

MAINE

HAMPDEN—*Adoptive Families of Maine,* P.O. Box 87, Hampden, Maine 04444

LIMESTONE—*Maine Council on Adoptable Children,* 45 Burleigh Street, Limestone, Maine 04750

MARYLAND

BALTIMORE—*Black Adoptive Parents of Greater Baltimore,* 1516 North Montford Avenue, Baltimore, Md. 21213

—*Open Door Society of Maryland,* 219 Altamont Avenue, Baltimore, Md. 21228

BEL AIR—*Families Adopting Children Everywhere (FACE), Main Chapter,* P.O. Box 102, Bel Air, Md. 21024

CLARKSVILLE—*Howard County FACE,* 7154 Route 32, Clarksville, Md. 21029

DISTRICT HEIGHTS—*Metropolitan Washington Council on Adoptable Children (COAC),* 1813 Glendora Drive, District Heights, Md. 20028

EDGEWOOD—*FACE,* 104 Palmetto Drive, Edgewood, Md. 21040

GLEN BURNIE—*Metro FACE,* 8108 Phirne Road, East, Glen Burnie, Md. 21061

LANHAM—*Southern FACE,* 6902 Nashville Road, Lanham, Md. 20801

SILVER SPRING—*Concerned Citizens for Black Adoption,* 9866 Hollow Glen Place, Silver Spring, Md. 20910

—*Families Like Ours,* 13106 Jingle Lane, Silver Spring, Md. 20906

—*Latin American Parents Association (LAPA),* P.O. Box 4403, Silver Spring, Md. 20904

WOODSBORO—*International Families by Adoption,* Box 1, Woodsboro, Md. 21798

MASSACHUSETTS

BOSTON—*Extended Family Institute,* P.O. Box 1040, Astoria Station, Boston, Mass. 02123

—*Open Door Society of Massachusetts,* P.O. Box 501, Essex Station, Boston, Mass. 02111

CANTON—*Open Door Society,* 48 Elm Street, Canton, Mass. 02021

EAST LONGMEADOW—*OURS of Massachusetts,* P.O. Box 128, East Longmeadow, Mass. 01028

NORTH QUINCY—*Single Parents for Adopted Children Everywhere,* 86 Edwin Street, North Quincy, Mass. 02171

PITTSFIELD—*"Adopt Me Please" Organization,* 154 Elm Street, Pittsfield, Mass. 01201

WABAN—*Adoption Counsellors,* 95 Dorset Road, Waban, Mass. 02168

WESTFIELD—*Massachusetts Adoptive Family Association*, P.O. Box 1542, Westfield, Mass. 01086

MICHIGAN

ANN ARBOR—*Ann Arbor Friends for International Adoption and Assistance*, 1213 Olivia Street, Ann Arbor, Mich. 48104

CANTON—*Michigan Aid to Adoption of Special Kids (AASK)*, 6514 Carriage Hills Drive, Canton, Mich. 48187

DETROIT—*Adoptive Parent Outreach*, 10014 Grandville, Detroit, Mich. 48228

—*Friends of Homes for Black Children*, 1140 Calvert, Detroit, Mich. 48202

FLINT—*OURS of Flint*, 4338 Crosby Road, Flint, Mich. 48506

GRAND RAPIDS—*Families for International Children*, 1307 Philadelphia, S.E., Grand Rapids, Mich. 49506

LAINSBURG—*International Adoptive Families*, 509 East Grand River, Lainsburg, Mich. 48848

LUDINGTON—*OURS of Mason County*, 204 North Gaylor Avenue, Ludington, Mich. 49431

MARQUETTE—*Adoptive Family Group*, 142 Fisher Street, Marquette, Mich. 49855

MOUNT CLEMENS—*McComb County Association of Adoptive Families*, 235 South Gratiot Avenue, Mount Clemens, Mich. 48083

PLYMOUTH—*Families for International Adoption and Assistance*, 254 Ann Street, Plymouth, Mich. 48170

PONTIAC—*North Oakland County OURS*, 2640 Hatton Road, Pontiac, Mich. 48057

RAPID CITY—*Grand Traverse Council on Adoptable Children*, Route 1, Box 469, Rapid City, Mich. 49676

ROYAL OAK—*Catholic Infant Society, County of Oakland (CISCO)*, 1421 Eleventh Mile Road, Royal Oak, Mich. 48067

SOUTHFIELD—*Families for Children*, 19100 West Ten Mile Road, Suite 104, Southfield, Mich. 48075

—*Michigan Association of Single Adoptive Parents*, P.O. Box 601, Southfield, Mich. 48037

SPRING LAKE—*Western Michigan Single Adoptive Parents*, 18754 Fruitport Road, Spring Lake, Mich. 49456

MINNESOTA

ANOKA—*OURS of Minnesota*, 20140 Pine Ridge Drive, N.W., Anoka, Minn. 55303

BLUE EARTH—*South Central Area OURS*, 225 East Third Street, Blue Earth, Minn. 56013

BUFFALO—*OURS Adoptive Parent Group*, 703 Eighth Street, N.W., Buffalo, Minn. 55313

DULUTH—*Duluth OURS*, 183 Beech Street, Duluth, Minn. 55804

ELY—*OURS of Northeastern Minnesota*, Box 33, Ely, Minn. 55731

HASTINGS—*Hastings OURS*, 9975—190 Street E., Hastings, Minn. 55033

LAKEVILLE—*Dakota County Adoptive Parent Group*, 17880 Jaguar Court, Lakeville, Minn. 55044

MCINTOSH—*Polk County OURS*, c/o Dennis Hammer, McIntosh, Minn. 56556

MINNETONKA—*Citizen's Coalition on Permanence for Children*, 17917 Cynthia Drive, Minnetonka, Minn. 55343

MONTEVIDEO—*Montevideo Area OURS*, Route 4, Box 272, Montevideo, Minn. 56265

NEW PRAGUE—*New Prague OURS*, Route 3, Box 149, New Prague, Minn. 56071

OLIVIA—*Olivia Area OURS*, Route 2, Box 19A, Olivia, Minn. 56277

PINE CITY—*Pine City OURS*, 229 Eleventh Street, Pine City, Minn. 56063

PINE ISLAND—*OURS of Rochester*, 318 S.W. Pine Crest Court, Pine Island, Minn. 55963

PINE RIVER—*Pine River OURS*, Star Route 60, Pine River, Minn. 56479

ROCHESTER—*Adoption Today*, Box 6003, Rochester, Minn. 55901

ST. CLOUD—*St. Cloud Area OURS*, Route 4, St. Cloud, Minn. 56301

ST. HILAIRE—*Thief River Falls OURS*, R.R. 1, St. Hilaire, Minn. 56757

STILLWATER—*Washington County Adoptive Parent Association*, 939 West Anderson Street, Stillwater, Minn. 55082

MISSISSIPPI

JACKSON—*Mississippi Advocates for Minority Adoptions, Inc.*, P.O. Box 71, Jackson, Miss. 39066

—*Mississippi Council on Adoptable Children (COAC)*, P.O. Box 1184, Jackson, Miss. 39205

MISSOURI

BOIS D'ARC—*Open Door Society of Missouri, Southwest Branch*, Route 1, Box 755, Bois D'Arc, Mo. 65612

CAPE GIRARDEAU—*Adoption Support Group*, P.O. Box 578, Cape Girardeau, Mo. 63701

CLAYTON—*Committee for Adoption Reform and Education*, 6401 Wydown, Clayton, Mo. 63105

FLORISSANT—*Parents of Oriental Children*, 14613 Petticoat Lane, Florissant, Mo. 63034

ILLMO—*Adoptive Mothers Club*, P.O. Box 382, Illmo, Mo. 63754

JACKSON—*Adoptive Parents of Special Needs Children*, 919 Odus, Jackson, Mo. 63755

KANSAS CITY—*Jackson County Adoptive Parent Support Group*, c/o Jackson County Family Services Office, 615 East Thirteenth Street, Kansas City, Mo. 64106

—*Parents Organized to Support Adoptive Black Children*, 8800 Briston, Kansas City, Mo. 64130

KIRKWOOD—*Friends of Children of Viet Nam (FCVN)*, 1460 Forest Avenue, Kirkwood, Mo. 63112

LEBANON—*Adoptive Parents of the Ozarks (APO)*, Brice Rte., Bennett Spring Hatchery, Lebanon, Mo. 65536

MEXICO—*Adoptive Parents' Support Group*, c/o Audrain County Family Services Office, P.O. Box 129, Mexico, Mo. 65265

MILO—*Open Door Society of Missouri, Kansas City Branch*, c/o Walker, Route #3, Milo, Mo. 64767

O'FALLON—*World Children's Fund*, Box 114, O'Fallon, Mo. 63366

PALMYRA—*Open Door Society of Missouri, Northeast Missouri Branch*, 222 East Lafayette, Palmyra, Mo. 63461

SPRINGFIELD—*Open Door Society*, 342 Landmark Building, Springfield, Mo. 65806

—*Pilot Parents Program*, 1772 South Kentwood, Springfield, Mo. 65804

—*Springfield Area Adoptive Parents*, 911 East Greenwood, Springfield, Mo. 65807

ST. JOSEPH—*Group for Adoption Interest Now (GAIN)*, 4106 West Haverhill Drive, St. Joseph, Mo. 64506

ST. LOUIS—*Adoption Parent Support Group*, c/o Adoption Unit, Division of Family Services, 3545 Lindell Boulevard, St. Louis, Mo. 63103

—*Children's Home Society*, 9445 Litzinger Road, St. Louis, Mo. 63144

—*New Horizons for the Behaviorally Disordered*, 13391 Walfield Lane, St. Louis, Mo. 63141

—*Open Door Society of Missouri*, 6127 Waterman, St. Louis, Mo. 63112

WARRENSBURG—*Open Door Society of Missouri*, 304 Jones Avenue, Warrensburg, Mo. 64003

MONTANA

ANACONDA—*Families for Adoptable Children*, P.O. Box 485, Anaconda, Mont. 59711

CONRAD—*Citizens Concerned about Adoption,* P.O. Box 644, Conrad, Mont. 59425

NEBRASKA

BLAIR—*Nebraska Foster & Adoptive Parents Association,* c/o Moore, R.R. #1, Blair, Nebr. 68008

COLUMBUS—*Our Family Plus,* R.R. #3, Box 5, Columbus, Nebr. 68061

COZAD—*Nebraska Foster & Adoptive Parents Association,* Route #2, Box 102-A, Cozad, Nebr. 69130

ELM CREEK—*Nebraska Foster & Adoptive Parents Association,* Route #1, Box 124, Elm Creek, Nebr. 68836

FREMONT—*Nebraska Foster & Adoptive Parents Association,* c/o Calta, Route #1, Fremont, Nebr. 68025

GERING—*Nebraska Foster & Adoptive Parents Association,* 1445 Gentry Boulevard, Gering, Nebr. 69341

GRAND ISLAND—*Nebraska Foster & Adoptive Parents Association,* 1408 North Ruby, Grand Island, Nebr. 68801

—*Nebraska Foster & Adoptive Parents Association,* 2307 Riverside Drive, Grand Island, Nebr. 68801

GRETNA—*Nebraska Foster & Adoptive Parents Association,* 205 Glendale Circle, Gretna, Nebr. 68028

HOWELLS—David Eurek, Box 406, Howells, Nebr. 68641

KIMBALL—*Child Saving Institute,* North Star Route, Box 17, Kimball, Nebr. 69145

LINCOLN—*Intercultural Families,* 800 Northborough Lane, Lincoln, Nebr. 68505

—*Interracial Families,* 435 South 29th Street, Lincoln, Nebr. 68510

—*Nebraska Foster & Adoptive Parents Association,* 2440 Southwest Eighteenth Street, Lincoln, Nebr. 68522

—*Nebraska Foster & Adoptive Parents Association,* 4920 Garland Street, Lincoln, Nebr. 68504

MADISON—*All in Our Family,* R.R. #2, Madison, Nebr. 68748

MAYWOOD—*Nebraska Foster & Adoptive Parents Association,* Route #1, Box 281, Maywood, Nebr. 69038

NORFOLK—*All in Our Family,* 508 South Sixth, Norfolk, Nebr. 68701

OMAHA—*Nebraska Foster & Adoptive Parents Association,* 5505 South 81st Street, Omaha, Nebr. 68135

—*Nebraska Foster & Adoptive Parents Association,* 5625 Pacific, Omaha, Nebr. 68106

—*Nebraska Foster & Adoptive Parents Association,* 11725 South 36th Street, Omaha, Nebr. 68123

—*Nebraska Foster & Adoptive Parents Association,* 3325 Woolworth, Omaha, Nebr. 68105

SUTTON—*Nebraska Foster & Adoptive Parents Association,* Box 117, Sutton, Nebr. 68979

WINNEBAGO—*Sharing Through Adoption,* Box 772, Winnebago, Nebr. 68071

NEVADA

LAS VEGAS—*Members and Advocates for Minority Adoptions (MAMA),* 6245 West Elmira Drive, Las Vegas, Nev. 89118

—*Nevada Families for Adoption,* 1858 Citation, Las Vegas, Nev. 89119

NEW HAMPSHIRE

CONCORD—*Frontiers in Adoption,* 65 Noyes Street, Concord, N.H. 03301

KINGSTON—*Open Door Society of New Hampshire,* R.F.D. 2, Box 211, Kingston, N.H. 03848

MERRIMACK—*Adoption Service League of Greater Nashua,* 8 Woodward Road, Merrimack, N.H. 03054

NEW JERSEY

CHERRY HILL—*South Jersey Council on Adoptable Children (COAC),* 134 Oakdale Road, Cherry Hill, N.J. 08034

HIGHTSTOWN—*Latin American Parents Association (LAPA),* P.O. Box 828, Hightstown, N.J. 08520

OCEAN—*Children Who Wait,* 1108 Berkeley Avenue, Ocean, N.J. 07712

TOMS RIVER—*OURS of New Jersey,* 1424 Colorado Drive, Toms River, N.J. 08753

WHIPPANY—*Concerned Persons for Adoption,* 200 Parsippany Road, Whippany, N.J. 07981

NEW MEXICO

ALBUQUERQUE—*IMPACT,* 4004 Camino de la Sierra, N.E., Albuquerque, N.Mex. 87111

HOLLOMAN, AFB—*Lincoln County Adoptive Parents Group,* 2041A Hanscom Place, Holloman Air Force Base, N.Mex. 88330

LOS ALAMOS—*Los Escogidos,* 4374 Ridgeway, Los Alamos, N. Mex. 87544

NEW YORK

ADAMS—*American Oriental Club,* R.D. #2, Adams, N.Y. 13605

BELMORE—*Adoptive Parents Committee of Long Island,* P.O. Box 71, Belmore, N.Y. 11710

BRONX—*South Bronx Adoptive Parents Organization,* 535 East 138th Street, Bronx, N.Y. 10454

CHAPPAQUA—*Westchester/Rockland Adoptive Parents Committee,* 12 Wynnewood Road, Chappaqua, N.Y. 10514

HIGHLAND FALLS—*Parents and Children Together,* 23 Webb Lane, Highland Falls, N.Y. 10928

ITHACA—*Adoptive Families Association of Tompkins County,* 220 Easter Heights Drive, Ithaca, N.Y. 14850

JAMAICA—*Family Dimensions, Inc.,* 106-60 Union Hall Street, Jamaica, N.Y. 11434

MORICHES—*Long Island OURS,* P.O. Box 637, Moriches, N.Y. 11955

MUMFORD—*Council of Adoptive Parents (COAC),* 110 Flint Hill Road, Mumford, N.Y. 14511

NEW CITY—*Rockland County OURS,* 4 Virginia Street, New City, N.Y. 10956

NEW HYDE PARK—*Concerned Persons for Adoption,* 222 Marcus Avenue, New Hyde Park, N.Y. 11040

NEW YORK—*Adoptive Parents Committee,* 210 Fifth Avenue, New York, N.Y. 10010. (212) 683-9221

—*Committed Parents for Black Adoption,* 271 West 125th Street, New York, N.Y. 10027

—*Council on Adoptable Children,* 875 Avenue of the Americas, New York, N.Y. 10001

—*Korean Families of Spence-Chapin,* 6 East Ninety-fourth Street, New York, N.Y. 10028

—*New York Council on Adoptable Children (COAC),* 875 Avenue of the Americas, New York, N.Y. 10001. (212) 279-4525

NIAGARA FALLS—*Black Homes for Black Children,* 1317 Niagara Street, Niagara Falls, N.Y. 14305

PITTSFORD—*Congress of Adoptive Children,* 624 Pinnacle Road, Pittsford, N.Y. 04534

ROCHESTER—*Black Children/Black Family,* 191 Troup Street, Rochester, N.Y. 14608

—*Congress of Adoptive Children,* 49 Dayton Street, Rochester, N.Y. 14621

—*Council of Adoptive Parents (CAP) of Rochester,* P.O. Box 9667, Rochester, N.Y. 14604

RONKONKOMA—*Open Door Society of Long Island,* P.O. Box 236, Ronkonkoma, N.Y. 11779

SEAFORD—*Latin American Parents Association (LAPA), Main Chapter,* P.O. Box 72, Seaford, N.Y. 11783

UNIONDALE—*Adopt Black Children Association*, 1027 Harding Street, Uniondale, N.Y. 11553

WESTBURY—*Adopt Black Children Association*, 42 First Avenue, Westbury, N.Y. 11520

NORTH CAROLINA

APEX—*Families for Adoptable Children*, Box 56A, Apex, N.C. 27502

CHARLOTTE—*Council for Adoptive Families*, 3127 Cambridge Road, Charlotte, N.C. 28401

—*Metrolina Black Adoption Task Force*, P.O. Box 16186, Charlotte, N.C. 28216

GREENSBORO—*Black Adoption Task Force*, P.O. Box 21542, Greensboro, N.C. 27406

HIGH POINT—*Adoptive Parents Together*, Route 1, Box 279, High Point, N.C. 27260

—*High Point Black Adoption Task Force*, 110 Orville Drive, High Point, N.C. 27260

JAMESTOWN—*Piedmont Council on Adoptable Children jj(COAC)*, 3032 Dillon Road, Jamestown, N.C. 27282

SHELBY—*Council on Adoptive Families*, 2946 College Road, Shelby, N.C. 28150

WILMINGTON—*Parents of Adopted Children Together*, 213 North Crestwood Drive, Wilmington, N.C. 28401

WINSTON-SALEM—*Black Action Committee on Adoptions*, 4283 Winnabow Road, Winston-Salem, N.C. 27105

NORTH DAKOTA

DICKINSON—*Southwestern North Dakota OURS*, 744 Tenth Street, East, Dickinson, N.Dak. 58601

GRAND FORKS—*Families and Friends of Adoption*, 1814 Lewis Boulevard, Grand Forks, N.Dak. 58201

OHIO

AKRON—*Black Adoptive Parent Outreach*, 1565 Thurston, Akron, Ohio 44320

CASSTOWN—*Caring Families through Adoption*, 2255 Rugged Hills Road, Casstown, Ohio 45312

CINCINNATI—*Citizens for Children of Hamilton County*, 4718 Winton Road, Cincinnati, Ohio 45232

CLEVELAND—*Families for Black Adoptable Children*, 2044 West Thirty-eighth Street, Cleveland, Ohio 44113

CLEVELAND HEIGHTS—*COACT,* 925 Woodview Avenue, Cleveland Heights, Ohio 44118

COLUMBUS—*Black Adoption Recruitment Committee,* 1882 Nason Avenue, Columbus, Ohio 43208

—*Single Adoptive Parents' Group,* 180 West Kenworth, Columbus, Ohio 43214

DAYTON—*Adopting Older Kids (AOK),* 7517 Yankee Street, Dayton, Ohio 45459

ELYRIA—*Helping Hands for Black Adoption,* 139 California, Elyria, Ohio 44035

MAUMEE—*Adoptive Family Organization of Northwest Ohio,* P.O. Box 502, Maumee, Ohio 43537

NORTH CANTON—*Forever Families for Kids,* 1670 Meadow Lane Drive, S.E., North Canton, Ohio 44709

RAVENNA—*Concern for Children,* 325 North Scranton Street, Ravenna, Ohio 44266

SHAKER HEIGHTS—*Cleveland Black Adoption Parent Support Group,* 18238 Van Aken Blvd., Shaker Heights, Ohio 44122

SPRING VALLEY—*Families through World Adoption,* 2933 Lower Bellbrook Road, Spring Valley, Ohio 45370

WOOSTER—*Area Adoptive Parent Association,* P.O. Box 311, Wooster, Ohio 44691

OKLAHOMA

OKLAHOMA CITY—*Oklahoma Council on Adoptable Children (COAC),* P.O. Box 18, Oklahoma City, Okla. 73101

OREGON

ASHLAND—*Planning Loving Adoptions Now (PLAN),* 1436 Butter Creek Road, Ashland, Oreg. 97520

—*Planning Loving Adoptions Now (PLAN),* 658 Valley View Road, Ashland, Oreg. 97520

—*Southern Oregon Adoptive Parent Group,* 368 Kent Street, Ashland, Oreg. 97520

ASTORIA—*Adoptive Parents Organization,* 216 Exchange Street, Astoria, Oreg. 97103

BAKER—*Planning Loving Adoptions Now (PLAN),* 1680 Clark Street, Baker, Oreg. 97814

BANKS—*Planning Loving Adoptions Now (PLAN),* Star Route, Box 75-F, Banks, Oreg. 97106

BEND—*Bend Adoptive Parent Group*, 66700 Gerking Road, Bend, Oreg. 97701

BONNEVILLE—*Planning Loving Adoptions Now (PLAN)*, 250 Star Route, Bonneville, Oreg. 97008

BORING—*Planning Loving Adoptions Now (PLAN)*, 13105 South East 197th, Boring, Oreg. 97701

CANABY—*Planning Loving Adoptions Now (PLAN)*, 1410 Northeast Oak Street, Canaby, Oreg. 97013

COOS BAY—*Planning Loving Adoptions Now (PLAN)*, 944 Flanagan Avenue, Coos Bay, Oreg. 97458

COQUILLE—*Coos County Parents for Children*, Fairview Route, Box 672, Coquille, Oreg. 97423

CORVALLIS—*Planning Loving Adoptions Now (PLAN)*, 236 Northwest 28th Street, Corvallis, Oreg. 97330

EUGENE—*Lane County Adoptive Parents*, 2231 Monterey Lane, Eugene, Oreg. 97401

—*Lane County Open Door for Adoptable Children*, 4801 Donald, Eugene, Oreg. 97405

—*Let's Adopt Resource Council*, 1247 Willamette Street, Eugene, Oreg. 97401

—*Planning Loving Adoptions Now (PLAN)*, 3160 Nob Court, Eugene, Oreg. 97404

—*Planning Loving Adoptions Now (PLAN)*, 3686 Revel Drive, Eugene, Oreg. 97404

FOREST GROVE—*Banks Parent Group*, Star Route Box 76-K, Forest Grove, Oreg. 97106

GLADSTONE—*Open Door Society*, 16801 Webster Road, Gladstone, Oreg. 97202

GRANTS PASS—*Planning Loving Adoptions Now (PLAN)*, 730 Northwest Kinney, Grants Pass, Oreg. 97526

—*Planning Loving Adoptions Now (PLAN)*, 2576 Harbeck, Grants Pass, Oreg. 97526

GRESHAM—*Planning Loving Adoptions Now (PLAN)*, Route 2, Box 411, Gresham, Oreg. 97030

HERMISTON—*Planning Loving Adoptions Now (PLAN)*, 235 Northeast Seventh, Hermiston, Oreg. 97838

HILLSBORO—*Planning Loving Adoptions Now (PLAN)*, 814 Southeast 36th, Hillsboro, Oreg. 97123

KLAMATH FALLS—*Planning Loving Adoptions Now (PLAN)*, 2113 Homedale Avenue, Klamath Falls, Oreg. 97601

LA GRANDE—*Planning Loving Adoptions Now (PLAN)*, Route 2, Box 2552 E, La Grande, Oreg. 97850

LAKE OSWEGO—*Planning Loving Adoptions Now (PLAN)*, 1575 Highland Drive, Lake Oswego, Oreg. 97034

LA PINE—*Planning Loving Adoptions Now (PLAN)*, 14901 White Pine, La Pine, Oreg. 97736

McMINNVILLE—*Family Opportunities Unlimited*, P.O. Box 194, McMinnville, Oreg. 97128

—*McMinnville Adoptive Parent Group*, 2920 Redwood Drive, McMinnville, Oreg. 97128

MEDFORD—*Planning Loving Adoptions Now (PLAN)*, 658 Canterbury Lane, Medford, Oreg. 97501

MYRTLE POINT—*Planning Loving Adoptions Now (PLAN)*, 1684 Eighteenth Street, Myrtle Point, Oreg. 97458

NEWBERG—*Be a Parent*, Route 3, Box 426, Newberg, Oreg. 97132

—*Give Us This Day*, Route #3, Box 140-C, Newberg, Oreg. 97132

NORTH POWDER—*Planning Loving Adoptions Now (PLAN)*, P.O. Box 175, North Powder, Oreg. 97850

NYSSA—*Adoptive Parent Group*, 915 East Mission Avenue, Nyssa, Oreg. 97913

OAK RIDGE—*Parent Support Group*, 47695 Commercial, Oak Ridge, Oreg. 97463

PHILOMATH—*Planning Loving Adoptions Now (PLAN)*, 362 Benton View Drive, Philomath, Oreg. 97370

PORTLAND—*Extended Family Outreach*, 4524 North East Ninth Street, Portland, Oreg. 97211

—*Planning Loving Adoptions Now (PLAN)*, 5802 Northeast Mallory, Portland, Oreg. 97211

—*Planning Loving Adoptions Now (PLAN)*, 4236 Southwest Hillside Drive, Portland, Oreg. 97221

PRESCOTT—*Planning Loving Adoptions Now (PLAN)*, 805 Prescott, Prescott, Oreg. 97211

ROSEBURG—*Planning Loving Adoptions Now (PLAN)*, 725 Southeast Haynes, Roseburg, Oreg. 97470

—*Team of Adoptive Parents*, 322 Arcadia Drive, Roseburg, Oreg. 97470

SALEM—*Marion and Polk County Foster Parents Association*, P.O. Box 12551, Salem, Oreg. 97309

—*Planning Loving Adoptions Now (PLAN)*, 483 Juedes Avenue North, Salem, Oreg. 97310

—*Salem Area Adoption Support Group*, 407 Browning Avenue Southeast, Salem, Oreg. 97302

SILETZ—*Coastal Network, Lincoln Adoptive Parents Group*, P.O. Box 362, Siletz, Oreg. 97380

SISTERS—*Planning Loving Adoptions Now (PLAN)*, P.O. Box 865, Sisters, Oreg. 97759

SPRINGFIELD—*Planning Loving Adoptions Now (PLAN)*, 2750 South M Street, Springfield, Oreg. 97477

SUMMERVILLE—*Families Adopting Children Together (FACT)*, Route 1, Box 41, Summerville, Oreg. 97876

—*Planning Loving Adoptions Now (PLAN)*, Route 1, Box 57 A, Summerville, Oreg. 97876

TERRABONNE—Genger Dowse, Route 1, Box 244, Terrabonne, Oreg. 97760

TIGARD—*Families Celebrating Individual Differences (FCID)*, 11780 Southwest 114th Place, Tigard, Oreg. 97062

TOLEDO—*Planning Loving Adoptions Now (PLAN)*, 360 East Graham, Toledo, Oreg. 97391

TROUTDALE—*Planning Loving Adoptions Now (PLAN)*, 537 Buston, Troutdale, Oreg. 97060

TUALATIN—*Oregon Chapter of OURS*, P.O. Box 332, Tualatin, Oreg. 97062

UNION—*Planning Loving Adoptions Now (PLAN)*, P.O. Box 523, Union, Oreg. 97883

VALE—*Planning Loving Adoptions Now (PLAN)*, 740 West Main Street South, Vale, Oreg. 98918

WALDPORT—*Planning Loving Adoptions Now (PLAN)*, P.O. Box 1196, Waldport, Oreg. 97394

WARRENTON—*Clatsop Adoptive Parent Group*, P.O. Box 58, Warrenton, Oreg. 97146

WEST LINN—*Southeastern Portland Adoptive Parent Group*, 19393 Kapteyns, West Linn, Oreg. 97068

PENNSYLVANIA

ALLENTOWN—*Open Door Society of Pennsylvania*, 1835 Troxell Street, Allentown, Pa. 18103

BEAVER FALLS—*Parents and Adopted Children Organization (PACO) of Beaver County*, 764 Blackhawk Road, Beaver Falls, Pa. 15010

BETHLEHEM—*Welcome House Adoptive Parents Group (WHAPG)*, 1437 Loraine Avenue, Bethlehem, Pa. 18018

BRADFORD—*Council on Adoptable Children (COAC) of McKean County*, 16 Welch Avenue, Bradford, Pa. 16701

BRYN MAWR—*Families for Black Children*, 138 Marlyn Avenue, Bryn Mawr, Pa. 19010

BUTLER—*PACO of Midwestern Pennsylvania*, 233 West Fulton Street, Butler, Pa. 16001

CORNWELLS HEIGHTS—*Bucks County Council of Adoptive Couples,* 6365 Powder Horn Court, Cornwells Heights, Pa. 19020

CORRY—*Parents for Overseas Adoption,* 158 Maple Avenue, Corry, Pa. 16407

DOYLESTOWN—*WHAPG,* Box 265, Doylestown, Pa. 18901

EDINBORO—*COAC of Northwestern Pennsylvania,* 114 Hillcrest Drive, R.D. 4, Edinboro, Pa. 16412

EMMAUS—*Pennsylvania Parents for Overseas Adoption,* Fifth Street, Emmaus, Pa. 18049

ERIE—*COAC of Northwestern Pennsylvania,* 327 Joliette Avenue, Erie, Pa. 16511

EXTON—*COAC of Chester County,* 124 Glendale Road, Exton, Pa. 19341

HAVERTOWN—*WHAPG,* 106 North Morgan Avenue, Havertown, Pa. 19083

HERMITAGE—*Mercer County PACO,* 1816 Rombold Road, Hermitage, Pa. 16148

HOMESTEAD—*INDABA,* 114 East Fourteenth Street, Homestead, Pa. 15120

KING OF PRUSSIA—*Tri-County Chapter of WHAPG,* 619 West Valley Forge Road, King of Prussia, Pa. 19406

LANCASTER—*PACO Lancaster County,* 2104 Willow Street Pike, Lancaster, Pa. 17601

LANDENBERG—*Adoptive Families with Information and Support,* R.D. 1, Box 23, Landenberg, Pa. 19350

MOUNTAINTOP—*Northeastern WHAPG,* 92 Naungola, Mountaintop, Pa. 18707

NEW CASTLE—*Black Adoptable Children of Western Pennsylvania,* 1020 South Mill Street, New Castle, Pa. 16101

—*PACO of Midwestern Pennsylvania,* 208 East Edison Street, New Castle, Pa. 16101

—*Lawrence County PACO,* 2907 North Mercer Street, New Castle, Pa. 16105

NEWTOWN SQUARE—*Adoptive Parents Group of Delaware County,* 146 Ashley Road, Newtown Square, Pa. 19073

NORTH IRWIN—*PACO Westmoreland,* 12 Madison Avenue, North Irwin, Pa. 15642

PHILADELPHIA—*Adoptive Parent Group of Delaware Valley,* 4917 Parkside Avenue, Philadelphia, Pa. 19131

—*Adoptive Parent Group of Philadelphia,* 14021 Faraday Street, Philadelphia, Pa. 19116

—*Latin American Parents Association (LAPA),* Philadelphia Chapter, P.O. Box 18107, Philadelphia, Pa. 19116

—*Metropolitan Philadelphia Minority Adoptive Parent Group,* 4917 Parkside Avenue, Philadelphia, Pa. 19131

—*Philadelphia Area PACO,* 2900 Queen Lane, Philadelphia, Pa. 19129

—*Philadelphia WHAPG,* 8638 Marigold Place, Philadelphia, Pa. 19136

PIPERSVILLE—*Bucks County WHAPG,* Box 150, Groveland Road, Pipers-ville, Pa. 18947

PITTSBURGH—*INDABA,* 545 North Fairmont Avenue, Pittsburgh, Pa. 15206

—*Southwestern Pennsylvania COAC,* P.O. Box 81044, Pittsburgh, Pa. 15217

—*Westmoreland County PACO,* 3837 Sardis Road, Pittsburgh, Pa. 15239

QUAKERTOWN—*WHAPG,* R.F.D. 4, Box 152A, Quakertown, Pa. 18951

READING—*Pennsylvania Coalition for Children,* 3101 Merritt Parkway, Wil-shire, Reading, Pa. 19608

ROARING SPRINGS—*PACO, Altoona,* 721 Main Street, Roaring Springs, Pa. 16673

WILKES-BARRE—*Child Advocates, Adoptive Parents,* 400 Bicentennial Build-ing, 15 Public Square, Wilkes-Barre, Pa. 18701

WILLIAMSPORT—*Northcentral Pennsylvania PACO,* 1029 Rural Avenue, Wil-liamsport, Pa. 17701

YORK—*Parents and Adopted Children Organization (PACO) Main Office,* 122 West Springettsbury Avenue, York, Pa. 17403

RHODE ISLAND

PROVIDENCE—*Ocean State Adoptive Group,* 170 Westminster Street, Provi-dence, R.I. 02903

SOUTH CAROLINA

COLUMBIA—*South Carolina Black Adoption Committee,* P.O. Box 2516, Co-lumbia, S.C. 29202

—*South Carolina Council on Adoptable Children (COAC),* 110 Coatsdale Road, Columbia, S.C. 29202

WEST COLUMBIA—*Parents Adoption Information Resource of South Carolina,* P.O. Box 1383, West Columbia, S.C. 29169

SOUTH DAKOTA

PIERRE—*Adoptable Children Information Exchange,* Part A, Pierre, S.Dak. 57501

RAPID CITY—*Contact: Adoptive Parents,* 1120 Farlow Avenue, Rapid City, S.Dak. 57701

TENNESSEE

HIXSON—*Chattanooga Council on Adoptable Children (COAC),* 2110 Ram-bler Lane, Hixson, Tenn. 37343

KNOXVILLE—*Knoxville COAC*, 2449 Brooks Road, Knoxville, Tenn. 37915

MEMPHIS—*Adoption–Foster Care Task Force of Shelby County*, 3359 Charlotte, Memphis, Tenn. 38106

—*COAC of Memphis*, P.O. Box 18951, Memphis, Tenn. 38118

NASHVILLE—*Adoptive Families of Nashville*, 6029 Sedberry Road, Nashville, Tenn. 37205

TEXAS

AMARILLO—*Catholic Family Service*, 1522 South Van Buren, Amarillo, Tex. 79101

—*Amarillo Council on Adoptable Children (COAC)*, 3306 Ostego, Amarillo, Tex. 79106

AUSTIN—*Austin COAC*, 3902 Holly Road Number 2, Austin, Tex. 78761

—*Texas Council on Adoptable Children (COAC)*, 6600 Bradley Austin, Tex. 78723

CORPUS CHRISTI—*Corpus Christi COAC*, 3809 Montego Drive, Number 8, Corpus Christi, Tex. 78415

EL PASO—*Adoptive Parents of El Paso*, P.O. Box 26712, El Paso, Tex. 79926

FORT WORTH—*New Hope Advisory Committee*, 2110 Hemphill, Fort Worth, Tex. 76110

HARLINGEN—*Rio Grande COAC*, 2614 Cypress, Harlingen, Tex. 78550

HOUSTON—*Adopt Black Children Committee*, 8602 Allwood, Houston, Tex. 77016

—*Houston COAC*, P.O. Box 2571, Houston, Tex. 77001

HUNTINGTON—*East Texas COAC*, P.O. Box 737, Avenue A, Huntington, Tex. 75949

KINGSVILLE—*Coastal Bend MAPLE of Texas*, 1830 Elizabeth, Kingsville, Tex. 78363

LEAGUE CITY—*Galveston County COAC*, 191 Loch Lomond, League City, Tex. 77573

LUFKIN—*East Texas COAC*, P.O. Box 742, Lufkin, Tex. 75901

McALLEN—*Concilio de Padres de Ninos de Adoptivos*, 2501 Maple Street, McAllen, Tex. 78501

MIDLAND—*Permian Basin COAC*, 3406 Princeton, Midland, Tex. 77903

NEW CANEY—*Montgomery County COAC*, Route 4, Box 1110-DP, New Caney, Tex. 77357

RICHARDSON—*Dallas COAC*, P.O. Box 1691, Richardson, Tex. 75080

SAN ANGELO—*San Angelo COAC*, 2807 Hemlock Drive, San Angelo, Tex. 76901

SAN ANTONIO—*Friends of Lutheran Social Services*, 112 Cotillion, San Antonio, Tex. 78213

—*San Antonio COAC,* 16503 Parkstone Boulevard, San Antonio, Tex. 78232

TEMPLE—*Temple COAC,* 208 South Twenty-seventh Street, Temple, Tex. 76501

UTAH

GRANGER—*Adoption Support Group of Utah,* 1863 West 3350 South, Granger, Utah 84119

LOGAN—*Families of Intercultural Adoption,* 1500 South 300 East, Logan, Utah 84321

PAYSON—*HOPE of Utah,* 190 East 600 South, Payson, Utah 84651

SALT LAKE CITY—*Families of Intercultural Adoption,* P.O. Box 15977, Salt Lake City, Utah 84025

VERMONT

ESSEX JUNCTION—*Room for One More,* 6 Lamoille Street, Essex Junction, Vt. 05452

VIRGINIA

ALEXANDRIA—*Metropolitan Washington Council on Adoptable Children (COAC),* 7018 Bedrock Road, Alexandria, Va. 22306

BLACKSBURG—*Adoptive Parent Group,* 2701 Chelsea Court, Blacksburg, Va. 24060

FALLS CHURCH—*Greater Washington Welcome House Adoptive Parents Group (WHAPG),* 5908 South Sixth Street, Falls Church, Va. 22041

MANASSAS—*Prince William County COAC,* 12413 Carrageen Drive, Manassas, Va. 22110

PRESTON—*COAC,* 11643 Newbridge Court, Preston, Va. 22091

RICHMOND—*People for the Adoption of Children,* 7649 Cherokee Road, Richmond, Va. 23225

—*Reach Out for Black Adoption (ROBA),* 9714 Laurel Pine Tree, Richmond, Va. 23228

VIRGINIA BEACH—*Tidewater COAC,* 512 Lavendar Lane, Virginia Beach, Va. 23462

WASHINGTON

ABERDEEN—*Aberdeen Washington Association of Christian Adoptive Parents (WACAP),* 202 East Eighth, Aberdeen, Wash. 98520

BATTLEGROUND—*Battleground WACAP,* 22608 Northeast Osman Road, Battleground, Wash. 98604

BELLINGHAM—*Northwest Adoption Services,* 2516 Henry Street, Bellingham, Wash. 98225

BOTHELL—*North King County WACAP,* 22198 61st Street Southeast, Bothell, Wash. 98011

BREMERTON—*Bremerton WACAP,* 143 Lebo Street, Bremerton, Wash. 98310

CHEHALIS—*Chehalis WACAP,* 440 Northwest Pennsylvania Avenue, Chehalis, Wash. 98532

CLARKSTON—*Lewiston/Clarkston WACAP,* 1215 24th Avenue, Clarkston, Wash. 99403

CLE ELUM—*Cle Elum WACAP,* 113 West Fourth Street, Cle Elum, Wash. 98922

COLVILLE—*Northern Adoptive Parents,* 152 North Walnut, Colville, Wash. 99114

EASTSOUND—*San Juan Island Adoptive Parent Group,* Route 1, Box 1598, Eastsound, Wash. 98245

EAST WENATCHEE—*Wenatchee WACAP,* 2410 I Street Northeast, East Wenatchee, Wash. 98801

ENUMCLAW—*South Puget Sound Adoptive Parents,* 1309 Lafromboise Street, Enumclaw, Wash. 98022

EVERETT—*Kids in Need,* P.O. Box 5449, Everett, Wash. 98206

GOLDENDALE—*Goldendale Adoptive Parents Association,* P.O. Box 756, Goldendale, Wash. 98620

KENNEWICK—*Tri-Cities Adoptive Parents Support Group of WACAP,* 3209 South Dennis, Kennewick, Wash. 99336

LONGVIEW—*Longview WACAP Support Group,* 129010 Mill Creek Road, Longview, Wash. 98632

MERCER ISLAND—*Eastside WACAP,* 3870 83rd Avenue Southeast, Mercer Island, Wash. 98040

MOUNT VERNON—*Valley Adoption Services,* 1625 Mt. View Road, Mt. Vernon, Wash. 98273

OLYMPIA—*Olympia Area Support Group of WACAP,* 401 West Seventeenth Avenue, Olympia, Wash. 98501

OMAK—*Omak WACAP,* P.O. Box 1632, Omak, Wash. 98841

PORT ANGELES—*Port Angeles Support Group of WACAP,* 527 Rose Street, Port Angeles, Wash. 98362

—*Western Alliance for Children,* P.O. Box 2009, Port Angeles, Wash. 98362

PORT ORCHARD—*Adoptive Support Group of Kitsap County,* 5408 Basswood Lane Southeast, Port Orchard, Wash. 98366

PROSSER—*Prosser WACAP,* Route 3, Box 3704, Prosser, Wash. 99350

RENTON—*South King County,* North Pierce County WACAP, 1814 Aberdeen Avenue, Renton, Wash. 98055

SEATTLE—*Adopt a Black Child,* 6846 38th North East, Seattle, Wash. 98115

—*Interracial Family Association,* 6925 56th Avenue South, Seattle, Wash. 98118

SPOKANE—*Singles for Adoption,* East 2212 Decatur, Spokane, Wash. 99207

—*WACAP–Spokane,* P.O. Box 475, Riverside Station, Spokane, Wash. 99210

TACOMA—*Little People of America,* Adoption Committee, 5302 East 138th Street, Tacoma, Wash. 98446

—*Tacoma WACAP,* 111 East 115th, Tacoma, Wash. 98445

VANCOUVER—*Southwest Chapter of Adoption Services of WACAP,* 7020 Louisiana Drive, Vancouver, Wash. 98664

VASHON—*Vashon WACAP,* Route 1, Box 788, Wash. 98070

YAKIMA—*Yakima Adoptive Parent Support Group,* 13706 Tieton Drive, Yakima, Wash. 98908

WEST VIRGINIA

CHARLESTOWN—*Adoptive Parents Group,* 1032 Valley Road, Charlestown, W.Va. 25302

PARKERSBURG—*Adoptive Parents Group,* Route 1, Number 36, Valley Mills Circle, Parkersburg, W.Va. 26101

WISCONSIN

EAU CLAIRE—*Northwest Wisconsin Open Door Society,* 225 Hudson Street, Eau Claire, Wis. 54701

GREEN BAY—*Northeast Wisconsin OURS,* 133 Apple Tree Court, Green Bay, Wis. 54302

HOLMEN—*Special Needs Adopters,* P.O. Box 17, Route 3, Holmen, Wis. 54636

MILWAUKEE—*Wisconsin Minority Adoption and Foster Parent Group,* 3460 North First Street, Milwaukee, Wis. 53212

—*Wisconsin Open Door Society,* P.O. Box 1352, Milwaukee, Wis. 53202

RIVER FALLS—*OURS of Western Wisconsin,* 212 South Eighth Street, River Falls, Wis. 54022

WAUWATOSA—*Greater Milwaukee OURS,* 2536 North Ninetieth Street, Wauwatosa, Wis. 53226

WYOMING

LARAMIE—*Adoption Advocacy Group,* 1414 Kearney, Laramie, Wyo. 80270

Index

Abandonment, state policies on, 172
Abortion, out-of-wedlock birth rate
    unaffected by, 28
Abuse. *See* Child abuse
Adjustment of adopted children to new
    status, 68–73, 203–205
Adopted children
  adjustment to new status by, 68–73,
    203–205
  biological children's problems with, 66
  knowledge of biological parents by,
    214–15
  meeting of, 74–75
  placement of, 75, 79, 108, 141, 189–90
  prejudice against, 20
  property of, 151
  truthfulness toward, 213–14
Adoption. *See specific subjects*
Adoption agencies, 38, 94–110
  adoptive-parent associations resisted
    by, 90–91
  approaching of, 96–99, 109
  arguments for using, 134–35
  case workers in, 90–91
    adoptive-parent relationship with,
      101–103
  clients served by, 35–36, 40, 62
  decision-making by, 105–107, 110
  decline in dominant position of, 25–26
  foster care and, 182–83
  open-list agencies, adoption process of,
    95–96, 108–10
  parent evaluation by, 103–105, 110, 187
  private, 94
  profiteering by, 29–30

  public, 94
  religious, 94
  reserved-list agencies, adoption process
    of, 95, 96, 98–108
  waiting children and, 73–74, 80–82,
    96–97
  waiting-list policies of, 94–96, 108–110
  See also Adoptive-parent associations
Adoption decree, 79–80
Adoption-exchange services, chart of,
    128–30
Adoption exchanges, 127–32
Adoption procedures, chart of, 155–58
Adoption record laws, chart of, 218–21
Adoption records, state policies on,
    217–21
Adoption Reform Act of 1978, 53
Adoption Resource Centers, 53, 59
Adoptive-parent associations, 85–89
  adoption process aided by, 26, 27, 38,
    204
  directory of, 223–48
  traditional agencies superseded by,
    25–26, 29
  See also Adoption agencies
Adoptive parents
  case worker relationship with, 101–103
  evaluation of, 103–105, 110, 187
  post-placement depression of, 203
  rights and responsibilities of, 150–51
  See also Biological parents
Advertising, finding children through, 138
Advocacy
  for adoptive parents, 86
  for children, 85–86

249